BUILD UPGRADE REPAIR YOUR COMPUTER

SECOND EDITION

Get *Exactly* What You Want

and Save *Serious* Money!

Michael Harris

Index Publishing Group, Inc.
San Diego, California

Build, Upgrade, Repair Your Computer

Published by
INDEX PUBLISHING GROUP, Inc.
3368 Governor Drive, Suite 273
San Diego, CA 92122-2936
(619) 455-6100; fax (619) 552-9050
E-mail: ipgbooks@indexbooks.com
Web Site: http://www.indexbooks.com/~ipgbooks

The purpose of this publication is to inform, educate, and entertain, and it is not intended to support, induce, or condone any activity that might violate local, state, or Federal law, nor to deprive any company of its lawful income. Neither the author nor Index Publishing Group, Inc. shall have any liability to any person or entity derived from any alleged loss or damage arising from the use or misuse of the information contained herein. The author and the publisher have exerted their best efforts to ensure the accuracy of the information presented herein, yet there are no doubt errors—which are sincerely regretted.

ISBN 1-56866-229-7 (Quality Paperback)
Library of Congress Card Number 98-85814

Publisher's Cataloging-in-Publication
(Provided by Quality Books, Inc.)

Harris, Michael L.
    Build, upgrade, repair your computer: get exactly what you want and save serious money! / Michael Harris. -- 2nd ed.
    p. cm.
    Includes bibliographical references and index.
    Preassigned LCCN: 98-85814
    ISBN: 1-56866-229-7
    1. Microcomputers--Maintenance and repair--Amateurs' manuals. 2. Microcomputers--Upgrading--Amateurs' manuals. 3. Microcomputers--Design and construction--Amateurs' manuals.   I. Title.

TK9969.H37 1998   621.391'6'0288
                       QBI98-66729

Cover design: R.J. Gough Designs
Text design: in house
Typeset: Cindy Cheek
Graphics: Michael Harris and Bill Cheek
Printed and bound by: Bang Printing

CONTENTS

This book is dedicated

to my mom, Phyllis, who always knew I had it in me,
to my dad, Adrian, who never let me forget,
to my children, Lisa and Tony, who inspired me with their successes,
and
to my wife, Linda Kay, who helped me accomplish this work and rebuild my life,
one day at a time.

Acknowledgements

I want to thank Linton Vandiver, Henry Eisenson, Bill Cheek, and Cindy Cheek
for their invaluable assistance in directing and polishing this effort.
Without the sum and total of their experience and help,
this book would have not been possible.

Michael Harris

INTRODUCTION

To The Second Edition

You purchased this book in order to evaluate your computer requirements, and to make a decision on building, upgrading, or purchasing a computer to meet *your* exact needs. Believe it or not, if you go forward, you have already performed the most difficult part of the task.

Most people have the misconception that a computer is internally similar to a television set, and the mere mention of opening the cover conjures up visions of unspeakable horror. The greatest fear is wondering if the darn thing will ever work again when (if ?) you ever get it back together. A look through this book will quickly put those myths to rest. **If you can operate a Phillips head type screwdriver, and follow instructions, you can build the most complicated PC, as the many users of the First Edition can happily attest.**

This book profiles the IBM-compatible PC, and covers the options and variations of the basic computer. You will learn about the spectrum of add-on items you can easily install to customize your computer, making it an individualized system to fit your special needs. Upgrades and customization are key subjects in this book, and these two topics will give you the power to keep your system current.

Many people have asked me if building a Pentium-based computer is much harder than creating a simple, but obsolete, 486-based system. The truth is that a Pentium system, or Pentium 2 system, is *considerably simpler* to build than its predecessors. The plug and play features in the new motherboard BIOS make a blazing speed system just as simple to build as the bare-bones systems of a few years ago. (BIOS is the instruction set built into the motherboard that allows the motherboard to recognize the add-on components you will install later). This is why this book was written. **The actual assembly involved is exactly the same for any processor or system speed, and the number and configuration of optional add-on components is the only set of variables to be considered.**

Let's talk about complexity again. The only tools you will need are a couple of screwdrivers, a pair of pliers, and a pair of tweezers. I built my first computer in 1986, and still use exactly the same screwdrivers, pliers, and tweezers today. The tools in question are a number two Phillips screwdriver, a small slot screwdriver, a medium slot screwdriver, a small pair of standard pliers, and a small pair of tweezers. Last month, I assembled a Pentium 120 computer in about 20 minutes with only these tools, and saved about $1000 or so compared to the best nationally advertised system with similar components.

Now seems a good time to mention a very important feature currently available to ease the task of building or upgrading the IBM-compatible computer. *Plug and Play*, or PnP, is the current standard built into many hardware devices and add-on components, and is the current standard in Windows 95. This single standard revolutionized the computer industry by severely reducing the hardware and software conflicts that installing new hardware once caused. *Plug and Play*, by definition, is a set of hardware recognition instructions residing on the motherboard that allows the motherboard to set up the hardware, such as modems or video cards, that you choose and install in your computer.

When I built my first computer, I had to manually configure each item with a unique *Interrupt Request, or* IRQ address. There are 16 different addresses available. There must never be two items with the same IRQ address. Many add-on components must also have a unique *Direct Memory Access*, or DMA setting. When I began building my first computer, I had to be certain that each item was unique in its IRQ and DMA settings. My tweezers came in handy for setting the switches on the components before installation. Fortunately, most newer components don't require this level of attention.

When I built my Pentium 200, all the items installed were PnP, and the first time I turned the computer on, it automatically configured everything. The record of each DMA and IRQ setting configured by the plug and play BIOS was saved, either on the motherboard or on each item installed. The beauty of this system is that one may never have to worry about DMA or IRQ conflicts, depending on the complexity of the computer.

PnP in Windows 95 goes one step further, and configures or specifies configurations for you to set on items not PnP compatible. The first time Windows 95 runs, it maps each installed item for conflicts, and notifies you if there is a conflict you must manually correct. The correction normally involves setting a component's jumper or switch to a different setting. Plug and play is a true blessing for the beginning computer builder or anyone interested in upgrading, and will eliminate hours of frustration.

Somewhere along the line you may ask yourself the big question: "What do I think I am doing?" Followed immediately by the statement: "I can't possibly build a computer!!" Ignore such concerns and let me show you how easy it can be.

Building instead of buying will save you a ton of money, and the experience will enable you to repair your PC, and successfully upgrade to keep it current, if you wish. Many people I know are satisfied with their existing computer, but would like a larger hard drive or more memory. The ability to perform upgrades yourself will save you even more money, since some retailers would rather sell you a new computer than provide the information you need to perform a simple upgrade.

One of the objectives of this book is to help you understand exactly what you want in a computer, before you spend a dime. Many people just need a basic system for word processing and running a few games, while those writing programs or performing operations with complex graphics, for instance, will require a more sophisticated and powerful system.

A couple of authors have stated that the buyer should purchase the most expensive computer that he or she can possibly afford, and their books reflect that belief. I have to disagree with their philosophy. l believe you should understand your computer needs right now, and make an educated guess at your future needs.

Project as far into the future as possible, but do not look beyond three years, as technology advances cloud up our crystal balls. Build the computer you want now, and upgrade storage, memory, speed, and other functions as required to match your advancing requirements. This realistic and cost-effective approach will not put you in the poorhouse.

With the help of this book, you will be able to decide on the computer you want, purchase and successfully assemble the hardware, and install the software. When you finish, you will have the system you need, and hundreds, even thousands, of extra dollars in your pocket.

This book covers upgrades for improved performance on widely used older machines, in easy-to-read language and with sufficient detail to let you easily master the task. Included are tips and basic troubleshooting techniques used by experts to repair and tune up computers and peripherals.

Chapter 1, **A Trip to the Computer Store**, details how to select the computer options you need: a realistic starting point. The biggest mistake first-time computer buyers make is letting a retail vendor decide for them what they need. Roughly thirty percent of all first time buyers return their first computer and leave the store angry and/or dissatisfied. This chapter details makes, models, options, and peripherals in easy-to-understand language, preparing you to pick the system to fit your current and possibly future needs, eliminating frustration and expense.

Chapter 2, **Performance and Price**, goes into detail on performance and price issues, outlining prices for systems from a basic 386 desktop publishing system to a full- blown multimedia data crunching Pentium system. Several sample systems are outlined, and price breakdown estimates for packaged systems and do it yourself systems are documented. When you finish this chapter, you will know exactly what hardware you want and how much it will cost.

Chapter 3, **Software for the PC**, covers commonly asked-for software, benefits, functionality overlaps, and basic pricing. Various software packages and the reasons for purchasing them are detailed, and software-hardware compatibility is discussed. Comparison between office suite packages is covered in detail.

Chapter 4, **Selecting Your Computer's Components**, is a trip to the retailers; this time you know exactly what hardware and software you need, and (more importantly) don't want. Check some of the packaged systems and get the best prices, then go to the component vendors and see what the system *really* should cost. Note: when you purchase components and build your own system, you have all the documentation, better components, and the power to fix your computer yourself. After this chapter, you will realize how easy it is to simultaneously save money and have a superior computer.

Chapter 5, **Putting It All Together**, is the heart of the book. You will assemble the purchased components and understand their interactions. You will learn to fix component conflicts, both software and hardware, and become proficient at spotting and correcting trouble spots. You will optimize the performance of your system, and be amazed at how easy it is. Most packaged systems are not optimized for performance, as documented in the addendum titled "**The case of the slow Pentium**," included in Chapter 2.

Chapter 6, **Upgrade Or Perish**, details examples of system upgrades, from simple add-on cards to complete processor and bus upgrades. The computer user will become familiar with the inner workings of the computer, and will be able to easily determine whether it is cheaper to upgrade or purchase a new system to get the performance needed.

Chapter 7, **Murphy's Law**, outlines the common hiccups that may occur when upgrading a system, or that even happen in a purchased system. You will be able to differentiate between hardware and software conflicts, make changes to system configuration files, and understand the reasons for the problems, including new software installation errors.

Chapter 8, **The Software Toolbox**, covers basic diagnostic software, repair tips, and tune up tricks, all to keep the computer in top condition.

Chapter 9, **Computer Terminology**, covers the computer dialect utilized in the industry today. The buzzwords can be the most confusing and intimidating aspect of computer shopping, primarily since the computer terms are the salesperson's best tool to gauge the customer's knowledge. This chapter gives the reader a compass to safely navigate the sales pitches to be encountered, and serves as a tool to determine exactly what your computer requirements will be. Readers have told me that the single most intimidating part of a computer sales pitch is getting past the computer-related terminology.

Chapter 10, **Where Do We Go From Here?** hints at the next generation of computers and software, and the tools needed to understand, build, and upgrade them. The next level of computer hardware and software is discussed, and possibilities beyond the year 2000 are suggested. This chapter includes source information on components and periodicals.

Who am I, and why did I write this book? I am currently a Test Engineer for one of the engineering companies designing the next generation of digital communications equipment, and specializing in high speed fiber optic communications links between computers. My interest in computers and instrumentation control software presses me to constantly update my computer hardware and software knowledge. You might have noticed that computers and related products are revised and improved upon on a monthly basis. The computer industry is constantly trying to convince the public that one year old products are obsolete!

One of the required parts of my job is to be just ahead of technological advances in the computer field. This spills over into my personal life, and my primary hobby is designing and building computer systems. On this subject, I serve in an advisory or consulting capacity with several progressive firms specializing in IBM-compatible hardware and software. *I have upgraded and repaired more than 5 thousand computers at this writing.*

I built my first IBM compatible computer in the early 1980s, to use as an engineering aid and typewriter. Saving money was high on my list, and by building my own computer, I saved about $1400. Recently, when I built my Pentium II-330, I saved about the same percentage of money, in 1998 dollars around $2000. Needless to say, I was *astounded* by the savings.

Today, due to the simplicity of design, a computer can be built by anyone with a modicum of dexterity and a bit of patience. Knowing this fact, I made the decision to share my 25 years of computer and electronic experience with you, especially since I realized there still exists potential for saving money by building your own system.

To confirm that the information presented in this text could help nearly anyone build a computer, I ran tests. The details are in the text, but to recap briefly, I took as subjects a lawyer, then an assistant manager from a local convenience store. I followed this experiment with a young Marine, a college undergraduate student, and a computer illiterate author as guinea pigs. With only the information in this book, all successfully built or upgraded their computers.

Putting a computer together might seem like an impossible puzzle right now. Read on, and solve the puzzle, one piece at a time!

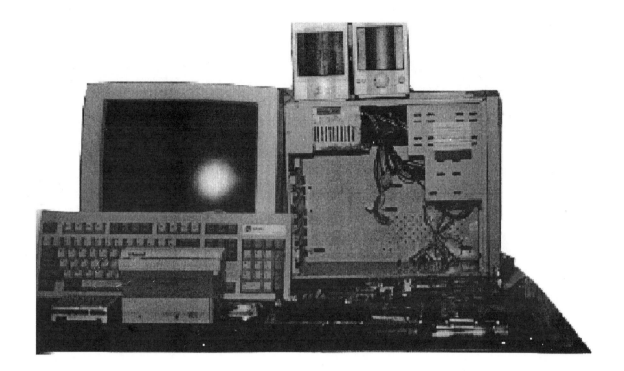

Your Notes

1

A TRIP TO THE COMPUTER STORE

Topics

What is a computer?
Bypassing the hype and getting to the truth
Which PC is right for you?
Processing speed, hardware, and options
How much computer do you really need or want?

External peripherals, printers, scanners, tape drives, and their uses
Selecting the components you want, and integrating them into a working system

Figures

WHAT IS A COMPUTER?

THIS BLOCK DIAGRAM WILL GIVE YOU SOME IDEA

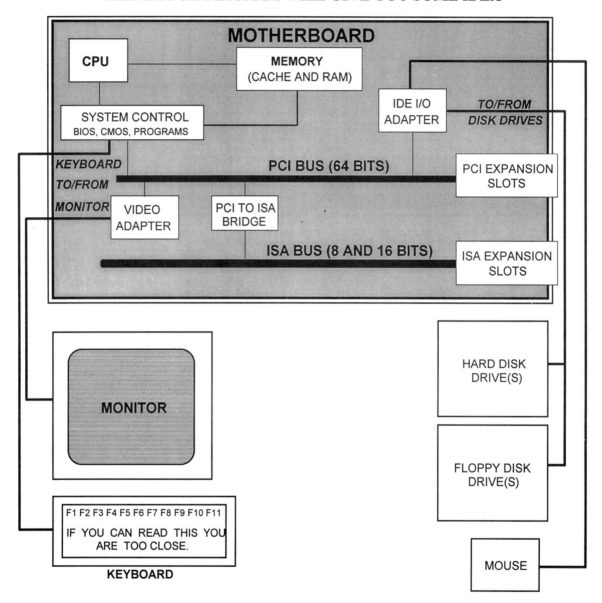

The first order of business in building your computer is to know what you want. The easiest way to understand your computer needs is to try someone else's system, and the easiest way to try lots of systems is a trip to the computer store.

The computer store mentioned may be a specialized computer and electronics outlet, a chain department store with a computer electronics section, or any other store with a moderate supply of varied computer systems.

Review this chapter on accessories and options, Chapter 3 on software, and Chapter 9 on terminology *before* you go shopping. You can get lots of mileage from sales personnel, whose objective is to keep your interest. They will, however, attempt to get you to purchase an expensive system you may not need. This is their sole purpose in life, and the reason so many people return their first computer purchase. Their intent is seldom to provide you the computer you need; rather, it is to offer you the computer they want to sell.

Try many computers of varying processor types, speeds, and with as many different accessories as possible. Get a feel for the IBM compatible computer, the wide variety of configurations and options, and the huge number of available software products. Do not be afraid to ask questions; get second opinions on everything any salesperson tells you.

After you cut through the sales hype, categorize the systems you have looked at into groups you can evaluate. I'll discuss my categories, and the reason for the groupings. Your individual requirements may necessitate making categories different than mine. The objective of this exercise is to determine which computer is right for you.

Bare Bones Systems

Beginning computer owners may wish to build a "basic system," to minimize expenditures as they develop an understanding of their total computer requirements. They can add hardware or software options later, as they begin to use the system and define their long term needs. A bare bones system will have a minimum of RAM, a small hard drive, a basic video card, basic I/O capability, a small monitor, a keyboard, and a basic mouse. Software operating systems may or may not be included. Bare bones systems are available in Cyrix 6x86, AMD K6, Pentium, Pentium Pro, or Pentium II models.

Desktop Publishing Systems

Compared to the above mentioned systems, the components that create a desktop publishing system include more RAM (at least 64 Megabytes), a larger hard drive (5.1 Gigabytes), a good video card, a larger monitor (15 inch digital), and a modem (56k fax/modem). The desktop publishing system typically has Windows 95, and one or more publishing or office suite programs included. A good quality laser or color ink jet printer is normally added to such a package.

Publishing and Multimedia System

In addition to the improvements listed above, the multimedia system adds a CD-ROM, a sound card, 64 Megabytes more RAM, an even larger hard drive, 6-9 Gigabytes, and often a 17 inch or larger digital monitor. Speakers to reproduce the stereo multimedia effects are added, and a joystick or flight controller or both are included. Few people need all of this functionality in a system, but many purchase a system like this, only to realize later they have made a mistake. Each one of these groups can have a 6x86, K6, Pentium II, or Pentium Pro microprocessor-based computer as the core system, and basically the only difference in performance will be the speed at which each system is capable of operating. Most of the software out there runs well on a 6x86, K6, or Pentium, and great on a Pentium II or Pentium Pro system. When deciding which speed is right for you, take everything into consideration, including the software you intend to run.

Processing speed is the biggest selling point of most systems. The data throughput, or actual processing speed, is measured in millions of instructions per second, or *mips*. It is useful to compare the speed of an old XT computer with today's Pentium. The XT processes data at 0.75 mips, while the slower Pentium processors run about 112 mips. A Pentium 200 microprocessor-based system is approximately 300 times faster than my first PC, and infinitely easier to build.

By this point in your exploration, you have hopefully tried out several computers, and probably know which processor best fits your needs and budget. Remember, 486 based systems can generally be upgraded to Pentium speed with the simple installation of a 5x86 chip, and that makes the 486 system a good place for the budget minded person to start. The Pentium system, though more expensive, is still open ended and has no speed limitation. Faster Pentium chips are constantly being offered. The Pentium 133 system is running about 420 times faster than my XT, and 200 MHz (and faster) chips are available as a drop-in upgrade for most motherboards. One final look at processor speed is available with this table of system benchmarks.

CPU DATA

	IBM XT 8086	IBM AT 286-16	AMD 386-40	AMD 486-100	INTEL 200 MMX PENT
≈ No. of Gates	30,000	135,000	275,000	1.2 Million	3.1 Million+
MIPS	0.75	2.7	11.5	54	400+
# BITS	8	16	32	32	64

The Clones of Note

Both Cyrix and AMD offer microprocessors that are compatible with motherboards that support Intel's Pentium line. The chips are both cheaper and faster than their Pentium counterparts, according to certain brands of benchmarking software.

5x86 processors, drop-in replacements for the 486 line, are still available in 120 and 133 MHz processor speeds, and can upgrade a 486 system to Pentium speed comparable to that of a Pentium 75. Be certain the BIOS of the motherboard will support the 5x56. Most PCI motherboards built after March 1996 will support the 5x86 processor.

The cost for a 133 MHz system with 8 Megabytes of RAM, a 1 GB hard drive, and no monitor, was about $300 less than for a comparable Pentium 75 system in 1997, and it was *faster*! Still available, this is a great low cost 486 upgrade option.

The Cyrix 6x86 is a drop-in replacement for Pentium chips on current Pentium motherboards. The BIOS on the motherboard must support the 6x86 chip. A Cyrix 6x86 P166 processor benchmarks about 40 percent faster than a Pentium 166 MHz processor with Norton Utilities.

How much CPU do you need? Weigh the options available to you against your budget. If a CPU selection drives you to the poorhouse, it's not the processor for you.

Build or buy the most open-ended system you can afford. "Open ended" means the ability to upgrade later. If you upgrade a 486 or 5x86-based machine, insist on a PCI motherboard with on-board *IDE I/O*. Both *Integrated Disk Electronics* and *Input/Output* are defined in Chapter 9 and are discussed in detail later in this chapter. "IDE" refers to the hard drive disk controller interface, and "I/O" to the input/output controller for printers, modems, and game adapters. The built-in interface is faster than an add-on card, and frees up a slot for more options.

If you build a 6x86 or Pentium-based system, buy the fastest motherboard you can, but don't buy one with an integrated sound card. You may not be satisfied with the level of sound card performance for the life of the motherboard. In general, do not lock yourself into a level of performance you may later regret. I mention this now because the price of a motherboard with an integrated sound card may influence you to purchase one, particularly if you associate a high price with a better motherboard.

Now is a good time to talk about hardware and options. I separate hardware into two groups. Things you have to install inside the case are **internal options**. **External add-ons** are the other options. Obviously, internal options require more work on your part, so we will look at them first.

Here is a list of the hardware required to build a basic computer, starting with the motherboard, case, and everything that goes inside. This is just a list. Detailed descriptions of the components, as well as pictures, can be found later in this chapter. Definitions of computer-related terms can be found in Chapter 9.

Internal Options

Motherboard

This is the *Central Processing Unit*, or CPU. The microprocessor, RAM, BIOS, cache, and all add-on cards plug into the motherboard. It is the heart of any computer, and determines the speed and flexibility of your computer. The microprocessor can be anything from a 5x86 to a Pentium, and beyond.

Case

All components except the monitor and external items fit inside the case, and operate from a power supply inside the case. A fan integrated into the power supply cools the power supply and all internally installed components. A small fan is often mounted on the microprocessor for more cooling.

Memory

The memory is installed on the motherboard, and consists of *Single In-line Memory Modules*. SIMM modules are discussed in detail later in this chapter. Included on the motherboard is cache memory, the fast RAM that stores information passing to and from the microprocessor.

IDE I/O

This function is often integrated into the motherboard, and all disk operations and all external input/output functions are controlled by it. The *Integrated Disk Electronics* and *Input/Output* functions are available as a separate add-on card for motherboards without a built in IDE I/O.

Video Card

This add-on card allows the computer to display text and graphics on your monitor. The range of performance in video cards is remarkable, and will be discussed later in this chapter.

HDD

(*Hard Disk Drive*) Most of the primary information, including the operating system, is stored on your hard disk drive. The basic exception to this is the setup information, which is stored in the BIOS ROM discussed later in this chapter. Most new motherboards and cases support multiple hard disk drives. All installed programs, and data you create, are stored and run from the HDD.

FDD

(*Floppy Disk Drive*) When installed, a hard disk drive has no information on it. You will install programs and operating systems on your hard disk using either a floppy disk drive or a CD-ROM. All programs you acquire will be installable using a floppy disk drive or CD-ROM.

Sound Card

To expand the computing experience, sound cards were invented. A sound card processes sounds from digital information. Certain programs and games provide sound and music during execution. The sound plays from either headphones or external speakers. A sound card is one of the most important pieces of a multimedia system, and most new games would be useless without one.

Modem

The primary way your computer talks to other computers is through the telephone lines using a modem. The MoDem gets its name from the operations it performs on communications signals passing through it to and from your computer. *Modulator* and *Demodulator* operations are discussed later in this chapter. The modem takes information from your communication program and converts it to analog signals for transmission over telephone cables. The signals are sent through the phone line to a destination you select. Most modems have FAX capability as well.

CD-ROM Drive

(*Compact Disk Read Only Memory*) Large amounts of data and visual information can be stored on a compact disk, and later accessed using a CD-ROM drive. This read-only type of media is the heart of the multimedia experience, because programs up to 650 Megabytes in size can be stored on a single CD-ROM. This fact opens up avenues for extensive graphics, including moving pictures and sound. The medium is similar to the compact disks you enjoy in your home stereo system.

Tape Drive System

The tape drive backup systems currently available are the most important protection available for today's computer systems. For under $100 you can protect the contents of your hard drive from data loss. A tape drive and the tapes are cost effective, easy to use, and reliable as well. Now, let's discuss the external components.

External Options

Monitor

The monitor is one of the most important parts of the computer, and one of the most expensive. You will see and use the monitor more than any other part of the computer, so it had better suit your needs. The monitor will outlive any other part of the system, since you may upgrade the motherboard, keyboard, mouse, and most of the internally installed components long before you upgrade or replace the monitor. The sizes and options will be discussed later in this chapter.

Mouse

Most programs today make use of the mouse-pointing device. It is primarily used to select options in programs and to start programs. Several options and configurations are available, and are discussed in this chapter.

Keyboard

The keyboard is the primary device you use to input data and control programs into a computer. It is set up similar to a standard typewriter keypad, but has several other options and keys to expand its capabilities for use on the PC.

Modem, CD-ROM, Tape Drive

These three devices, discussed above as internal parts, are common items you can also purchase as external. They interface through cables attached to I/O ports on the back of the computer.

Now let's take a more detailed look at the options within each component category. This is where you make an informed decision on exactly how much computer you will build. Remember, maximum performance usually means more cost, but weigh your requirements against the future and your pocketbook when deciding. Remember, *you normally do not have the option to select any of the components if you purchase a packaged system from a retail outlet*.

The Case

The cabinet and included power supply constitute the case. You will find several different case styles available, such as mini, medium, and full tower cases. Still available are flat desktop styles commonly used in older systems. Choose the case type only after you have selected everything else, since the case size can limit your options. A mini-tower case, for example, will not house two floppy drives, a CD-ROM drive, and a tape backup system, and neither will most basic desktop cases.

Power consumption is also a factor, but case designers typically take this into consideration when they make the cases. A mini-tower case should be rated at 200 watts minimum. A medium case should be rated at 250 watts, and a full tower should support at least 300 watts of accessories. The larger cases have more drive and accessory bays, so the power supply must provide more power.

IMPORTANT NOTE: some tower system cases, when packaged, do not have the power switch installed. It typically interferes with the type of packaging used to ship the cases. To install the switch, follow the wiring information carefully. This is the only part of the installation that can cause you harm! **If you have any doubt whether the switch is wired properly, consult the sales personnel where you purchased the case.**

The power supply inside the case takes the 117 VAC from your wall socket and converts it to the +5 volts, +12 volts, -5 volts and -12 volts the computer requires.

The power supply fan must be kept free of dust and obstructions to airflow, so don't let anything block the part of the case where the fan is mounted. Blocking the air flow through your computer will result in heat damage to one or more of the internal components. This fan is the only source for cooling in most computers.

As is true with all computer components, prices for cases cannot be depended upon to remain constant. Advances in technology and market forces drive costs down steadily. Use the following prices for reference only.

Desktop cases run about $22 with a 150 watt power supply. You can get a 200 watt version for about $37. Mini tower cases start at around $30 with a 230 watt power supply. Both mid tower and full tower cases with 230 watt power supply go for about $45. The same case with a 300 watt power supply is $55.

You can spend more for cases with special colors, styles, or other gimmicks, but I don't recommend it generally. If you spend a few dollars more for a case with an extra fan, however, it is money well spent, since two fans are **safer** than one. *Nothing kills a great computer faster than an uncorrected fan failure.*

The Motherboard

The biggest difference between PC models is the motherboard and central processing unit, or microprocessor. The CPU type commonly gives its name to the system. A *Pentium* system has a Pentium CPU loaded on a PCI bus motherboard. (More about the PCI bus later in this chapter.) *486* and *386* computers have 486 and 386 microprocessors and motherboards installed. Both the 486 and Pentium motherboards will support various clone processors, since the clone processors use the standard pin arrangements. Though many clone processors use different voltages, the motherboard documentation covers any configuration issues you may encounter.

Compatibility among processors and motherboards breaks down as follows:

A 486 PCI motherboard built after March 1996 will support the 5x86 clones. The only requirement is the BIOS on the motherboard must recognize the 5x86 processor.

The Basic Input Output System, or BIOS, is information stored in a programmable memory device on the motherboard. It is configuration information to allow you to initially set up your motherboard's configuration for various options. More on this in Chapter 9.

The manual included with the motherboard will tell you if your BIOS will support a 5x86 microprocessor. 5x86 clone processors, like the AMD 5x86 133, are as fast as a Pentium 90. Try to get this type of upgrade information in a computer store!

The Pentium PCI motherboards will support several clones, but a good choice is the Cyrix 6x86. This is a very fast upgrade for any Pentium motherboard built after March 1996. Ensure that the BIOS on the motherboard will support the clone processor. *Figure 1-1* shows a typical clone-compatible PCI Pentium motherboard with on-board IDE I/O functions.

I have found no clone for the Pentium Pro or Pentium II yet, though both AMD and Cyrix are competing actively against the fastest Pentium processors. Neither the Pentium Pro nor the Pentium II processor will fit on normal Pentium motherboards because of their size and heat dissipation. Remember, the Pentium Pro processor was designed primarily for 32 bit processing. The average home user will see no performance improvement running typical applications. Normally, consumer software development lags behind hardware advances, so invest in the newest and greatest hardware **after** the rest of the system is available.

Why does a fast processor like the P6 run slowly on the *average home user's system*?

Most of us use programs written in 16 bit code embedded in the programs and operating systems and we use or plan to use. Even Windows 95 has both 16 bit and 32 bit code. Windows NT, however, is a true 32 bit operating system. How many of you use or plan to use Windows NT? Not many, I'll bet.

The bulk of PC software available is 16 bit software, written in 16 bit code with 16 bit compilers, and using 16 bit drivers. Many hardware devices do not have 32 bit drivers or software available.

The average home system must be capable of efficiently processing both 16 and 32 bit code. The Pentium can do this, but the Pentium Pro, optimized for 32 bit code, slows down considerably running 16 bit code. It normally runs **slower** than a Pentium-based system running the same 16 bit program.

If you are an NT user running only 32 bit code, you will enjoy significant improvement in speed with a Pentium Pro. If not, stick to a Pentium or Pentium II processor. With the advent of the Pentium II, fewer Pentium Pro systems are being sold today.

Some motherboards have a feature for energy savings called the *green feature*. You can set the shutdown time in BIOS. The motherboard will shut down the hard drives and other accessories after the time you set in BIOS. This can save quite a bit of energy on a system left unattended.

The *green* feature is in many peripherals for today's computers, including monitors, printers, scanners, and some high-end cases.

Figure 1-1, ahead, has both ISA and PCI bus slots. The next few paragraphs describe the bus types. These slots are for the various add-on cards. Add-on cards provide video display capability, sound support, hard disk control, and many other functions. These cards and others are discussed in detail later in this chapter. Most of the add-on cards used in different system types are similar. The primary difference between cards is the bus type, which we will discuss later. This is why it is just as easy to build a Pentium screamer as a 386 system. It is actually easier! Why?

The primary reason is current motherboards for all processor types are more flexible in ease of configuration, and support an increasingly large number of add-on cards. The only real differences in computer architecture are determined by the motherboard. The architecture mentioned above refers to the parallel data bus to and from the components on the motherboard. Data in an XT computer travels on an 8 bit parallel bus. Imagine 8 lanes of traffic. To increase data throughput, a 286 system doubles the bus to 16 bits of parallel data.

The 386 and 486 have a 32 bit bus, and the Pentium has a 64 bit bus. Even if there were no other advantages, the 64 bit bus (64 lanes of traffic), moves data 8 times faster.

The ISA (*Industry Standard Architecture*) bus was introduced in the first PCs, and remains

one of the standards. This standard, however, limits the I/O bus size to 16 bits and the I/O speed to 8-10 MHz. Current motherboards still have several slots of this bus type, primarily to offer support for the large number of ISA add-on cards currently available.

Data throughput on the motherboard has vastly improved since the XT days. To preserve compatibility with older hardware, the I/O bus speed remains at 8-10 MHz, for the ISA lots. The VLB, *VESA Local Bus*, addition to the 486 motherboard eliminates the 8-10 MHz bottleneck.

VESA stands for *Video Electronics Standard Association*. VLB motherboards and add-on cards have a 32 bit path added in line with the existing 16 bit connector. This connector allows local bus cards and motherboards to communicate at the speed of the CPU clock, increasing the speed of the system nearly 10 times with a 66 MHz CPU clock. The VLB connector is also downward compatible to 8 and 16 bits.

Some 486, 586, and all Pentium motherboards have a *peripheral component interconnect*, or PCI bus, that is 64 bits wide. This bus is stand-alone and is not downward compatible to VLB, 16 or 8 bit busses. It has one great feature: it supports PnP, or *Plug and Play* compatible add-on cards. As previously mentioned, PnP means you install the card and the computer interface sets the DMA and IRQ settings for you. Fortunately, all PCI motherboards also include several 8 and 16 bit bus slots for your 8 and 16 bit add-on cards.

Speed is the most significant difference among CPUs, and the reason faster processors are more expensive. One factor in CPU speed is how the CPU handles instructions. Of the CISC processors, the Pentium is king. CISC, or *complex instruction set* processors, have a large instruction set built into the chip. When the CPU is asked to

Figure 1-1 A TYPICAL PENTIUM PCI MOTHERBOARD WITH IDE I/O

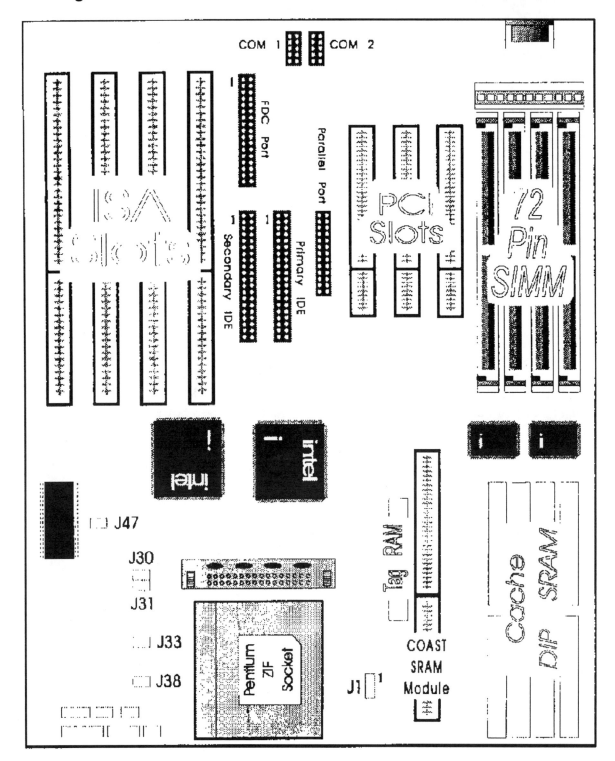

perform a task, it must sift through a built-in list of instructions to find the ones necessary to perform the task. RISC processors, like the DEC Alpha AXP and Apple's PowerPC, have a much smaller instruction set. They can process data at speeds of 150 mips *(million instructions per second)*. These *reduced instruction set* processors are *faster* than the Pentium, but...

There are more than 75,000 programs that run on a Pentium. Nearly all of these programs must be *translated* to run on a RISC machine, because the RISC processor only understands instructions written in its unique language. The chore of translation slows the program to a crawl, so the RISC processor running a Pentium-based program is up to 50% slower. In other words, the Indy race car runs great on a closed racetrack, but will never survive New York's pothole-laden city streets. For the time being, **if you want speed and compatibility, select a fast Pentium motherboard.**

This is true even after the release of the P6, or Pentium Pro, a superscalar processor optimized for 32 bit programs. It is extremely fast using 32 bit code or programs, but slows down like a RISC processor when running 16 bit applications like Windows 3.1. It seems that the home user is restricted to Pentium K6 or 6x86 machines if he or she wants a fast and compatible machine for home use.

Or so we thought. Intel, in its infinite wisdom, decided to utilize its 0.25 micron technology, MMX instructions, and the finest aspects of both the Pentium and the Pentium Pro, and go back to the drawing board. What evolved from these efforts is the currently unsurpassed CPU called the Pentium II. With speeds exceeding 400 MHz, **the Pentium II is the current state of the art for the high-end computer owner.**

Built-in functions available on the newer motherboards include the EIDE, *Enhanced Integrated Disk Electronics* interface for IDE hard drives. A floppy disk controller and support for four IDE devices, including IDE CD-ROM drives, is part of this package.

Support for two serial ports, a 16550 UART, (*Universal Asynchronous Receiver Transmitter)*, one parallel port, and one game port complete the IDE I/O functions built into this group. This group of built-in connectors eliminates the need for an I/O add-on card and an IDE add-on card, freeing up one or two PCI slots in your computer for other options.

Some motherboards include a SCSI adapter as well, but most people I know prefer the IDE interface as their disk controller. However, the *Small Computer System Interface* has additional uses, including support for external scanners, backup systems, and sound card add-on peripherals. The SCSI interface is widely used in Macintosh computers, but the lower cost and easier installation of IDE components makes the IDE system more attractive to most PC users.

Avoid on-board video adapters. The video standard industry is advancing rapidly, and six months sees a new generation of accessories. You need the flexibility to upgrade video performance by spending less than $100 to drop in the latest upgrade. Many software packages spell out a level of video performance required to run the program, and you need the option of easily upgrading to keep up with your future needs.

Sound card options are often added to the motherboard. If you want to keep up with high end performance in this department, **do not buy a motherboard with integrated sound.** Sound systems are increasing in capability, yet they require fewer computer resources. Keep this portion of your system open to easy upgrading with a plug-in sound card.

Another built-in feature of the motherboard is the ability to self-test when you turn on the computer. This POST, or *Power On Self Test*, is one of the many features stored in the BIOS, or *Basic Input Output System* chip. In addition to self-testing, other features are loaded into the BIOS, such as the entire configuration map you create the first time you power up a new system. This configuration information is the only portion of BIOS you can change or modify without a chip or disk from the manufacturer.

Support for larger hard drives and PnP add-on cards is included in newer BIOS. When you purchase a motherboard, look for one with plug and play BIOS which supports mode 3 and mode 4 EIDE HDD. This is necessary to have support for the newest generation of hard drives and the plug and play add-on cards. Fortunately, the BIOS chip is normally installed in a socket, and can be replaced.

The motherboard manufacturer will be able to upgrade your BIOS by sending you an updated BIOS chip if you request it. As new features are added to the BIOS, you can easily update your motherboard. The newest motherboards support flash BIOS, which can be updated with a floppy disk provided by the motherboard manufacturer. With this capability, *you don't have to open the case!*

When you build a computer and turn it on for the first time, it has to be configured. The system configuration setup program needs information about the hardware present in your system. You input this information the first time, then it is stored and reused every time you turn on the computer. This subject is addressed in detail at the end of Chapter 5.

The configuration information is stored in volatile memory, which is kept alive with a small battery installed on the motherboard. If this battery fails and has to be replaced, you must reconfigure the computer. Keep a record of your CMOS, or *Complementary Metal Oxide Semiconductor* setup in writing, taped somewhere inside the computer case, to prevent real headaches later. A PnP motherboard will often configure the computer automatically the first time you turn it on.

As you can see, the motherboard is the heart of your computer system. A basic upgrade to a faster computer starts here, and many upgrades require only changing the motherboard or CPU. Simple upgrades, like improving video quality, sound support, or increasing memory require only changing add-in modules on the motherboard.

Memory Types

Without memory to store instructions and intermediate results, a computer would be a high-speed typewriter. When a computer compiles data while running a program, portions of the program and data are loaded into *Random Access Memory,* commonly called RAM.

The CPU accesses the RAM, extracts portions of the data, performs operations on the data, and sends it back to the RAM. This interaction may occur thousands of times during the execution of a program. Only after all the processing is completed is the data sent to a more permanent storage device; your hard disk or floppy. Often, the data is used to display something on the monitor, send information to a printer, or prompt you for more input.

Another type of memory is the ROM, *Read Only Memory,* which holds the BIOS information mentioned in the motherboard section of this chapter. This memory is read only, and is utilized on power-up to configure your computer for use.

Most computers have between 1 MB and 32 MB of RAM installed on the motherboard.

The RAM normally consists of integrated circuits mounted on a small 30 or 72 pin *Single In-line Memory Module*, or SIMM. Larger SIMM modules are being utilized, but these are the most popular sizes currently.

Each SIMM contains between 256 KB and 32 MB of RAM. The most common type of RAM is *dynamic RAM*, called DRAM. DRAM must be refreshed often during program execution, or the information stored in it will vanish.

Still another type of RAM is SRAM. *Static RAM* holds data until it is changed, eliminating refresh cycles. RAM is used for temporary storage primarily because each element of information can be accessed and changed as often as necessary. This is what random access means. Random access memory can be modified in part or in whole, depending on the program you are running and its requirements at the time. Any memory location can be addressed, read, or written to independently of all other memory locations.

Data stored on a hard drive or floppy disk, on the other hand, is stored sequentially. It cannot be accessed or changed one byte at a time. This makes access to floppy and hard drive memory a much slower process than RAM access. This is noticeable when you run a large program, and the program runs out of RAM. The computer will use part of your hard drive to temporarily store information normally stored in RAM. You will notice the computer slow down while it searches the hard drive for the temporary results to process. When you hear someone talk about a swap file, they are referring to this process.

There is another reason Pentium machines are faster. Information is stored in RAM in 8 bit increments called bytes. The XT can process one byte of information at a time. The 16 bit 286 can handle 2 bytes. The 32 bit 386 and 486 can process 4 bytes simultaneously. The Pentium, with its 64 bit bus, can handle 8

bytes at a time, which is 8 bits per byte, or 64 bits, simultaneously.

Memory utilization is important, particularly for DOS-based programs. DOS, the *Disk Operating System* prevalent on most PCs, requires its core programs to live in RAM the entire time you use the computer. DOS, unfortunately, only allows you to use the first 640 kB of memory in your computer. It reserves the next 384 kB for programs you specify in setup files to run in upper memory. Anything above that, unless specially addressed by certain programs, is invisible to DOS. This includes all the additional SIMM memory you can install on the motherboard.

This means large programs will not run fast (if at all) in DOS. Special programs called memory managers allow large DOS-based programs to run. Memory managers give DOS programs the ability to use the additional memory installed in your computer by allocating portions of it to programs normally resident in DOS, or low memory.

Windows, OS/2, and Windows 95 are three operating systems that get around the 640 KB limit imposed by DOS. These programs have memory managers, and all three make use of the expanded and extended memory available. Refer to *EMM, Expanded Memory*, and *Extended Memory* in Chapter 9 for more details on these subjects.

We talked about SIMM memory earlier, and mentioned the common sizes. Now let's talk about configuration on the motherboard. Memory on the motherboard is configured in banks of SIMM. Usually, a motherboard will have between two and four banks of SIMM. The banks are usually numbered from 0 to 3, and loaded sequentially with SIMM, normally from the lowest numbered bank to the highest.

You can load any number of banks with SIMM, but each bank you load must be filled. Note: some motherboards auto-detect memory, enabling you to load any bank, instead of the lowest first.

The 30 pin SIMM modules must be installed in groups of 4, but the 72 pin SIMM modules can be installed in pairs. Some motherboards support both formats of SIMM, but most support only one. The 72 pin SIMM is newer, and has replaced the 30 pin type on current motherboards. Most Pentium machines have two or three banks for 72 pin SIMM. Most new motherboards also support 132 pin *DIMM. Dual Input Memory Modules* come in both EDO and *SDRAM* configurations.

EDO RAM has arrived in force, and in a fast machine it can be 10% faster than conventional memory. This *Extended Data Output* RAM also costs about 10% more than normal DRAM. Mixing EDO RAM and regular DRAM is like mixing matter and anti-matter, so don't. If you need speed, buy it. The difference is evident in extremely fast games and complex graphics programs.

Finally, *SDRAM* is a current evolution from EDO RAM. With 10 nanosecond access speed, it is 6 times faster than EDO RAM. Don't consider operating a 200 MHz or faster computer without SDRAM.

Cache memory is one way to speed up a computer. Many times during program execution a program must loop several times through the same steps. Cache memory is used by the computer to store these repetitive operations. It consists of 256 kB or 512 kB of very fast SRAM memory chips. Considering that a fast DRAM memory chip runs at 60 ns, or *Nanoseconds*, the SRAM processing speed of 8 ns to 15 ns is quite impressive.

Pipeline burst cache is a recent addition to the high-speed improvements for faster machines. It is significantly faster than SRAM cache, and improves the benchmark of a Pentium 120 by 20%. Refer to Chapter 2 to see how much improvement pipeline burst cache makes in 32 bit performance, as reported by Norton Utilities for Windows 95.

Memory is the easiest upgrade you can perform on a computer. You just find the lowest numbered open bank, and fill it with SIMM. Be advised, however, that memory can be the single most expensive item in the computer.

IDE I/O Cards

The IDE hard disk interface and I/O functions are normally paired in a single assembly. This is true whether they share the same add-on card or are incorporated into the motherboard design. The input/output functions normally supported include game controller and printer support. The primary I/O function is support for two serial-controlled devices, the mouse and the modem.

Most enhanced IDE I/O cards support 2 floppy disk drives, 4 IDE hard drives or CD-ROM drives, 2 serial communication (COM) ports, 1 parallel printer port, and 1 game controller port. The non-enhanced versions normally included in purchased computers only support 2 hard drives or CD-ROM drives. We will look at the devices that connect to the I/O portion of your computer later in this chapter. *Figure 1-2* shows an enhanced local bus IDE I/O CARD.

Figure 1-2 AN ENHANCED IDE I/O LOCAL BUS CARD

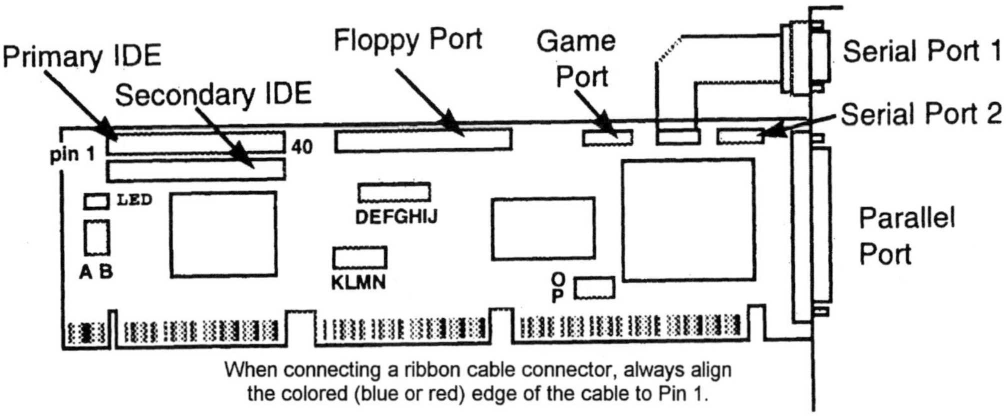

Primary IDE
Secondary IDE
Floppy Port
Game Port
Serial Port 1
Serial Port 2
Parallel Port

pin 1   40

LED
DEFGHIJ
A B
KLMN
O P

When connecting a ribbon cable connector, always align
the colored (blue or red) edge of the cable to Pin 1.

Video Cards

The monitor is useless without a video adapter card. This card takes the digital information from your programs and converts it to analog information in a format your monitor can display. Most video adapters have both text and graphics support.

To display text, the adapter looks up a typed character in its library, then displays it. Video graphics is a bit more complicated, so most video graphics display is a function of programming. Video adapter software allows the user to put lines, graphs, pictures, and most any type of image on a computer screen.

Certain video cards are referred to as *graphics accelerator cards*. They perform certain graphics display functions without interrupting the CPU. This is possible because they have special functions built-in, and can handle many operations called out by programs without processing data over the

bus. Any operation processed without bus interaction is very fast. Certain video cards even have their own built-in microprocessor.

Figure 1-3 STEALTH VIDEO IN VLB AND PCI FORMATS

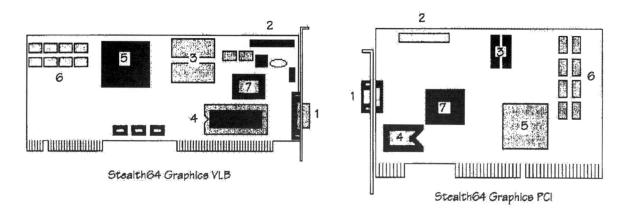

Stealth64 Graphics VLB

Stealth64 Graphics PCI

Video cards normally have RAM installed, to save having to go through the bus to use the motherboard RAM. Standard video RAM size is 1 Megabyte, which allows you to display 256 colors at 1024 × 768 pixels resolution. Two Megabytes of RAM is a better choice, because you can display 64,000 colors at the same resolution. This is a must for 15 inch and larger monitors.

Most high quality video cards are available both in VESA and PCI bus types. *Figure 1-3* shows a good quality video card in both local bus and PCI formats. Though 16-bit video cards are available, they typically have limited graphics support, and are not generally considered viable purchases for today's computers.

Speed is an important consideration in video processing. Purchasing a PCI or VLB video card will produce a considerable speed improvement over a 16 bit video card. Even greater improvement can be obtained by purchasing a video card with VRAM, *video RAM*, instead of DRAM. The advantage lies in the architecture. Video RAM has dual ports, and can be written to while being read, but single port DRAM has to accept one operation at a time. You will notice the difference, particularly if you use graphics-intensive games or CAD programs.

To work with a SVGA monitor, *Super Video Graphics Array*, a video card should have video accelerator functions and 1 to 2 MB of memory. Never buy a SVGA monitor without also purchasing a VLB or PCI bus video accelerator adapter card. For true colors and depth, a good video card is necessary.

If you have interest in running video graphics from CD-ROM or external video sources, consider a MPEG, *Motion Pictures Expert Group*, video adapter. This adapter supports video compression and decompression, allowing you to capture and display true motion video. Video adapters that support 3-D games and movies are available as well.

Hard Disk Drives

The hard drive installed in your computer is the primary storage and retrieval device. Most of the programs you run will be executed from the hard drive. Programs are read into memory, then executed. Data from the programs is stored on the hard drive to be used later. Any permanent data you save is stored on the hard drive in a format that allows you or the program to retrieve it when needed.

The hard drive, when new, is formatted into concentric tracks, that are divided into sectors. Each sector is 512 bytes in length. Since many files are larger than 512 bytes, the system will record as much of a file as will fit in one sector, then look for the next available sector. The remainder of the file will be stored in available sectors as they are located.

During formatting, sectors are grouped into allocation units. No more than one file can be written in the same allocation unit, but a file may span several allocation units. The number of sectors per allocation unit varies with the size of the hard drive. A 200 MB hard drive has allocation units composed of 8 sectors, but a 100 MB hard drive allocation unit is only 4 sectors in size. Note: you can get more data on a large hard drive if you partition it into several logical drives. This is particularly true if you have lots of small files. More on partitioning can be found in Chapter 5.

With all of this data stored on a hard drive, how does the computer find it? A portion of the hard drive is reserved to store a *File Allocation Table*, or FAT. The FAT stores the location of each part of every file, and updates itself each time the hard drive is accessed. The computer is smart enough to make a copy of the FAT, in case the original is damaged, if you have a disk manager utility program, as mentioned in Chapter 8.

A hard drive may be made of several disk platters, and many heads, to read from and write to the platters. This makes the hard drive fragile and sensitive to rough handling. Hard drives are factory sealed, to prevent dust from entering. The smallest dust or cigarette smoke particle can destroy a hard drive by becoming lodged between one of the heads and a platter. If this happens, all data on the affected disk surface will be unreadable, and lost. Care should be exercised when moving your computer or handling a new hard drive prior

to installation. The hard drive is also sensitive to motion, especially when the computer is turned on. Avoid moving a computer unless it is turned off.

The two primary specifications used in small computer disk interfaces are EIDE and SCSI. The recently added EIDE specification improves the IDE format to handle larger hard drives, and improves the transfer rate of data to 13.3 Megabytes per second. All IDE hard drives are supported by the EIDE format. There are other formats for disk control, but they are either obsolete or seldom utilized.

Figure 1-4 HARD DRIVE CONFIGURATION JUMPERS

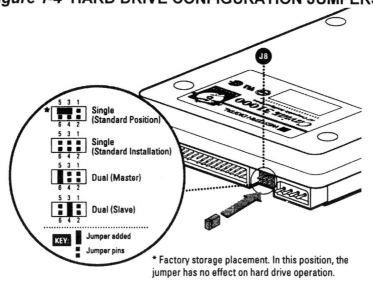

* Factory storage placement. In this position, the jumper has no effect on hard drive operation.

IDE hard drives are often recommended for several reasons, including ease of configuration, and standardization. The IDE control system is inexpensive, and is often included on the motherboard. IDE drives can be chained on the same controller, and up to four IDE drives can be easily installed. More are possible, but the installation becomes somewhat complicated. More on configuration in Chapter 5, and refer to *Figure 1-4* for a quick look now.

Regarding IDE standardization, some IDE hard drive manufacturers bend the standard a

bit. Occasionally different brands of IDE hard drives may not be compatible when installed together. The best approach is to install drives from the same manufacturer.

Who uses SCSI hard drives and why? The primary reason some people move to SCSI hard drives seems to be the capability of installing seven logical devices on one adapter. You can install up to four interface boards, but can only have a maximum of 24 SCSI devices. Each device must be hardware addressed with jumpers to a unique *logical unit number*, or LUN address.

Other reasons are some SCSI hard drives are a bit faster than equivalent IDE hard drives, and SCSI hard drives are available in extremely large sizes. A friend of mine recently installed a 9.1 Gigabyte SCSI hard drive! Why eludes me. The safer approach is to spend less on each hard drive, and use multiple drives. A hard drive crash is less traumatic if you have multiple drives. You only have to replace a portion of your total storage capacity, and the cost is much lower.

While on the subject of hard drives, here's a useful offshoot from the basic hard disk storage system: the removable disk drive system. Several types are available, and each one has its own noteworthy features. The Bernoulli drive, from Iomega (801-778-1000) is a popular choice, and among the first removable drives. It is one of the most popular removable drives, in sizes ranging from 20 MB to 1 GB. One feature of this drive is its nearly indestructible mechanism. It can be dropped from a height of 6 feet with no internal damage to the drive.

This drive could be the only drive in your system, which would allow you to remove your work and store it somewhere safe when you leave your computer. It can also be used in conjunction with an existing hard drive. The drive comes in both IDE and SCSI formats, as well as Iomega's proprietary interface. This drive normally takes one standard bay in your case. It is also available as an external drive, but is more expensive in that format since you have to pay for the additional hardware and power supply.

One disadvantage of this system is the lack of access speed. It is slower than newer hard drives. It is a smaller capacity storage medium, much smaller than the 2 to 3 GB drives commonly utilized. The clear advantage is the built in crash protection. The Bernoulli drive has flexible disks, and even if the head comes in contact with the disk, it

seldom damages it. You can even send the drive to another user through the mail without concern for damage, if properly packaged.

The Iomega Company's zip drive uses a 3.5 inch cartridge. Similar in appearance to a standard 3.5 inch floppy disk, this system can store up to 100 MB on each cartridge. The Zip drive is inexpensive, at about $140, and the cartridges run about $15. This system could replace your hard drive, but capacity is a limitation. A better use is as a backup system.

Another popular removable hard storage medium is the SyQuest drive. SyQuest (800-437-9367) has a line of removable hard drive cartridges with capacities up to 270 MB uncompressed. Disadvantages include small capacity, slow access speed, and the requirement of a SCSI interface for the drive.

Zone bit recording, ZBR, is the recording method utilized to reach the 270 MB capacity. Each disk is divided into zones. The longer outside tracks are divided into a smaller number of sectors, with a large number of bytes per sector. The inner tracks are divided into a larger number of sectors, but have a smaller number of bytes per sector, which increases the storage capacity significantly. Nearly all other systems stick with 512 bytes per sector.

SyQuest offers both internal and external SCSI drives, and several drives that operate from PCMCIA TYPE III slots. The *Personal Computer Memory Card Industry Association* bus is found in laptop and notebook computers, but this standard occasionally is found in desktop machines. These drives are small in size and capacity. They measure about 1.8 inches across, and the capacities are 60 and 80 MB.

These plug-in drives, mounted on add-on PC cards, can be removed and installed while your computer is running. Some US government offices use this method of storage, because such drives can be removed and locked up for security purposes.

Several companies offer tiny hard drives from 60 MB to more than 340 MB in size. The drives are so small they offer an easy and safe way to secure confidential data and back it up. Look for the greatest advancements in hard drive storage capacity in this type of drive.

While SyQuest is still fresh in your mind, consider their parallel port drives. They borrow the computer's parallel printer port, or supply an additional connector. The primary use I have seen for this type of hard drive is backup, but you can use it to secure sensitive data also. If you share data with another computer, this is a good way to do it. Several other companies use this type of interface.

MO, *magneto-optical* hard drives, were designed to resist the tendency of hard drives to lose data. Even the best magnetic hard drives will not hold data stored on them magnetically longer than several years. MO drives store data by using a laser to preheat a small section of the disk immediately prior to data storage. This is performed on a material with a high resistance to being demagnetized. The high heat produced by the laser reduces the material's resistance to being magnetized, enabling you to store data on it. When the area cools down it regains the resistance to being magnetized or demagnetized. This gives your stored data a lifetime five times the life of normally stored data. Common shelf lives exceed 10 years.

These drives have a relatively small storage capacity, normally 120 MB to about 250 MB. Unless you never backup your data, you will not need this level of protection for your data.

The *Write Once, Read Many times*, WORM drive is an optical storage device similar to a CD-ROM recorder. It typically stores data in the same fashion as hard diss, with concentric circles of sectors and tracks. The CD-ROM recorder stores data in a single winding track from the center of the CD to the outside.

There are no standards for WORM drives that all manufacturers follow. The size of this system varies from a standard 5.25" bay in your computer up to 12" desktop models.

Floppy Disk Drives

Your basic resource for installing computer software and transferring data to and from your computer will probably be your floppy drive system.

Floppy drives come in several sizes. The most popular physical size is the 3.5 inch, which will fit in either a 5.25 inch standard bay or the smaller half-height bay in your case. The older and less popular size is the 5.25 inch. Another common drive is the combination drive, which consists of a 5.25 inch and 3.5 inch, both driven by the same drive motor.

The first personal computers had no hard drive, but had two drive bays that housed one 12 inch floppy disk each. The boot drive was the upper floppy disk, and the bottom disk was the *working* disk. The only disk I could modify data on was the working disk. The storage capacity of these floppy disks was 150 kB and 300 kB.

Floppy drives have advanced significantly. The first small 5.25 inch drives were single sided, and could only store 140 kB on each disk. The current 5.25 inch drives support media densities of 360 kB and 1.2 MB. The 3.5 inch disk drives support 720 kB and 1.44 MB. A 2.88 MB version is available, but most prefer the less expensive 1.44 MB standard.

Since the specifics of data storage on a floppy drive represent a book in itself, let's greatly simplify description of the process, as in the hard drive section. The recording medium is different than a hard drive, and is made up of a thin, oxide coated polyethylene film. Hence the name *floppy*, or flexible disk. The 5.25 inch floppies are housed in a flexible case, while the 3.5 inch floppies have a hard plastic case. Unlike most hard drives, the floppy disk medium is removable. The two read-write heads remain in the floppy drive unit mounted in the computer.

The disk surface is written to by magnetizing a small portion of the surface by generating a magnetic pulse in one of the write heads of the disk drive. When the disk is read, that spot causes a magnetic flux to occur in the read head, producing a small electrical signal. This signal is added to other bits and decoded to reassemble the data you stored on the disk. This process occurs thousands of times per second during data storage and recovery.

How does the computer know where the data is stored on the disk? A floppy disk must be *formatted*. Formatting magnetically divides the disk surface into concentric circular tracks, of which each is divided again into sectors. In a 1.2 MB double sided high density floppy drive, there are 80 tracks per side.

1.44 MB 3.5 inch disks are the same. Each track on the 1.2 MB disk is divided into 15 sectors, while each track is 18 sectors for the 1.44 MB. Each one of these sectors constitutes an allocation unit. An allocation unit is a spot *allocated* on the disk for data to be stored.

Only single files or parts of a single file can be stored in an allocation unit.

The difference in the number of sectors between the 1.2 MB and 1.44 MB disks is the reason for the difference in capacity. During formatting, a *File Allocation Table*, or FAT, is created on track 0 of the disk. This track is where the index for the disk is stored. Each time a sector is written to, a record of the task is placed in the FAT. This is how the computer knows where data is stored on the floppy disk surface.

The 5.25 inch floppy drive, though obsolete by current standards, is still available. The floppy disk media comes in 360 KB and 1.2 MB. The 1.2 MB disks are labeled *double sided high density*.

The 3.5 inch floppy drive is the current standard. The media available for it consists of 720 KB *double sided double density* and 1.44 MB *double sided high density floppy diskettes*, which are readily available and inexpensive.

The 2.88 MB 3.5 inch *extended density* drive has been out for several years, but hasn't really caught on. Affordable CD-ROM equipment, with 600+ MB capacity, minimized the importance of the 2.88 MB floppy for program installation. The ED drive is a good concept, but may have been introduced too late. The added expense of a special 1 MB controller may also have influenced its lack of popularity.

A floppy disk overview

FLOPPY DISK CAPACITIES

disk size	tracks per side	sectors per track	capacity preformat	used by system	# available	max # dirs
360 KB	40	9	368640	6144	362496	112
1.2 MB	80	15	1228800	14898	1213952	224
720 KB	80	9	737280	12800	724480	224
1.44 MB	80	18	1474560	16896	1457664	224
2.88 MB	80	36	2949120	33792	2915328	240

Note that the maximum number of root directories is the same for the 1.2 MB, the 720 KB, and the 1.44 MB disks. The limitation is in the DOS file allocation table. To put more directories on a floppy disk, you must create subdirectories beneath the root directories. More on subdirectories is in Chapter 5.

Sound Cards

To enhance the computing experience and add complex audio to projects, games, and presentations, the multimedia sound card accessory was created. Sound cards often come as part of a *multimedia* kit, that normally packages a sound card, a CD-ROM, software, and speakers. They can be purchased separately, normally for less money. *Figure 1-5* shows a Sound Blaster compatible 16 bit sound card with wave table and SCSI interface. The Sound Blaster product line is the defacto standard in sound card performance and standardization. The MediaVision family of sound cards is a good alternative, because of the extensive MIDI support available, and the higher power output they provide. MediaVision cards also support Sound Blaster compatible modes.

Figure 1-5 16 BIT SOUND CARD WITH SCSI INTERFACE

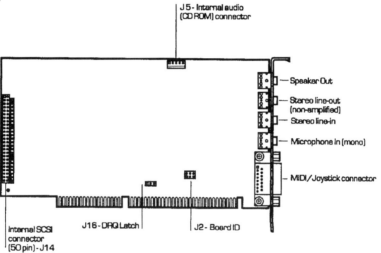

Most sound cards can record high quality sound from a variety of sources. These include a compact disk, remote stereo, video camera, or any MIDI device connected to your computer. *The Musical Instrument Digital Interface* built into most sound cards allows you to capture sound bits from keyboards, synthesizers, and a variety of input devices.

FM synthesis built into the sound card allows you to accurately reproduce up to 128 MIDI sounds and more than 45 percussion instruments. Some have actual samples of instrument sounds built in, and use a wave table for FM synthesis.

Mixer capabilities are a useful addition to sound cards. An audio mixer allows you to control sound levels, bass, and treble in program material you wish to record. A microphone jack is a normal addition to most sound cards, and so is voice recognition software.

Voice recognition software allows you to operate your computer by talking to it, by creating a voice-to-text table using samples of your voice reading certain words. After the computer stores your voice, it can recognize commands you dictate through the microphone attached to your sound card.

The sound card is a digital to analog interface that converts digitally stored information to analog sounds that speakers and headphones can play. Many sound cards double as an interface for a CD-ROM. If the interface is SCSI, the sound card will also control up to six other devices. The interaction between a CD-ROM and a sound card is digital. The only time the sound card provides analog output is when you are playing something through the speakers or headphones.

The technique sound cards use to record music and voice onto your hard drive is called *digital sampling*. The analog sound is broken into small fragments, and only a portion of these fragments is stored. If the fragments are small enough, and the space between the stored fragments is small enough, the sound can be reliably reproduced.

Most sound cards are at least 16 bit cards. A 16 bit card can break an analog wave into 65536 (or 64 K) fragments. If you use a 44 kHz sample rate to store stereo music, you will need more than 10 MB of disk space to store 1 minute of sound. This is why the average compact disk, with over 650 MB of storage capability, can only store about 1 hour of music, *but it is stereo!*

When recording high fidelity sound, it is necessary to go well beyond the limits of ordinary hearing. The reason is that many audible sounds are made by mixing sounds outside the range we can hear. We would notice if sound cards limited sample rates to the 20 kHz limit of normal hearing; in fact, you must sample at more that twice the normal hearing range upper limit of 20 kHz to obtain good quality reproduction. A 44.1 kHz digital sample produces a 22 kHz analog signal when converted.

The greatest advantage provided by digital processing in a sound card is the absence of noise. There is no tape hiss or static. Digital processing normally gives a signal-to-noise ratio of -90 dB. At this level, noise is inaudible.

The on-board *Digital Signal Processor*, or DSP, helps reduce any added CPU traffic by keeping most sound-related operations on the sound card. With no bus traffic to and from the processor for sound-related functions, there is less possibility for CPU slowdown when running complex sound and graphics operations.

The obvious advantage the DSP offers is speed, since the processor is not interrupted to handle sound processing. The DSP also handles the music synthesis and specialized digital effects required by many high end programs. Assembling the many notes for a variety of instruments would be an imposing task for the processor otherwise.

The minimum sound card you should get is a 16 bit type with a DSP function. Anything else is already obsolete, and will not handle future requirements. Expect to spend around $40 to $75 for basic sound support, and up to $225 for 3D full-featured wave table 32 bit sound and 64 MIDI voices.

The Modem

Communication with others is a principle requirement for today's computer users. The primary tool required for this task is a fax modem. Without a modem, you would have to hardwire computers together in a network to communicate with other users.

The modem gets its name from its principle functions: *MOdulator* and *DEModulator*. A modem has the task of modulating the digital information a computer provides into analog signals the phone system understands. When the analog signal is received on the other end of the communication link, the receiving modem demodulates the signal to digital information the computer understands.

The phone line, being an analog system, is full of noise. This noise affects the quality of transmission to and from the modem. Most modems have error correction functions built in to clean up poor quality communications, and can adjust the communication speed on both ends to optimize response quality.

Baud rate is a measure of the communication speed between modems. A baud rate of 300 means the computers are talking at about 27 characters per second. This number is derived by adding the 8 bits that define a character to 1 start bit, 1 stop bit, and the next start bit. We then divide 300 by the total (11) to get about 27 characters per second. *"Baud" is an outdated term now; bits and bytes per second is more accurate and correct.*

Two modems, when communicating, must operate at the same baud rate, and use the same communication protocol. Fortunately, faster modems are downward compatible with slower ones. Modem speeds can vary from 300 bps to over 56 kbps. A 28.8 kbps modem transmits at approximately 2800-3300 characters per second.

One protocol of choice is Zmodem batch, which sends data as a continuous stream. Error checking codes are inserted at certain intervals. If an error is detected, the affected portion of data is sent again.

Other protocols include Kermit, Xmodem, and Ymodem. These three send a block of data with error checking code attached and await a positive response from the recipient before sending the next block. This is very slow. Since Zmodem batch is a bi-directional protocol, error detection and correction is a continuously ongoing process.

Let's discuss **ITU-recommended standards**. The *International Telecommunications Union*, formerly the *Comité Consultatif Internal de Telegraphique et Telephone* (CCITT), was established to standardize worldwide telecommunications. The committee makes recommendations only, and companies can accept or ignore these suggestions.

All suggestions for standardization in small computers have a V or X prefix, for switched or non-switched phone networks respectively. Most systems are switched. All revisions or alternate suggestions have either *bis* (for second) or *ter* (for third) following the standard type. An example is V.32bis.

A V32bis modem can communicate at 14.4 kbps, but a V.32 modem can only run at 4800 or 9600 bps. The V.32bis standard is a modulation method. The V.34 standard is for the 28.8 bps modems. The V.42bis standard is a method of combined error checking and compression. Two V.42bis modems can communicate at speeds up to 57.6 kbps.

All modems use **communications software** to operate. When you get a modem, it normally comes with a stripped down version of a popular communications package. You may want a high performance software package to optimize use of your modem.

Some communications packages worth note are Qmodem (Mustang Software Co. 805-873-2500), Procomm Plus (DataStorm 314-474-8461), and WinComm Pro (Delrina 800-268-6082). There are also numerous shareware packages available, like Lcom, and BBS software like Wildcat, WWIV, and others.

Hayes compatibility is an important data requirement for modems. Nearly all modems are Hayes compatible; Hayes set the standard.

There are **two types of modems, internal and external**, each with its advantages and disadvantages. Both have a speaker to allow you to hear busy signals or ringing. External modems have a switch to turn them off. If you are security conscious, it makes sense to prevent access to your computer by turning your modem off when not in use.

External modems show activity with status LEDs on their front panel, so you always know what's going on. The disadvantages of external units are higher cost and the requirement for an external COM port. Internal modems are the most popular. They are their own communications port when installed, and do not require additional desk space. They do not have status indicators and cannot be switched off, however. They also eat up one of the valuable add-on card slots in your computer.

Fax capability is normally included on most modems available today. Any document you create can be faxed to a recipient with a fax modem or conventional fax machine.

CD-ROM Drives

Since the middle 1990s, a CD-ROM has become a necessity. The device that was once a nice option has become a key part of nearly everyone's computer requirements. The CD-ROM provides numerous benefits for home computer users, and the host of software available is endless. *Figure 1-6* depicts a CD-ROM drive.

The uses of CD-ROM for business are significant, but this book focuses on the home user. Since the price of CD-ROM games and entertainment packages has dropped significantly, people purchase computers with CD-ROMs already installed.

Home entertainment is one of the principal targets for CD-ROM software developers. Games, encyclopedias, music, art, and movies are transformed to CD-ROM software. Educational software is quickly and easily learned from a CD-ROM, and kids are quick to acquire the skills necessary to use the system. Several hundred books, or three hours of compressed video, can be stored on a single CD-ROM.

Figure 1-6 THE CD-ROM DRIVE

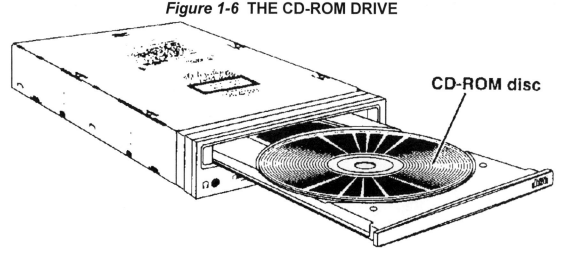

CD-ROM disc

The total sensory experience of a CD-ROM system makes learning easier. With more avenues to the brain, topics can be easily assimilated and retained. School topics become multimedia experiences, and learning becomes fun.

The CD-ROM has recently become a convenient medium for software installation, including operating systems, legal programs, medical software, pharmaceutical reference books, and desktop publishing software. The uses for this medium seem to be endless.

The CD-ROM was first marketed in the 1980s by Sony and Phillips Corporations. Its initial use was recording music without the analog noise common in existing systems at that time. Of course, home units could only play music. The recording system cost at that time was prohibitive.

A CD-ROM disk is made by burning microscopic depressions in the disk material with a miniature laser, in response to program data digital logic levels. This creates a pattern of *pits* and *lands.* Data is read from the disk by another type of laser. When the read laser is focused on the programmed portion of the disk, the pits do not reflect as much light back as the lands, allowing the read laser to easily distinguish the programmed bits. The digital *ones* and *zeroes* represented by the pits and lands are decoded, and the data is recovered.

Data on a laser disk is encoded in one large spiral track, winding outward from the disk's center. This single track is divided into about 270,000 sectors, if the laser that programmed the disk is a low frequency red laser. More than 5 times that many sectors are available with a green laser, but this technology is not yet commonplace. Each sector in both types is 2048 bytes. The sectors are numbered in .001 second increments, which allows the data to be easily located.

The rotational speed of a laser disk constantly changes with respect to distance from the disk center. This CLV, *constant linear velocity* method allows uniform data acquisition with respect to time, and is similar to the zone bit recording method used in some hard drives.

Like a hard disk, the speed at which a laser disk can transfer data to memory is far slower than direct memory access. The first CD-ROM drives had a data transfer speed less than 100 sectors per second. Since a sector is 2048 bytes, or 2 kilobytes, the first CD-ROMs could transfer (2 kilobytes times 100 sectors), or 200 kilobytes (200 thousand bytes) of data per second. By comparison, current IDE hard drives can transfer between 4 Megabytes (4 Million bytes) and 13 Megabytes of data in the same amount of time.

This category of computer accessory has improved substantially. Transfer rates for CD-ROM drives have been the primary performance increase. To put transfer rates in perspective, an old drive was rated about 150 kilobytes per second. A good 4X drive will transfer 600 kilobytes per second. A 6X CD-ROM increases this number to about 900 kilobytes per second.

Access time, the length of time the drive takes to find any sector, is the other measurement of CD-ROM performance. An old drive took 600 *milliseconds*, or ms, to locate data, and a 6X drive only takes about 100 ms to perform the same operation.

Remember cache memory? A good CD-ROM drive has a built in cache buffer. When data is transferred from the CD-ROM drive to the computer, it is temporarily loaded into cache on the drive. The data transfer to the computer can occur much faster and smoother this way. Most inexpensive CD-ROM drives have a 256 kB buffer, but a good drive has 2 MB.

Several companies offer CD-ROM caching software. These programs set aside memory in your computer to use as a temporary storage cache, for use while running programs on CD-ROM. The memory they set aside can be either on your hard disk or on your motherboard. Either way, the access time of the cache memory will be much faster than the CD-ROM access time, so your program will run faster.

There are other differences in CD-ROM drives. The most significant is the internal or external option. An external drive will cost more, but performance should be similar. Stay away from CD-ROM drives with their own proprietary interfaces, and pick a good IDE or SCSI drive that fits your requirements.

New and faster drives are constantly being designed. Stay at least one speed behind the pack to get the best deals. That $200, 36X CD-ROM drive will cost only $50 when the 48X drive becomes commonplace.

The CD-ROM recording system has become inexpensive enough for home use. You can bring a recorder home for less than $300. Many companies have their paper records scanned and put on CD-ROM, then use the recorder to archive duplicates of the data. With 650 Megabytes (or up to 4 Gigabytes of storage capability using compression) you could archive the complete records of a large hospital on a few disks.

CD-ROM recorders are becoming popular as backup systems, and for copying systems from one computer to another. Remember, if you purchase software, you normally agree to install the software on only one machine. You can get into serious trouble if you violate your software license agreements.

Please do not use a CD-ROM recorder to illegally copy or transfer software. To do so is copyright infringement.

Tape Backup Systems

The move to larger hard drives in computers today necessitates a backup system with large capacity. A good tape backup system will save you hours of frustration and yards of gray hair. Tape backups are inexpensive, too.

You can purchase a tape backup system that supports 350 Megabytes of storage on each tape for around $70. A good external drive that puts up to 800 MB on each tape is under $140. The tapes are also constantly coming

down in price. A five pack sold recently for about the price of a single tape one year ago. 250 Megabyte tapes go for about $7, and the 800 Megabyte Travan cartridges run $20. Tape backup systems operate between 4 MB and 12 MB per minute, depending on the hardware. A tape system accelerator card such as the Colorado Memory Systems FC-20 will give 12 MB performance to a 4 MB system. It works with any Colorado or HP tape drive designed for use on a PC. *Figure 1-7* is an example of a good tape accelerator card.

Most home users will not be interested in a tape backup accelerator card. The hardware compression utilized by the accelerator card is not compatible with most other backup systems, so you cannot transfer data on a compressed tape to another tape drive without the card. However, a tape accelerator card does help with two things: it decreases by at least 50% the time required to back up your computer, and it improves the data compression of your backup software.

These are parameters that only power users or office computer managers are normally interested in. *Do not buy a tape backup accelerator card if you don't plan on weekly system backups*. It's a necessary $50 to $150 investment only if you back up often.

The best part of a tape backup system is the ease of use. Most tape drives come with DOS and Windows backup software, which automatically configures the tape system for use. In the event of a massive hard drive failure, your tape backup system will save you hours of stressful data recovery.

Consider the 3 hours required to restore a system crash from tape backup. If you had to rebuild 1.6 gigabytes of installed software without a tape backup system, it might take several days, if you can accomplish it at all.

Figure 1-7 **A TAPE BACKUP ACCELERATOR CARD**

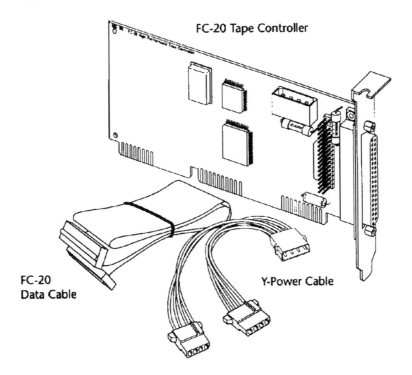

FC-20 Tape Controller

FC-20
Data Cable

Y-Power Cable

A backup system is only good if you use it. Do a full system backup as soon as you install the tape drive. Perform incremental backups weekly if you use the computer daily. Since the tape backup system is easy to use, take advantage of it. You will be ecstatic the first time you have to recover data, or must rid your system of a computer virus by re-formatting your hard drive.

The Monitor

By now, you know how important a good monitor is. Your monitor will probably outlive everything else in your system, so get exactly what you want. If you will be happier with a larger monitor, get it now. They normally go down in price slowly, unlike other computer accessories.

It is necessary to mention the monitor sizing scheme. When you buy a 14 inch monitor, you can only use a portion of that 14 inches. There is a border of up to one inch all the way around the monitor screen. This border masks

a portion of the monitor deemed unusable due to screen curvature. Even a good 15 inch flat screen monitor has only 13.5 inches of diagonal viewing area.

Size is the most important feature. Get the monitor most comfortable to view, considering your software requirements. If you plan to do any CAD or schematic work, do not get a monitor smaller than 17 inches. Desktop publishing or heavy 3-D gaming requires a minimum of a 15 inch monitor. The standard 14 inch monitors are simply inadequate.

What To Watch Out For

Bench test your monitor before purchase at a computer retailer. Check the outside corners for fuzzy display areas, or distortion. Ensure that you can set brightness and contrast controls for comfortable viewing without overdriving the screen. Overdriving is evident as poor focus and excessive glare, and will prematurely age the monitor. Reflected glare from the monitor face can also be a problem, though many monitors come with a anti-glare screen.

Get a *green* monitor if possible. A green monitor has circuitry that makes it *sleep* if left unattended for a period of time. A *sleeping* monitor consumes very little energy. Since an average monitor can consume 150 watts of energy, a green monitor can save you money. The EPA Energy Star seal is on each green monitor, identifying it as a energy conserving computer accessory.

Be sure to get a good quality .28 dot pitch or better SVGA monitor. Many vendors will try to get rid of their obsolete .39 dot pitch monitors, so don't be the next victim. You *will* notice the difference.

The Mouse

In the beginning of personal computing, a mouse was a rarity on a DOS computer. The keyboard was the primary input device. With the advent of sophisticated graphics-intensive programs, the mouse has replaced the keyboard as the primary input device.

The advent of Windows and Windows-based programs occurred primarily because of the Macintosh success story. If you give someone an easy-to-use computer without a maze of commands to learn, they will learn quickly and enjoy using it. A clean graphic user interface with icons, a mouse, and very little memorization makes for a comfortable computing environment.

When choosing a mouse, consider the fact that a $10 mouse will do most of the things a $100 mouse will. If you have no particular reason to choose one mouse over another, consider saving money and purchasing an inexpensive Microsoft compatible mouse instead of the high priced spread.

If you have applications that require a high resolution mouse, like engineering, drafting, or design, you will have to purchase a more expensive alternative. You might spend a few bucks more and buy a stationary TrackBall. A primary reason is you might have no desk space for a conventional mouse and pad. The other reason is the increased resolution obtained. A TrackBall is nothing more than an upside down mouse. The ball is rotated with the thumb, and the rest of the mouse just lies there on the table.

The mouse plugs into a serial port on your computer. As you move the mouse, the ball moves two or more wheels. The wheels have holes or indentations, which interrupt a light path to photosensitive diodes or transistors. This creates a data stream, which enters the computer through the serial port. Using the buttons causes additional data bits to enter the data path into the computer. The I/O card or built in function decodes the data stream, to know exactly what the mouse pointer is pointing at when you make a selection. The mouse, like all accessories, must be configured in software to be useful. Windows 95 and several other operating systems have embedded plug and play software functions to detect and configure your mouse. Other software requires you install a driver for the mouse, and one normally comes with it for that purpose.

When purchasing a mouse, be certain to get a high resolution mouse if you will be doing high level design work. If you just want a pointer, and don't need the resolution, you can get off inexpensively. Since even the inexpensive type lasts a long time, do not buy a high end one if you don't need it.

The Keyboard

The keyboard is the most abused part of your computer. You will bang on it when things don't work, spill your drink of choice into it, and fall asleep on it occasionally. It will, however, give you the least trouble of any part of your computer.

Unlike the typewriter, the computer keyboard has no real standardization. You can blame the independent manufacturers for this. Everyone has their own idea of which keys should be placed where, and how many function keys are necessary.

Newer keyboards are almost microcomputers themselves, with a ROM based operating system and processor installed on their main boards. They store keystrokes and generate unique codes for each key pressed. They even know when you want to repeat a keystroke.

So many specialized keyboards exist, and you may go crazy trying them out, but try you must. This keypad will be in front of you for a long time. Purchase your keyboard only after trying out many different types. Like the mouse, you can spend $100 or more on a keyboard, or as little as $9. Pick a keyboard you will be happy with many years, since they last a very long time.

Extras

Now for the fun stuff. Have you ever looked at a picture and thought you would like to see it every time you turned on your computer? You may have several pictures you like enough to view often. All you have to do is scan the pictures into your computer.

A **scanner** is an option used a lot. You can make a multitude of flyers for friends and clients, and a basic color scanner makes this easy. The price of a usable single pass color scanner is in the $100 to $300 range, and it makes an economical and enjoyable addition to your system.

When you look for a scanner, insist on a TWAIN-compatible scanner. *Technology*

Without An Interesting Name is an *Application Programming Interface*, or API specification several large corporations jointly developed. This helped standardize the device drivers for the scanners, so you will not have configuration headaches using your scanner in different programming environments.

The Printer

To round out the computer peripheral and accessory section of this book, let's look at printer types. Remember this one point, however. Printers typically outlast most of your computer accessories, so get one you can live with a long time.

The first color printers **were dot matrix printers** with a color kit. The color kit consisted of a special ribbon with three color bands and a black band. Special software was necessary to drive the print head up and down the ribbon to produce color images.

The advantage of current dot matrix printers is cost. The lower initial cost is added to the lower cost per page of printed material. A good dot matrix printer can be purchased for around $140 with the color ribbon and software. Dot matrix printers come in narrow and wide styles. The wide style can handle the 11 by 14 inch paper commonly used to print ledgers and spreadsheets. Most dot matrix printers use fanfold continuous feed paper.

Disadvantages of this type of printer include lower print quality than other types of printer and extremely slow color printing. The noise of a dot matrix printer can be uncomfortable. They have a very small print buffer and are generally without scaleable fonts, too. Scaleable fonts are text styles that can be made larger or smaller by newer printers.

Ink jet printers normally cost from $140 to $600, and are a quantum leap from the dot matrix printer. Hewlett Packard invented the ink jet printer, and holds a vast portion of the current market share. A color ink jet printer from HP will cost about $200 with the color kit included. A competitor, Digital Equipment Corporation, or DEC, often advertises their color ink jet printer for about $180 and includes a $40 mail-in rebate.

Several ink jet printer manufacturers include a fax machine in their printers. They can be used as a copier or printer. HP and Ricoh both make these machines.

Laser printers do premium black and white printing. They normally have resolution of 300 to 600 dpi (dots per inch). The common resolution for a low cost ink jet printer is also 300 to 600 dpi, but the laser image always looks better. Today's laser printers are available for $250 and up.

Laser printers, at 4 to 25 pages per minute, are the fastest printers available for home computing. The technology behind the laser printer is a book in itself, but this description fits most of them. A laser printer utilizes complex optics and mirrors to write text and graphics onto a photosensitive rotating drum assembly. The laser beam is swept across the drum, pulsing in intensity to identify light and dark areas. The dark areas, where printable material is encoded, are sensitized by the laser beam onto the drum. As the drum rotates through the toner material, the sensitized areas pick up the carbon toner. Paper is pressed against the drum, picking up the toner. The paper is heated, fusing the toner to the paper. Except for the laser, this system is similar to a standard copy machine.

The prices range from about $250 for a good 4 page per minute 600 dpi unit to around $2500 for a 24 page per minute unit with 1200 dpi quality. They can not commonly do color at an affordable price. If you wish to spend $2000 to $10,000, you can have a Xerox or QMS

laser color printer. This price is ten times the cost of a good color ink jet printer.

Laser printers can use lower quality paper easily, but some paper will eventually clog up the printer. The high level of solid particulate material associated with cheap paper eventually impairs the workings of the laser printer, so clean the paper path often, if you use cheap paper.

Laser printers format data before printing, so a print buffer of 1 to 2 Megabytes is a necessity. Most laser printers have built in scaleable fonts for more flexibility in printing. These two options add to the printing speed.

A typical laser printer will get 2000-4000 pages or more from a toner cartridge. Most ink jet printers can only print about 300-600 pages per ink cartridge. The average price for a laser toner cartridge is between $40 and $100, while color ink jet cartridges cost $20 to $40. Expect to spend more time maintaining an ink jet printer than the average laser printer, because of the difference in toner and ink capacities.

In summary, if you only print an occasional letter, get an inexpensive dot matrix printer. If you often print in color, and don't need laser quality resolution, get a good ink jet printer. If you print tons of high quality black and white letter quality documents, get a laser printer. The most versatile setup is to have a 600 dpi laser printer and a color ink jet printer.

Power and Line Voltage Conditioning

Nearly everyone has experienced a power blackout or brownout, which can be harmful or destructive to your computer. If you live where lightning strikes are commonplace, you know the amount of damage they can cause.

Plan on purchasing a power strip with surge protection for your computer. Power surges, caused by line voltage fluctuation, often damage or destroy home electronics. They can be caused by lightning strikes, power pole damage, or any sudden load on the power grid in your area. This will add $30 to the price of your system, but this is an inexpensive insurance policy, considering the investment.

An *Uninterruptible Power Supply*, or *UPS,* is a necessary purchase if you live in a environmentally challenged area. Blackouts, brownouts, and electrical storms are largely ignored by a computer plugged into a UPS. A UPS is a stand-alone power source that converts direct current voltage from a set of internal batteries into 60 cycle 120 VAC. The UPS is plugged into the wall socket, and the computer draws power through the UPS from the wall socket. If power is interrupted for any reason, the UPS starts up immediately and supplies power to anything plugged into it, without any interruption in service.

When choosing a power-conditioning device, be certain that you assess your needs honestly. Trying to save a few dollars now can cost you hundreds later.

We have looked at truth in advertising in the computer store, studied types of systems, and examined in reasonable detail the components of a computer system. We have reviewed peripherals and accessories. With the information presented up to now, you can make intelligent choices regarding the specific components you want in your system. When you decide on your components, you will have created an integrated working computer model. This model will serve as your dream machine, for comparison with store bought systems.

Put together on paper the system you desire. Compare your dream system to actual hardware on sale at a retail vendor. Try out a system that closely matches your model, and be certain your plan has omitted nothing important. When you finish this exercise, you have removed all doubt that you will be satisfied with your system.

Now, let's move on to Chapter 2, and see how much money you are about to save.

Your Notes

PERFORMANCE AND PRICE

Topics
How much can you save?
Packaged systems and beating their prices with better components
Building the computer you want
Outlining some basic examples

Figures

How Much Can You Save?

This is the real question, and the reason for writing this book. Let's look at some sales literature…

Another big sale weekend and I have the advertisements for the weekly sales in front of me. Disregarding the department store advertisements because the prices I see are too high, I peruse the electronic specialty stores and computer outlets for the best current prices on several systems.

Electronics superstore #1:	System price: $1499.97, a complete MMX and MPEG system: Pentium 200 system with 4.3 gigabyte hard drive, 15 inch .28 dot pitch monitor, mini tower, 2 Megabyte Trident video card, 56k fax/modem, 64 megabytes of RAM, 24 speed CD-ROM and sound card, satellite speakers, 3.5 inch 1.4 megabyte floppy drive, mouse, and keyboard. *Software:* Windows 95 (without manuals), Microsoft Encarta, several generic shareware programs worth $20.00.

Let's try to beat it.		
	Motherboard with pipeline burst cache and CPU:	179.00
	Case (mini-tower):	19.00
	64 Megabytes of EDO RAM:	110.00
	3.5 inch 1.44 Megabyte floppy drive:	20.00
	Internal 56k fax/modem:	40.00
	101 style keyboard and 3 button mouse: 15.00	
	PCI PnP Stealth 2 Megabyte video card:	49.00
	4.3 Gigabyte hard drive:	165.00
	15 in. digital super vga monitor .28 dot pitch:	159.00
	32X multimedia CDROM pkg. with 16 bit stereo sound card, speakers, and 10 CD ROM titles:	115.00
	Software: DOS 6.22 and Windows 95 pkg.:	99.00
	Microsoft Encarta 96 and 10 titles:	39.00

Grand Total: **$1009.00**

Difference in price: **You save $ 490.97**

You also get much more software, 10 titles with the Encarta bundle and 10 titles with the CD ROM bundle. The important hardware improvements in your package are the better PnP motherboard, the pipeline burst cache, the EDO RAM, and the fast Stealth PnP video card. Remember, most fast food systems will not come with the best components. It is difficult for the average fast food computer store to get good prices on high performance components. Also, you will not experience the nightmare of chasing down a hardware interrupt or DMA conflict because of these components. You also get a 32X CD-ROM!

The superstore's offering is a fairly good price on a system, but can be easily beaten, and without doing a lot of running around. Now, let's look at some more locally advertised bargain priced systems, and see if we can beat them, too.

The Hot Rod System

John Q. Public just won the lottery, but not big enough to quit his job or buy that new Rolls. He must reward himself, however…

The catalog shows a full-blown Pentium II-333 system. He knows Pentium II chips are out that clock at 400 MHz and faster, but realizes they are not cost effective, and benchmark about the same as the 333 MHz chip when installed in a system, so he goes the safe route. He will get the 400 MHz chip when prices fall.

Computer catalog price:	System Price: $3119.00, full MMX and MPEG system: Mid tower Pentium II-333 system with 64 megabytes of SDRAM 512k of pipeline burst cache, 5.1 gigabyte hard drive, 17 inch SVGA monitor with .28 dot pitch, 4 megabyte video card, 32 speed CD-ROM multimedia system with speakers, 56k fax/modem with voice capability. Mouse and keyboard. Software: Microsoft Windows 95, Office 97, Bookshelf.

He comes to you gloating, informing you this is a one of a kind super sale, and you will never find a system this good for the price. It is a good price indeed, but let's just see.

Do it yourself:	Motherboard with pipeline burst cache and CPU:	595.00
	Case (medium tower):	45.00
	64 Megabytes of 10 NS SDRAM:	122.00
	3.5 in. 1.44 megabyte floppy drive:	20.00
	Internal 56k fax/modem:	40.00
	101 style keyboard and 3 button mouse:	15.00
	PCI Diamond Stealth 3D MPEG with 4 MB of VRAM (high quality video card):	75.00
	Western Digital 5.1 gigabyte IDE hard drive:	209.00
	17 in. Shamrock digital monitor, .28 dot pitch:	299.00
	32X multimedia pkg. with AWE 64 sound card:	115.00
And, optionally, add these:	Altec Lansing sub-woofer and powered speakers (Price shown later, on next page)	
	Software: DOS 6.22 and Windows 95 package:	99.00
	Microsoft Office Pro7.0 with Bookshelf:	189.99
	Total, to match John's system:	**$1823.99**
	Difference in price: You save $1295.01	
	Now, add the optional explosive speakers mentioned above:	109.00
	Total, to blow away John's system:	**$1932.99**

And so, once again, we beat the unbeatable price, with quite a bit of margin.

Beating A Bargain Priced Pentium System

Why would anyone want a bare-bones Pentium computer today? Ask any student who needs a computer, but doesn't have $1000 to spend.

Most stores have the come-on computer attractively priced. It is usually not processor-upgradeable, and comes with a minimum of bells and whistles. Here's a sample.

Local computer outlet:	System price: $799.99
	Mini tower or desktop Pentium 166 computer with 16 megabytes of RAM, 14 in. .39 dot pitch monitor, 1.2 gig hard drive, 3.5 in. 1.44 Megabyte floppy drive, windows pre-installed, DOS 6.22 pre-installed, 2 megabyte RAM video card, mouse and keyboard included.

I wouldn't even think of buying a new system with these parameters. There are too many places that sell used systems like this for $500 to $700, as excellent starter systems. You can even find good 486 systems for around $350, if your needs are simple. Our objective now is to beat the price, with margin, while maintaining the option to easily upgrade to a faster computer later. The add-on components will also be Pentium II compatible. We will also include a much better video card and larger hard drive as well as more RAM.

Do it yourself:	
PCI motherboard with built in IDE/IO, including Pentium 166 MMX CPU: (upgradable to Pentium 200)	149.00
Case (mini-tower):	19.00
32 Megabytes of SDRAM:	50.00
3.5 in. 1.44 Megabyte floppy drive:	20.00
101 style keyboard and 3 button mouse:	15.00
PCI plug and play 2 Megabyte video card:	29.00
2.1 Gigabyte hard drive:	119.00
14 in. SVGA monitor .28 dot pitch:	135.00
Software: DOS 6.22 and Windows:	99.00
Grand Total:	**$635.00**
Difference in price:	You save **$164.99**

The real importance isn't savings, but the ability to upgrade this system later. Everything is PCI, which means all components will work with the fast Pentium processors. For example, the 200 MHz MMX is a drop-in upgrade, and will hop up this system beyond Pentium Pro speed. If you would rather upgrade to a Pentium II instead, the motherboard and processor are all you need to change, since the video card and all other components are already Pentium II compatible. *The items in bold print on the quote sheet are components that are better than those in the store-bought computer.*

The three systems whose cost we beat are priced about 10 to 30 percent below similar systems at most retail outlets. Nobody looks for the most expensive system when selecting a computer. That is why these systems were selected for comparison pricing. By building, you will save 10 to 30 percent more than this on typical computer prices.

By now you're probably convinced it is possible to build a computer and save money. I have looked at this reality through the years, and come to the same conclusion each time. Every time I see an advertised deal on a super system, I find it easy to beat the price by building it myself. Hence this book.

The most important fact remains undisclosed. We have been pricing complete systems that have generic components from inexpensive parts wholesalers. The components in most of these systems are not what you would pick if you had the choice. In fact, when I price components for a system to build, *I use prices of components I want in my system.* I purchase high quality components that can be upgraded if possible. PnP components and current model items are the standard.

My systems normally are 3 to 6 months more current than the computers sold in the stores. Why? I buy the newest components available at reasonable prices. Systems in most stores have been assembled and put in storage somewhere, then are bulk purchased by the retailers. I buy components a matter of hours before I build the computer.

Innovations are slow to filter into the retail computer marketplace. A recent example is pipeline burst cache. The article I wrote to local retailers and a local news group follows, and explains my frustration with some computer retail outlets.

The following article discusses a commonly overlooked motherboard characteristic that improves overall performance significantly.

The Case Of The Slow Pentium

Nowadays, the hot thing is to buy the fastest machine on the market when you upgrade, to eliminate being obsolete before you reach the parking lot.

There are, however, some other serious considerations often ignored by the need-for-speed crowd who buy the 'fast' systems.

When purchasing a packaged system designated as 'upgradable', assume your purchase is set up with some of the slowest components available, and consider the cost of faster RAM, faster cache, and a faster video card in the projected upgrade cost. Why? Because it is not cost effective for computer retailers to put the fastest and most expensive add-in components in their systems.

Never purchase a system based on processor speed alone. The benchmark data provided with this document shows why.

Note the top benchmark. This is a purchased Pentium 133 MHz system compared to a Pentium 90. The difference is insignificant, and certainly not worth the significant difference in price.

The bottom benchmark compares a Pentium 120 against the same Pentium 90 tested above. This is the expected increase in performance one would like to see from a faster processor. The primary system difference is I have set up my system BIOS parameters for faster performance and purchased the faster pipeline burst cache memory. The 7 Ns cache memory is a necessary addition to any processor faster than 90 MHz, and is seldom provided on the cookie cutter 100 MHz and faster systems. The cost of upgrading cache memory runs about $85.

The moral: Don't buy until you have a clear idea of the actual performance improvement you can expect, and never buy a system based on processor speed alone.

Shadows_Lair@msn.com

Benchmark 1

The below graphs show the speed of a system (*CPU, memory, motherboard*), compared to the speed of other systems for running common 32-bit applications. For example, a typical 90-MHz Pentium system is 20.4 times faster than a typical 16-MHz 386SX system for these types of applications.

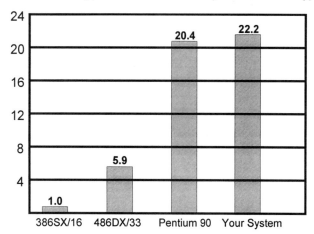

This Pentium 133 is not really optimized, as you can see. Tested while running 32 bit applications, the primary code it was designed to run, it performs barely better than a one year old Pentium 90.

Read on to find out why.

Benchmark 2

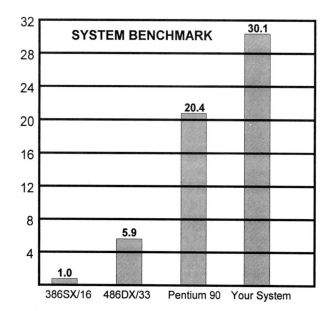

This is more like it. The computer benchmarked here is a Pentium 120. I wonder why the store-bought Pentium 133 benchmarked so poorly in the test above?

We know why, upon opening the case. The Pentium 133 does not have pipeline burst cache! It still has the obsolete dip cache, but the Pentium 133 is six months *newer* than the Pentium 120 used here.

This is exactly why I build my own systems. Don't get the idea I am a supreme expert whose intuitive senses ferret out the best deals. I am a horribly impatient shopper, and will spend five dollars more if I can avoid going to the store next door. The deals out there scream in every component distributor's handouts and in the computer magazines. Note: there is an extensive list of computer and trade magazines listed in Chapter 10.

Building The Computer You Want

We have examined how much can be saved by building our computer, and found out that some packaged systems are not what they seem to be. We have taken a good look at hard performance data from a recognized software company proving a take-out computer does indeed have that fast food quality. Now, let's take a good look at what is out there in the component categories, and then buy the components we want in our custom system.

An attorney came to me last year wanting a good, fast computer. He was primarily interested in a Pentium system, but thought a fast Pentium system was too expensive. I had been interested in several clone systems, strictly from a performance standpoint, and suggested he build one.

This is the computer he wanted, at the best price he could find on sale:

System price: $2199.00
Pentium 200 MHz mini-tower multimedia system.
32 MB RAM, 2.5 Gigabyte hard drive, 3.5 in. 1.44 floppy,
16X CD-ROM drive, 16 bit sound card,
PCI 2 MB video card, speakers, mouse,
keyboard, Win 95 and MS Works, mouse and keyboard,
15 inch .28 dot pitch monitor, 33.6 fax modem.

He already had a good laser printer; after all, he is a lawyer!

A couple of quick moves with a screwdriver opened the case to reveal the inner workings. We found a Trident 2 megabyte video card, which is an inexpensive, moderate speed video adapter. Two other cards were installed. One was a generic brand modem, the other a generic Sound-Blaster compatible 16 bit sound card. This motherboard was a good one, with enhanced IDE I/O on-board. It had 16 Megabyte of EDO RAM; the fast stuff. There was a slot for pipeline burst cache, but none was installed. This computer had 256 K byte of DIP cache. So much for a "fast machine"!

Do not plan on getting a look inside a fast food computer before you buy it. We were just lucky someone did not throw us out of the place. Once we knew what a packaged system had inside, it was time to go shopping. I suggested a 6x86 P166+ 133 megahertz system with a Cyrix microprocessor and the Intel Triton chip set. I knew this was a good system, having played with one about a week before the lawyer's urgent request.

I outlined the minimum requirements for a Pentium type system. The case, a mouse, a keyboard, a motherboard, the RAM, a floppy drive or two, the modem, a video card, a hard drive, a monitor, and a CD-ROM. Speakers and a sound card wrapped up the package. *Figure 2-1* is the benchmark for the Pentium killer processors commonly available. We were building faster! *We?* I don't *think* so!! I decided to let John go it alone this time.

Figure 2-1 BENCHMARK FOR CYRIX BASED COMPUTERS
(Motherboard includes Intel Triton chip set and pipeline burst cache.)

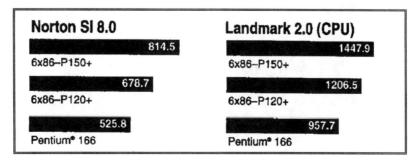

Needless to say, this system is extremely fast. Even the slower 6x86 chips are very fast.

Dear John was beside himself. He was torn between buying, out of fear, the much slower system, or jumping into the exciting world of building his own system. Deep inside, I knew his killer instincts would kick in, especially where money was concerned. He knew he would save money, and get a better system.

I helped him with the shopping, my *least favorite* part. He taught me some patience in this department, so I learned, too. I prefered to go one place and get all the components, but John is a miser, and got some great deals.

Motherboard with 6x86 P166+ processor and pipeline burst cache and IDE I/O and Intel Triton chip set	180
32 Megabytes EDO RAM	110
Case	20
Floppy times 2 (both 3.5 in., for disk copying office records)	50
56k fax modem	99
Keyboard and mouse bundle	20
Diamond Stealth 3D MPEG PCI 2 MB video card	59
15 inch .28 dpi Shamrock digital monitor	219
Toshiba 16X CD-ROM, IDE	89
DOS 6.2 and Win 95: (free with stuff)	00
Western Digital 3.1 Gigabyte hard drive	210
Sound-Blaster 64 (one of the best) (This is a great sound system):	125
Sony speakers:	30
Grand Total:	**$1211.00**

John just saved nearly $1000, and got a superb system he picked and designed himself.

Now comes the **easy** part. To give John an idea of what he was undertaking, I showed him *Figure 2-2.*

If that didn't terrify an attorney, nothing would. This array of components is the computer that Lisa, an assistant manager for a local drug store, built for herself using old spare parts and this book. In Chapter 5, the mess pictured below becomes a fully functional 486-based multimedia system.

Figure 2-2 **THE COMPONENTS OF A BASIC COMPUTER**

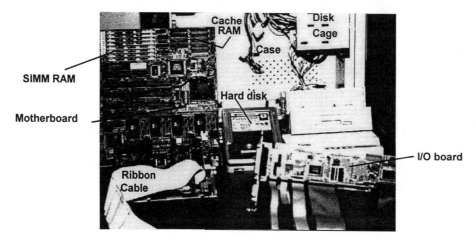

Before I go any further, I want to discuss one source for components. Most vendors advertise in publications distributed at no cost. The advertisers support the magazines, and the people get the publications free at local software and component vendor locations. Magazines like these are a primary source for components. Refer to *Figures 4-3* and *4-4*.

Figure 4-3 ONE GOOD PARTS SOURCE

Figure 4-4 ANOTHER PARTS SOURCE

Magazines like these are readily available at local component stores and computer outlets. Displaying these periodicals is not an endorsement. I am showing you sources commonly used for component procurement. Another good source is local swap meets. Many vendors increase their public exposure by renting booths at local swap meets and user group gatherings. Many computer shows also have a vendor section, where the latest available components are shown. Watch the local newspapers to find out when these shows pass through your area.

Back to John

Like Lisa, two weeks before, John had a pile of unfamiliar parts in front of him, and no idea of what to do with them. That is where this book came into play. John read Chapter 1 to review what he bought and why. (He already had read Chapter 2 out of context. That's why he knew to pick up a good video adapter and sound card.)

He performed the steps in Chapter 4 to procure the components, then read Chapter 5 on Lisa's exploits in building her computer.

Then he was ready. He installed the Pentium motherboard per the directions in the included manual, added the RAM, double-checked the jumper settings, then installed the video card, modem, and sound card.

He installed both 3.5 inch floppy drives, the hard drive, and CD-ROM. When he finished this portion, I took a look at his progress, and found every jumper and cable properly placed.

He finished connecting up the IDE hard drive cable and IDE CD-ROM cable, then wrapped up internal installation by connecting the I/O cables to the rear panel of the case. I suggested he leave the cover off.

He was one hour into the project when he finished connecting up the mouse, keyboard, and monitor. That's how long I take to build one, I thought to myself. I noted that Lisa took 45 minutes to get to this point, and wondered if it would be this easy for anyone.

He turned the computer on, and went into the setup routine. (He had done this before, when he installed a new hard disk in his old 386.) (All initializations and setup procedures are discussed in Chapter 5.) He set up the hard drive, floppy drive parameters, date, and time.

He booted up on his DOS 6.22 disk, ran fdisk, then formatted his hard drive. He installed DOS, then Win 95, and **had a perfectly operational computer within 2 hours.**

Everything worked the first time. I have built many computers, and have only returned two defective items, so I was not surprised. One was a hard drive that died after 24 hours, and the other was a motherboard with a bad CMOS battery. With today's quality control, you can be reasonably certain your components will work properly, if you follow basic handling precautions.

Chapter 5 has pointers on handling static-sensitive components, hard drives, CD-ROM drives, and other items that can be damaged with improper handling.

Now, let's move on to Chapter 3 and look at the software currently available. Remember, your choice of software may affect your hardware selection.

3 SOFTWARE FOR THE PC

Topics
Buying new software for less money
Reasons for buying certain types of software
Function overlaps between programs
Getting a good price

Figures

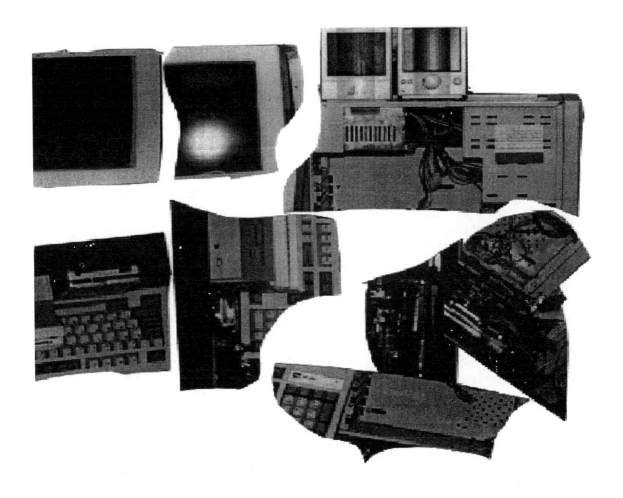

Software is the principal reason people buy computers. Without software, a computer is merely a box of hardware. Nothing was ever done with a computer without software programs running things. At today's prices, the software you purchase can cost more than the computer, but, unless you have software in your computer, the only thing you have to show for your expenditure is a high speed moron.

Just a quick interjection: *software* consists of lists of instructions written in computer language that tell the hardware in your computer what you want it to do. The *firmware* instruction sets written into your system BIOS as permanent memory configure the hardware to operate properly, but you must install programs to exercise any control over your hardware. As you must have guessed by now, the *hardware* in your computer is everything else, including memory and the case.

Thousands of software companies are hungry for your money and support. There are so many programs out there you could never install all of them in a single computer. You must choose the programs that support what you want to do with your computer. This chapter will help you do that, and in the process, you will save hundreds or even thousands of dollars.

Computer software is categorized according to basic functions. There are word processing programs (like the one building this book), database programs, DOS programs and utilities, Windows programs and utilities, games, and the list goes on. We will take a detailed look at many common categories later in this chapter.

Software prices vary significantly depending primarily on where you purchase it. There are also discounts for upgrades, if you already have (or can buy) a previous version of the software installed on your computer. You will find that good software packages often cost more than a computer, but never buy software until you get several price quotes.

WANT TO SAVE LOTS OF MONEY? TRY THIS TRICK

I read about and then tried a neat trick to reduce my software expenditures. Several local vendors in my area make a good business of buying outdated software from retail vendors. They pay pennies on the dollar. Then, they offer the software at substantially reduced prices to people who are not interested in the latest and greatest.

Here's the trick. You can qualify to receive substantial discounts on great software packages if you have older versions of either the same software, or a competitor's version.

Step by Step

Find a vendor of obsolete software. If you can't find one, call (800)-753-7877. The phone operator will take your address and send you a catalog of older software. You have just called Surplus Software, and it is a legitimate and very helpful company.

Then, identify the software packages you want. Look for software that offers either a competitive upgrade or special price for upgrades. Example: I bought an old version of *Microsoft Visual Basic* for $30. I never installed it. Instead, I ran over to **Egghead Software** with the unopened box, and bought the new *Visual Basic 4.0 Pro* for $94. The regular price for this software is $498.

I wrote this book with *Microsoft Office 97*. How did I get it? I bought *Word 2 for Windows* at $29.95, then went to a local computer warehouse where I paid $280 upgrade for the $540 software package.

By the time I was finished, I had *saved* over $1500, by purchasing either outdated competitor's software or older versions, then upgrading. I also had a cache of older software, unopened and unregistered, that I could sell to friends who were less upgrade conscious. I kept the old stuff, just in case.

Where do I buy software? I live in a very competitive area for computer products, so my possibilities are endless. I use various computer stores, depending on who offers the best upgrade discount. Other good sources I use are the many catalogs available. Here's a short list, but there are many more.:

Computer Discount Warehouse	(800) 330-4239
Computer World	(800) 221-8180
Dell	(800) 847-4051 or 4113
Desktop Publishing	(800) 325-5811
Egghead Software	(800) 344-4323
Global Software	(800) 845-6225
Image Club	(800) 661-9410
Insight	(800) 488-0002
Micro Warehouse	(800) 367-7080
MAC and PC Connections	(800) 800-1111 or 5555
PC Zone	(800) 258-2088
Power Up!	(800) 851-2917
Shareware Express	(800) 346-2842
Tiger Software	(800) 888-4437

I mentioned several types of software available. Now, let's take a closer look.

Every computer uses an *operating system* of some type. Many systems have more than one. DOS, Windows, Windows 95, OS-2, and Windows NT are the systems commonly used on the IBM-compatible family of computers.

Utilities are programs used as tools, to correct problems or tune your computer from a software standpoint. Spinrite, Norton Utilities, Checkit Pro Analyst, and PC Tools are examples.

Word processors, *spreadsheets*, *database programs*, and *drawing programs* are programs necessary to most computer users. I will go into detail on some of these later in this chapter. Suites are combinations of the above mentioned programs built into one large program. More on these later, too.

Figure 3-1 shows a sample of the programs used by a typical desktop publisher.

A desktop publisher often must utilize several programs to achieve a given task, and will purchase many more programs than the average user. Of course, he or she will have Windows 95 or NT. *Figure 3-2*, on the next page, shows a Windows 95 opening screen. We have looked at several aspects of software, including where to buy and tricks to get better prices. Now let's take a detailed look at the software types and programs within each common type.

Remember, there are more programs than we could possibly talk about. The ones I discuss are the most often utilized programs, according to the sales personnel I know.

Figure 3-1 A GOOD WINDOWS 98 ENVIRONMENT

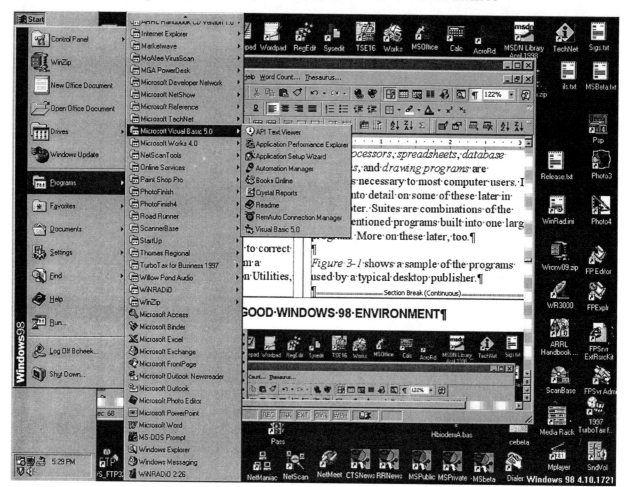

The best approach to deciding on the software you will be purchasing is the *try before you buy* technique. Several options are available to you. The best option is finding a computer in a store with the software you might be interested in purchasing.

Obviously, you will have to try several different stores, to get a good sample of software types, but it is worth your time. Many software titles fall short of your expectations, and software is **very difficult** to return to the store.

Try it before you buy it!

Operating Systems

DOS

I always start discussions of operating systems by talking about DOS, the *Disk Operating System* used by the industry for many years. Many people learned DOS long before Windows and other operating systems were developed. My DOS operating system has over 70 commands, but, like most people, I use only a few of them.

I recommend installing DOS regardless of the operating system you prefer. DOS is excellent for repairing problems in other systems, especially if you cannot properly initialize Windows or Win 95. The editing features of DOS allow you to edit the initialization files

Figure 3-2 WINDOWS 95 OPENING SCREEN

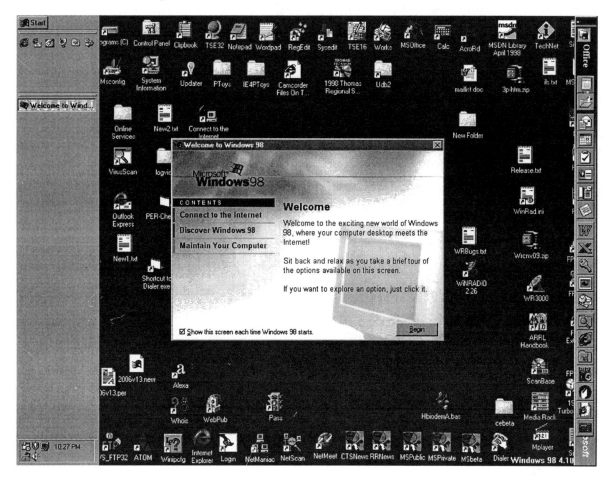

win.ini and system.ini and fix many problems caused by improper installation of Windows.

DOS is an excellent tool for emergency backups if you have a tape drive. (And you will have one, if you follow my recommendations!) In the event of a destructive crash, where you must format or replace your hard drive, you need only install DOS and the tape backup software to recover. DOS plus your tape software will finish the reinstallation of your software, and restore your old configuration.

If you install Win 95, be sure to keep DOS running under it. Win 95 allows you to restart in DOS mode, if you have to. Some older programs do not properly run in a Windows environment.

Windows 3.1

Though obsolete, this program will die hard. Many people refuse to make the jump to Windows 95. Windows 3.1 is a stable environment with which many people are very comfortable, and it will be around for a long time. It is a 16 bit operating system, however, so it is inherently slower than Win 95.

Windows 95, Windows 95b

This upgrade from Windows 3.1 is a hybrid system, with both 16 bit code and 32 bit code. It is measurably faster than Windows 3.1, and even more stable, especially running older DOS programs. The memory management is superior to any other operating system, and multitasking is easier also. You will find it easier to use, and upgrades are much simpler under Windows 95. Both hardware and software installations move much smoother.

Windows 95b, a product available only by purchasing a pre-built system, offers several improvements over Win95, but some compatibility issues occur. These are discussed in detail on page 70, since they will not apply to most readers of this book.

Windows 95 has its own programs, and 32 bit upgrades for most Windows 3.1 software are now available. I outfitted my Win 95 system with upgrades for Microsoft Office, Visual Basic, Microsoft Works, and Microsoft Publisher. Of course, I got them for a fraction of the new list price by using the competitive upgrade technique mentioned earlier in this chapter.

OS/2 WARP

This true 32 bit operating system includes multitasking, full DOS program support, full support for programs written for Windows, and large memory addressing. It is a good alternative to Windows 95, but takes getting used to. It has a bit less functionality than Win 95, but runs on less of a computer, and with a smaller RAM requirement. A 286-16 with 4 Megabytes of RAM (*there's one in the Smithsonian!*) will run this software.

Windows NT

Look for Windows NT to be the operating system of the future. It will run *very fast* on the RISC machines mentioned in Chapters 1 and 2. Though it is designed for high end users and work station environments, it will soon be in the home. Advancements by Microsoft will focus on Windows NT.

Why? It works on both CISC and RISC machines equally well. It is a true 32 bit operating system, with all the functionality of Windows 95. New software written with

Windows NT in mind will be streamlined and fast, and the NT front end is very easy and comfortable to use. It is also the most stable operating system in use today.

Now let's look at some useful program types other than operating systems.

Utilities

Utility programs are your personal in-computer toolbox. They do everything from clean out and organize your file system to repair damage to your hard disk.

SpinRite, from **Gibson Research**, 714-363-8800 is the first disk repair utility I used. The original version for MFM and RLL hard drives could repair bad portions of your hard drive. *MFM* and *RLL* are two obsolete hard drive technologies. Due to changes in hard drive architecture (like sector translation), SpinRite is limited to recovering data and moving it to a safe part of your hard drive. *Sector translation* is one way of fooling DOS and older computer BIOS into recognizing very large hard drives.

The *Norton Utilities* from **Symantec** at (800) 441-7234, encompass a large set of unique capabilities. Norton can repair damaged or lost files, recover recently erased files and directories, back up your computer, and run in the background. By running as a background process, Norton allows you to continue using your computer while it does its work.

The Windows 3.1 version 8 has a package of utilities for DOS and Windows, and sets up icons for both when you install it. The Windows 95 version includes a protected recycle bin, which means even when you empty the trash you still can recover most deleted files. Both include a feature called *image*, which creates a mirror image of your file archive table and stores it safely. If you lose your original FAT, you have a backup.

Remember (from Chapter 1), the FAT is an index to all the files in your computer.

Norton Utilities has the ability to automatically correct problems as they happen. You are prompted for this option when you install it.

Another utilities program is _PC Tools_, also by Symantec, which has embedded anti-virus tools, backup support, a shell program, and data recovery capabilities.

Checkit Pro, from **TouchStone Software**, (714) 969-7746, is an analysis program that keeps you updated on your computer's configuration. It can test performance and benchmark your system as well.

You will notice a lot of functionality overlap in the utility programs. It is not necessary to own more than one of these specialized tools. Personally, I prefer the Norton package. It has the most functionality in one program for my personal requirements.

Virus Detection And Protection

Now's a good time to mention computer viruses. A virus is a program designed by jerks, who know quite a bit about computers and software, to corrupt some aspect of your computer's performance. The virus is placed on a public access domain, like the Internet or an online service like Prodigy. When you access the infected file, the virus can be transferred into your computer.

Some viruses have completely shut down military defense systems, automatic payroll systems, and computerized phone systems all over the country. A virus in a company computer can wreak all kinds of havoc. In your home computer, a virus can format your hard drive, erase some or all of your data, modify the way some programs run, print obscene messages on your screen, or just make your speaker go off at unusual times.

Viruses can be tricky, and it takes special programs to get rid of them. Symantec offers a great anti-virus program in Norton. Another to check out is _F-Prot_, from **Command Software Systems**, (407) 575-3200, a program that finds as yet unknown viruses by looking for their characteristics.

McAffee, (408) 988-3832 is a pioneer in anti-virus programs, and constantly updates their _Virus Scan_ as new viruses arrive. Finally, try _Invircible_, from **CPC Limited**, (708) 729-3565. This program scans for polymorphic (moving) viruses by cleaning main and video memory, then searching quickly through all files by checking them against their signature. If a virus is hitchhiking on any of your programs, this program will find it.

Other programs have anti-virus routines embedded in their program set. DOS 6.22 is an example.

Note: To be effective, an anti-virus program must be updated regularly. Be certain you have a program **newer than 3 months old**.

Home Office Programs

Suites

If you're going to buy a publishing program, a database or spreadsheet program, and a graphics package I recommend purchasing a "_suite_". A suite "packages" several useful functions, or programs, in one package, and delivers a better bundle price than the individual elements. A suite includes a common interface between the packages, making it simple to move tables, graphs, and pictures from one document to another.

The _Lotus Smartsuite_ includes the latest _Lotus 1-2-3_ spreadsheet, the _Word Pro Approach_ publisher, _Freelance Graphics_, and _Organizer_ programs. It also includes a _SmartMaster_ template and _Lotus Assistants_, to merge the separate programs into a seamless system.

Separately, the programs would be very expensive, but you can find this package for under $400. Or, if you can find an older version, you can walk away with the upgrade for less than $170. This is less than any one of the included programs would cost.

Microsoft Office 97 suite is available in Windows 3.1, Windows 95, and Windows NT versions. It combines *Microsoft Word*, *Excel*, *Powerpoint*, *Scheduler*, and *Access* into one seamless system. The Windows 95 version is 32 bit, and at least twice as fast as the Windows 3.1 version.

To purchase Word, Excel, and Access separately, you would have to pay $900. The five program package retails for $550, but the upgrade price is only $330. (Less if on sale).

Obviously, if you need any two of the programs, it's cheaper to buy the suite. Purchasing the suite also buys you the seamless interactivity of the Office program, with its many wizard programs. These page wizards will auto-format any type of presentation document you wish. There is even the capability of placing moving pictures and sound in your presentation.

Since **Novell** and WordPerfect become synonymous, **Corel** took over the suite and renamed it to *Corel WordPerfect Suite 8*. The suite includes *WordPerfect 8*, *Quattro Pro 8*, *Presentations 8*, and a host of value-added applications and applets.

Envoy is a publishing program, *GroupWise* is an E mail, scheduling, and task manager. Presentations, like the Office program's PowerPoint, is a presentation designer. Quattro Pro, like Lotus 1-2-3, is an excellent spreadsheet, and WordPerfect is an excellent word processor.

Since the acquisition of Ventura Publisher, **Corel** created a suite of its own. *CorelDRAW* incorporates *CorelDRAW*, *Ventura Publisher*, photos, fonts and clip art. Less comprehensive as other suites, it's a good start.

Another basic suite is *Microsoft Works*, one of the many "freebie" programs normally bundled in the "*software package valued at $1000,*" included with a fast food computer system. At less than $80 retail, it represents a good start for a budget-minded user.

We should now go into depth on several of the programs that build a suite. Some people may not wish to buy all the programs in a suite, but rather own just one. Most programs in a suite are available individually.

Example: Microsoft Office includes Microsoft Word, Excel, and PowerPoint. If you only need Microsoft Word, just buy it, and save hundreds of dollars.

The following programs are suite elements broken out separately:

Spreadsheets

Business applications often require a method to display and manipulate large amounts of numeric related data. Programs designed for this purpose are called spreadsheets. They have the ability to handle accounting tasks, expenses, provide forecasting results, display and change inventory numbers, and create presentations of the results. Most spreadsheets will automatically perform math operations on large databases, as you require. Most will display data in graphic format if you request it. If you are like me, and your work sometimes follows you home, a spreadsheet program is critical.

Examples of feature-filled spreadsheets are *Microsoft Excel*, *Corel Quattro Pro*, and *Lotus 1-2-3*. Lotus is the original spreadsheet of choice for the PC, functioning as a spreadsheet, graphics package, and database. Microsoft Excel doubles as a database, and provides easy to use menus for the inexperienced user.

Quattro Pro looks and works like Lotus 1-2-3, so much so that Lotus attempted (and failed) to sue the former owner, Borland. The Borland package had several features that made it unique. Like Excel, Quattro Pro has pull-down menus, but unlike Lotus, Quattro Pro can print sideways. It can, however, manipulate Lotus spreadsheets. Hmmm....

Database Programs

Like spreadsheet programs, database programs are designed for the office environment. Most people will not need this at home, unless the *work fairy* loads your trunk with something special to take home with you. Like a spreadsheet program, a database can store and manipulate large amounts of data. Most have built in search and sort functions. Database programs store information, allow you to perform calculations on it, sort it, and create reports from the data.

Microsoft Access allows you to work with replicated copies of database files, then synchronize the changes with the master document. You can grab flat file data from a wide variety of different formats and create a relational database from the data. Application performance can be monitored and improved with the on-board performance analyzer wizard. This menu-driven application allows you to optimize spreadsheet manipulation. If this means nothing to you, do NOT buy this program because you don't need it.

I tried the DOS version of *dBASE* years ago, and abandoned it. The Windows version is much more user friendly, and an extremely powerful program. The on-board tutorials and help menus enable you to quickly learn the program, a real plus in today's stress-filled office environment. It's easy to click and drag forms, and reports are much simpler to create.

People who use **Corel** *Paradox 8* claim it has features that make it uniquely easy to use and learn. The main menu is full featured, and each menu item opens up sub-topics associated with the item, a great feature for the novice and casual user.

Word Processing

Processing data and thoughts into readable documents, and manipulating text, are the primary reasons computers are used today. That means word processing software is the most used software currently available. More than 30 word processing software packages are available in a variety of languages.

Spelling and thesaurus sub-programs are useful. Multiple formats are a necessity, including page layout, outline, and full page views. The ability to easily import graphics, text, and pictures is essential in today's desktop publishing environment. Let's look at some programs.

Microsoft Word is the program that stole me away from WordPerfect 5.1. Why? First, I had to work using Word for Windows in my occupation. The first thing I found out is you can use WordPerfect commands in Word. I thought, if they made things this easy for a WP nut like me, how hard could the program be to learn? I decided to try it at home, where I had the luxury to learn at a leisurely pace.

I never opened the book. When I wanted to know what action an icon performed, I put the mouse pointer on the icon, and the computer told me the function. After I wrote my first report, I tried the auto-format function, and achieved great results automatically.

I erased WordPerfect from my hard drive the next day, and upgraded to Microsoft Office.

Briefly, Microsoft Word 6 and Word for Windows 95 both have drag and drop for adding charts, graphs, and pictures to documents, and a full find and replace routine, spell check, thesaurus, and the capability to print or fax within the program.

I hate to admit it, but I haven't been back to the WordPerfect environment since version 5.1. It has the ability to do most of the functions of Microsoft Word. The interface has always been an easy one to learn, and the ease of importing text and graphics is wonderful.

Since the buyout by Corel, I'm certain WordPerfect will become one of the top contenders for the desktop publishing and word processing marketplace. Tremendous improvements have already occurred. Power users of the Windows version or WordPerfect insist that the program is more comfortable to use than any other desktop publishing program.

One of the first word processors was *WordStar*. I wrote my first fiction novel on it. It still resides on my old XT, and is the only word processor this machine will support today. I still use it sometimes, when my other machines are tied up.

Special note: I recently read that WordStar has one of the most full featured dictionaries available, so don't expect me to get rid of this very special program. Though WordStar has fallen behind the others in the bells and whistles category, I believe it is one of the easiest programs to learn and use for basic publishing.

Now, let's stray from the office environment, and look at some good software for home use.

Home Accounting

Home accounting is an important part of daily life, and programmers have recognized this. Two packages jump out at you.

Peachtree Accounting Windows version is the multi-user solution. Though it is a popular home accounting solution, it is network ready upon installation. It handles invoicing, general ledger, budgeting, receivables, and numerous other operations. The price is less than $120, making it a realistically priced package for your home office.

Microsoft Money, sometimes a freebie, is a more basic program catering to the casual home user. You can schedule, manage, and pay bills with this program. You can even print your own checks. It has a retirement planner built in. If you have to pay for the program, it is under $15 for the Win 3.1 version and under $30 for Win 95. Be certain you give it a try, especially if it's free.

Quicken, from the co-op created by the merger of **Intuit** and **Chipsoft**, is a full-featured home and office accounting package. Properly kept records will merge with *Turbotax* at tax time, and create a complete tax return with minimal input from you. Your primary contribution will be the signature at the end of the tax form.

Quicken offers full-featured interaction with your banking institution. With a modem, you can perform most banking tasks through the phone lines. Quicken has investment advice, home inventory, and a full video tour, all in one package.

A quick note on the subject of banking over the internet. You can be certain that someone is watching every aspect of any transaction you make. Keep your banking transactions private by using a modem along with the phone number supplied by your banking institution. Do not use the Internet. Also, keep in mind the lack of security on the Internet when you are tempted to give out your charge card number. Many people have had their number needlessly stolen.

Now, step into my office. These are the two programs I use the most.

Programming And Development Tools

Microsoft Visual Basic for Windows 95 revolutionized the programming environment of Basic. The interactive tutorial is a modular, completely interactive course with flexible search routines, good notes, and sample code. This program is the fastest way I have seen to create clean good code and state of the art solutions to programming issues.

Microsoft Visual C++ is for C programming what Visual Basic is for Basic programming. Version 4.0 introduces the Component gallery, a one step storage area for reusable objects. The *Microsoft Foundation Class Library*, or MFC, contains more than 120,000 lines of code in 150+ classes. This proven and tested code enables you to get on line quickly. The application wizards you can create easily will double your throughput.

Print Shop Programs

There are quite a few graphics programs that allow you to design and print color cards, posters and envelopes. Examples include:

The Print Shop Deluxe CD Ensemble, from **Broderbund Software**, comes on one CD-ROM or a large handful of 3.5 inch floppies. You can pick the project you wish, then choose graphics from a long list of candidates. This program supports greeting cards, labels, signs, calendars, and more. With more than 4500 graphic images to choose from, you may never use the same one twice. Note: you can custom design envelopes, too. It runs in Windows and Windows 95.

The special option that *Announcements*, from **Parson's Technology** offers, is the capability of making large format posters. The program

divides the poster into 8.5 x 11 inch modules, and configures your color printer to print each module separately. You can attach the pages together to make a large banner if you wish. Thus, you can make great announcements and large banners with relative ease. It is available in CD-ROM format, or on 3.5 inch floppy disks, for Windows or Windows 95.

Studio M is a program that allows you to introduce multimedia to your presentations. You can create speaking greeting cards and moving e-mail. It has an easy to use interface, so learning the program is simple. You can personalize sounds and morph between two different photos. Available in 3.5" floppies.

Random Acts of Programming

There are so many programs out there! Here are just a few that caught my eye.

Anything that can create a television image can be captured in your computer with *Snappy for Windows*. Camcorder images, VCR, and Laser disk outputs become inputs for your computer enjoyment. A morph program is included to further manipulate the images. Stills can be created from any of the inputs listed above, and more.

Easy to use movie file editing, more than 70 filter effects, and a multiple document interface makes *Corel Photo Paint* an excellent addition to your computer. Though this is a full-featured paint and edit program, you will find it easy and convenient to use.

Autodesk's *Animator Studio* has the ability to create animated presentations for games, web site logos, and audio visual presentations. The true color environment enhances the full motion and sound creations you generate. This program requires a CD-ROM.

Learn about the body with a true 3-D full motion movie program. See the human anatomy as you have never seen it before. Rotate 3-D representations, zoom in, and out. _BodyWorks_ is probably the best reference module of its kind. You will need a 4X CD-ROM or faster to get full benefit from the solid model rotation capability of this program.

The _Microsoft Encarta_ encyclopedia is extremely easy to use. It has pull down menus, full color video presentations, and stereo sound. Microsoft Encarta is available exclusively on CD-ROM.

Over six hours of multimedia entertainment is available with _Grolier Encyclopedia_. Full narration on complex topics is included. This program is available on CD-ROM only.

This heavily endowed and well-animated multimedia screen saver is a favorite. You will spend hours just viewing some of the many options available while using the _After Dark_ screen saver. This program can be found living on 3.5 inch disks or CDROM.

Several packages are available for this screen saver, including the "Outer Space" and the "Sierra Club" collection. With _Microsoft Scenes_, you can customize your own screen saver using pictures you choose. I have included several dozen scanned photographs in my collection. Available on 3.5" disks.

A must if you have Quicken, _TurboTax_ is an easy way to handle even fairly complicated tax preparation. I have legitimately saved many thousands of dollars on my taxes using TurboTax, and can recommend no better program for doing personal taxes. Like _BodyWorks 5_, _It's Legal_ comes to us from **Parson's Technology**. _It's Legal_ is an excellent source for legal documents of all types. I have saved many hours of a lawyer's time using this program.

Parsons Technology also has a great _PDR_. A _prescription drug reference_ is a necessary product, notably if you have small children.

While on the subject of Parsons software, I want to mention their tax software. Their _Personal Tax Edge_ program is less costly than TurboTax, and will suit many individual tax preparers just as well.

If you have kids in school, consider _Mathcad_. You can make full graphic representations of math equations, enabling you to get an easy grasp of complex problems. Inserting math equations and graphs into existing documents is easy with Mathcad.

Though the Internet is a library in itself, perhaps the best way to surf the net is _Netscape Navigator_. Available in 16 bit for Windows and 32 bit for Win 95 and NT, this program is full of single click options. Get the _PowerPack_ for additional functionality.

There are so many programs available, this chapter barely scratches the surface. There's software for just about anything you want to do with a computer.

Decide carefully on your software purchases. Read the reviews, literature, or box carefully before you make your purchases.

Check for functionality overlap between software packages. It is expensive to buy two packages that provide the same functions.

One more thing about software: I like to try before I buy. In most cases, this is impossible, unless your friend has the program, or a computer salesman gives you a demonstration of the program.

The **Software Dispatch Company**, (800-289-8383), will send you a CD-ROM with programs on it. You can try them out with a *software key* for a limited time. A software key is a program that allows you to use the programs you might like to purchase. If you like them, you buy them, and the company "unlocks" the programs so you can install them on your computer. This is one CDROM that the manufacturer welcomes you to pass around to your friends.

When you want to buy a program, they give you a password over the phone that allows you to install the program. The package they offer is expansive, but not expensive, and you may find many of the programs that you want are on the disk.

For those who have more than one computer, and have Windows 95 installed on one of

them, please review the compatibility issues on the following page. **Note: these issues will not affect most computer builders, unless they purchase Windows 98**.

Now is a good time to shut the door on software and move on to Chapter 4.

In Chapter 4, we get a look at components and prices for our new system. As you consider software, and begin laying out your inventory plans, keep track of the hard disk and RAM requirements for the programs you wish to install. After choosing your specific components, you will be ready to jump into building your computer.

Shadow's Rules

WINDOWS 95b OEM RELEASE

FAT32, And What It Means To YOU

Imagine buying a second computer, with the intention of sharing resources between the two, and finding out, through experimentation, that it is impossible. What has happened, and why? This article attempts to answer your questions.

A little History

The FAT, or *file allocation table,* was invented as a means to store and retrieve data to and from both floppy and hard disk assemblies. Very few improvements in the technology of the FAT structure have been implemented, at least up to now.

The only major improvements in file allocation of note have been to modify the FAT to allow use of larger hard disk assemblies. From its invention for use on floppy disks through the adaptation that supports 2 Gigabyte hard disks, support for larger hard drives has been the principal concern.

That Is, Until Now.

Microsoft, in its infinite wisdom, broke the FAT16 barrier by introducing FAT32, in its newest release of Windows 95, a version available to the home user ONLY if purchased on a new computer. (This version is available only to OEM suppliers, and cannot be independently purchased.) This introduction has its good and bad points, and we will examine them now.

The Good

Many new computers new come with 2.5 Gigabyte and larger hard drives, which must be partitioned into two or more virtual drives to make use of any space beyond 2.0 Gigabytes. I have built computers with 9.1 Gigabyte hard drives, and had to make a bunch of 2 Gigabyte partitions to use the drive. FAT32 increases the allowable hard disk size to 2000 Gigabytes.

Now, the answer to: "Why does my 1.6 Gigabyte hard drive only hold 1.1 Gigabytes of data?" I asked myself this question many times, until I called Western Digital, a hard disk manufacturer.

Cluster size is the answer. Each file stored on a hard disk must take up at least one cluster, or allocation unit. An allocation unit, or cluster, is the smallest amount of room a file can occupy on your hard disk. Cluster size increases

with the size of your hard disk partition. The following table gives more information.

DISK OR PARTITION SIZE	CLUSTER SIZE
0 TO 127 MEGABYTES	2 kilobytes
128 TO 255 MEGABYTES	4 kilobytes
256 TO 511 MEGABYTES	8 kilobytes
512 TO 1023 MEGABYTES	16 kilobytes
1024 TO 2047 MEGABYTES	32 kilobytes

What Does This Mean?

This means, if you have a 2 Gigabyte hard disk and it is not partitioned, each file, no matter how small, will occupy at least 32 Kilobytes of hard disk space. A small batch file that is only 100 bytes will waste 30,000 bytes of your valuable hard disk space!

FAT32, as you must of guessed, gets rid of this problem too. The user can configure FAT32 to set cluster size at 4 Kilobytes, allowing the user to increase usable disk space by 15-30%.

Other improvements include the ability to eliminate the current limitation on the number of directories you can create in the root directory. Since FAT32 treats the root directory as just another cluster chain, it can be any size, and located anywhere on the hard disk. You can eliminate the annoying need to run FDISK and destroy all your hard disk's data when re-sizing partitions, too. Sounds too good to be true? Let's look further.

The Bad

Everything in life has advantages and disadvantages. FAT32 is no exception. Microsoft does **NOT** intend to test FAT32 on older hardware, so no guarantees of compatibility will be implied or stated.

At this time, nobody has released utilities that will convert your existing hard disk to a FAT32-compatible hard disk, and Microsoft will not assume that responsibility.

Even on new computers with pre-installed FAT32-compatible systems, problems can occur. As of now, no other operating systems, including win 3.1 and Win NT, are guaranteed to work. Forget using your dual-boot machine with FAT32.

Legacy hardware and software may be incompatible. If you have older external hard disks, backup systems with accelerator cards, zip drives, or other external peripherals that read and write to the hard disk, you may be out of luck.

Existing Drive-Space and Microsoft Plus applications are out. You cannot compress file systems formatted with FAT32. According to what I have read, It seems that disk maintenance features will be supported by updated versions of FDISK, FORMAT, DEFRAG and ScanDisk.

I suggest using FAT32 only if your new computer comes with it, and **NEVER** hook up any older peripherals to the new system.

SELECTING YOUR COMPUTER'S COMPONENTS

Topics
Your shopping list
What to watch out for, and why
High performance for less
Special handling to avoid electrostatic damage

PRICES OF COMPUTER COMPONENTS RELATIVE TO THE WHOLE COMPUTER'S COST

COMPONENT	PRICE*	% OF WHOLE
MOTHERBOARD, PENTIUM II	$159	11.60
CASE, MID-TOWER	$29	2.07
MICROPROCESSOR, PII 300	$449	32.80
RAM, 64 MB. SDRAM	$102	7.44
VIDEO CARD,DIAMOND 8MB	$79	5.76
HARD DISK, 6.4 GIGABYTES	$210	15.31
FLOPPY DISK, 1.44 MB.	$25	1.82
KEYBOARD, 101 STYLE	$12	0.88
MOUSE, 3 BUTTON	$7	0.51
MONITOR, SHAMROCK 17"	$299	21.8

* Your prices will be lower, but this is representative of the ratios you will find at any time. A comparable pre-built system costs $2299, but this one is $1371. Build it yourself and save money!

The above prices are for a typical Pentium II 300 MHz system with 64 Megabytes of SDRAM and a Diamond Fire Gl 1000 AGP video card with 8 Megabytes of VRAM. A Western Digital 6.4 Gigabyte hard drive and 3.5 inch floppy drive are included.

The rest of this chapter will show you how to select the components for your computer. You will be shown how to make your shopping list, and given the information to allow you to intelligently select the accessories you need.

When you finish this chapter, you will have a list of the components to build exactly the computer you want.

One necessary consideration is your software requirement. *Be certain, after selecting your software, that the computer you are building will support the software you plan to use.*

This is a common mistake often made by people who buy packaged systems. The system looks good enough, but unless the buyer has done his or her homework, the buyer goes home with a system that does not fit his or her needs.

Keep your current and future software requirements in mind as you select your components, and you will not be disappointed or unpleasantly surprised.

Making Your Shopping List

I have never seen any book or periodical that gives you information on exactly what to buy to make a computer. Other books discuss some features of a few necessary components, and leave the rest as guesswork. *This book is the exception.*

My objective in this chapter is to eliminate any doubt in your mind that you are buying exactly what you want and need. You will wind up with the best possible computer for your requirements, and have more money in your pocket than you expected.

Minimum components required to build a computer are the *case*, a *motherboard*, the *microprocessor*, the *RAM*, a *video card*, either *on board IDE I/O or an IDE I/O card*, a *hard disk*, a *floppy disk*, a *keyboard*, a *mouse*, and a *monitor*. More details are listed in Chapter 1, and a preview with prices relative to the whole computer cost is on the previous page.

The Motherboard

Start with the motherboard. The motherboard determines the required characteristics of the rest of the components. *Figure 4-1* on the next page shows a 486/5x86 motherboard with the PCI bus. The PCI slots are the short slots next to the 72 pin SIMM connectors.

This PCB does *not* support pipeline cache. Refer to *Figure 1-1* in Chapter 1 for a Pentium motherboard with the single slot for a pipeline SIMM. The pipeline cache SIMM on this motherboard is installed between J1 and the empty SRAM sockets shown on *Figure 1-1*.

The motherboards readily available today are, from slowest to fastest, the 486/5x86 PCI, the Pentium/6x86 PCI, the P6, or Pentium Pro, and the Pentium II. Pricing is approximate, but here are some guidelines.

Expect an upgradable 486 PCI motherboard with BIOS support for 5x86 processors to cost $49 to $69 with a 5x86 133 MHz processor and DIP cache. This motherboard without the processor is about $40. It has on board EIDE I/O, and 256 kB of cache memory.

A fast Pentium PCI motherboard with pipeline burst cache and on board EIDE I/O will cost about $55 without CPU, but remember, the pipeline cache is included, and the BIOS has support for the 6x86 processor family.

Now, hold onto your pocketbook. The Intel Aurora motherboard which supports the Pentium Pro, or P6 microprocessor, runs about $105 *without* the processor, which is about $200 for a 200 MHz processor. This motherboard has full support for EIDE I/O and, of course comes with pipeline burst cache. These prices will generally fall with time, of course, and serve as references only.

The hottest processors on the market today are Intel's Pentium II models. The CPU assembly looks more like an add-on card than a CPU, and the motherboard is unique, costing about $150. The processors range in price from $200 to $800, at frequencies from 233 MHz to beyond 400 MHz.

Someone asked me about mechanical configuration and quality issues recently, so they will be addressed now. Quality between different manufacturers is very similar. The primary reason is component vendors have no sense of humor when it comes to returned items, and they will not tolerate any manufacturer who does not conform to their standards. The quality issue is resolved before the customer gets involved. It is necessary, when doing large volumes of business, to start and maintain a good quality control system.

This should be enough information to pick a motherboard for your needs and budget.

Configuration between different manufacturers of motherboards and components is tightly controlled by the standards to which each component has to adhere. Without going into extensive detail, let it suffice to say that the parts that are used to make an IBM compatible PC are for the most part completely interchangeable within the families. When choosing add-on cards, remember the bus type of your motherboard and choose only cards that fit your motherboard. Whether you choose the PCI or VESA bus family, either will support, in addition, the 8 and 16 bit ISA bus cards.

The Case

Get the case that suits your future needs. If you want a desktop case, you are somewhat limited in what can be put inside. Remember also; the *primary* reason for moving from the desktop case is your health. A monitor placed on a desktop case is too high to view without neck and back strain.

Figure 4-1 A 486/5x86 PCI MOTHERBOARD WITH ON BOARD IDE I/O

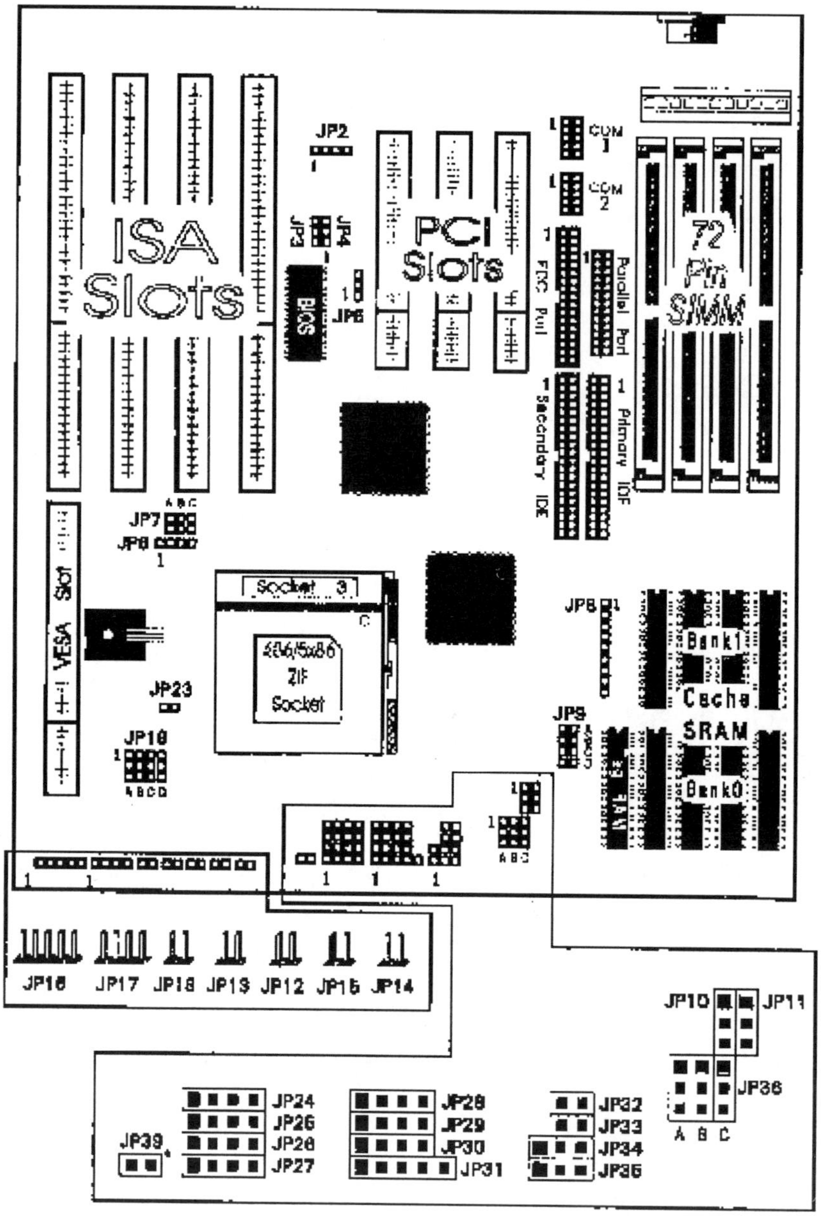

The medium tower case is a good buy and is suitable for adding extra goodies later. It has a larger power supply, more connectors, a larger fan, and room for tape drives, CD-ROMs, extra hard drives, and additional floppy drives.

Mini towers are generally the best buy, and around $25 buys a good mini tower. If you do not plan on the combination of a 5.25"

floppy drive, an internal tape drive, and a CD-ROM, a mini tower will suffice. Figure 4-2 on the next page shows a mini-tower case.

This case is suitable for the majority of computers, but the larger medium tower allows an additional bay for an internal tape drive.

There are so many types and styles of cases, it would take hours to describe them all. Since it is one of the most visible parts of your computer, make your choice carefully. The case will generally outlive upgradeable items like the motherboard and internal components, so get a case you are comfortable with, and one that will serve your current and future requirements.

When you evaluate computer cases, consider future expansion. Most people select a mini-tower case, and most purchased computers come with one, but you may decide to add enough peripheral equipment to make a mini-tower useless.

Tally up the equipment you will be adding to your computer over the next several months **before** you firm up a decision on your case requirements.

Example: you want two hard drives, a tape backup, a CD-ROM drive, and two floppy drives. You have one more device than you have drive bays. A medium tower is your most viable choice with these peripherals.

Most vendors have good selections of cases. Ask for the advantages and disadvantages of each case that interest you before you decide to buy. Buy enough case for your predicted future requirements, and be certain to look at a sample case to confirm it will actually suit your needs before making the purchase.

The mini tower and full tower cases have the same configuration. The difference is the medium tower has an additional 5.25" bay. The mini tower supports 2 hard drives, 3.5" drives, and 5.25" drives. The medium tower adds a third 5.25" bay.

RAM

The type of motherboard you purchase will determine the RAM you buy. You may have

banks for 30 pin and 72 pin SIMM, 72 pin only, 72 pin and 168 pin DIMM, or 168 pin DIMM only. *Dual Inline Memory Modules* are primarily utilized on Pentium MMX and Pentium Pro motherboards for SDRAM.

Figure 4-2 A MINI TOWER CASE

You need 8 to 16 Megabytes of RAM to run most 32 bit applications, including Windows 95 and Windows NT with any degree of speed. You need at least 5 Megabytes of RAM to run most office and desktop suites, and 8 Megabytes is better.

The most common memory capacity today is 8 Megabytes. Soon, due to 32 bit applications, the most common size will be 16 Megabytes. Get 16 Megabytes now, and you will be glad you did.

Plan on buying EDO or SDRAM if you are making a Pentium machine. The 10-30% increase in speed is worth the price difference. 486/5x86 computers will show less of a performance increase, so the 60 Ns or 70 Ns non-parity SIMM is appropriate.

You now have the case, motherboard, CPU, and RAM specified for your system. The next item to weigh is the video adapter card.

Video Adapter

Remember, the video adapter is an add-on card that converts digital information from your computer into signals that display information on your monitor. The range in video performance for a computer is staggering. You can purchase a basic VESA or PCI video card for as little as $22. The Cirrus Logic, Trident 9xxx, and Tseng Labs cards fall into this category and they provide true color performance at an affordable price. These are 1 Megabyte video cards, and adding another Megabyte of RAM generally adds 30 percent to their price.

The next step up is the Diamond Stealth and ATI Mach series video adapters. These are faster, have VRAM capability, and the option of 4 Megabytes of RAM. Though a 2 Megabyte video card from any manufacturer will display the same graphics, these cards are much faster at video processing. They cost under $60 with 4 Megabytes of VRAM.

The next generation of video card is the *AGP* video card. The Diamond Fire Gl 1000 series dominates this category, introducing *Accelerated Graphics Port capability*. Expect to spend $165 for the 8 MB version.

There are dozens of game video adapters available. Beware of a video adapter that supports only one or two 3D games. It will be expensive, and perhaps not compatible with forthcoming software packages.

The average Pentium or 6x86 user should purchase a Diamond Stealth 2 MB video card, or comparable. If you have a 486 or 5x86, the Cirrus Logic is a good choice.

Why spend more money for a better video adapter? The reasons vary, but support for graphics-intensive programs is the primary reason. The speed of a VRAM video adapter is significant in high end 3-D applications like solids modeling and CAD programs.

The other primary user of high end graphics adapters is the extreme game player. The new 32 bit video games use MPEG video compression to store embedded video clips in computer games. Only the best video adapters can smoothly display the video clips. If your requirements fit in these categories, consider a high end video adapter a necessity.

The Hard Disk

Hard disks come in all shapes and sizes, in capacities from 100 Megabyte to over 8 Gigabytes in IDE format, and well beyond 9 Gigabytes in SCSI format.

What do you need and why? If your intended applications are considerable, your hard disk capacity requirements will match. Consider the software you will be installing, and get a hard disk with a minimum capacity of twice that much.

Access times are similar for most hard disks today, so this factor is not significant in selection. You will find the prices are pretty similar, too.

The most popular hard drives today are high capacity IDE hard drives. Conner, Maxtor, Quantum, Seagate, and Western Digital all make hard drives in excess of 5 Gigabytes. Conner, Maxtor, and Western Digital make drives in the 6 Gigabyte range and beyond.

Both Conner and Seagate make large capacity hard drives in SCSI format. The larger Conner 2.1 Gigabyte and 4.3 Gigabyte drives have access times in the 9 millisecond range. This is comparable to the Western Digital IDE 5.1 Gigabyte hard drive. This fast access time is essential in the faster Pentium and 6x86 machines.

What to Buy...

If I were assembling a budget minded computer, I would purchase a smaller IDE hard drive, such as the 5.1 Gigabyte IDE hard drives available for about $180. If I were making a fast Pentium or clone machine, I would double up a pair of Western Digital 6.4 Gigabyte hard drives for about $200 to $220 each. There are many variations in size and price between these two extremes, and also 9 Gigabyte hard disks and beyond. Just look at everything available before you decide, and remember that the newest hard disks are overpriced in comparison with drives a few months older.

Floppy Drives

Most people will buy only one 3.5" floppy drive for a first time computer. The only people who should even consider a 5.25" floppy drive are older style computer owners with previous data or software on 5.25" disks. Some people, like me, duplicate data disks for clients, and a pair of 3.5" floppies makes this easy. The DOS Diskcopy program supports dual identical drives, and makes exact duplicates of a disk in one pass.

Important things to consider when buying a floppy drive are price and adaptability. Though floppy drives once cost hundreds of dollars, today's prices for floppy drives range from $15 to $30. *Never* pay more than $25 for a Sony or Teac 3.5" 1.44 MB floppy drive. For adaptability, the floppy drive should include a 5.25" mounting kit, so you can install the drive in either 3.5" or 5.25" bays in your case. Since floppy drives are so similar in all other respects, including longevity and quality, these are the two primary issues to keep in mind.

Keyboard and Mouse

Like your pillow and mattress, your mouse and keyboard are individual and personal.

Nobody touches my mouse without my permission! Since most of the operations you perform on a computer require one of both of them, you should purchase wisely.

There are numerous designs, types, and configurations of the keyboard. Ergonomic keyboards suit the power user, because they conform to the individual requirements of someone who spends hours on a computer. A casual user may be happy with a $12 keyboard conforming to the AT specification. The best place to test drive keyboards is a computer store, or even a large department store. They will have a selection of computers available, with choices of a wide variety of peripherals.

There are as many types of mice as keyboards, and I recommend trying out several before purchasing. Try the stationary trackBall mouse as well; a good choice for limited desk space. Evaluate both two and three button mice. The middle of a three button mouse allows you to customize certain applications, to save hours of typing.

Prices on mice and keyboards varies widely from store to store. I purchase inexpensive ones for people I build for, because I know they will be the first things the new owner replaces with his own personal types.

$20 can buy you a keyboard and 3 button Microsoft compatible mouse. You can also spend $75 for a Logitech trackBall and upwards of $100 for an ergonomic keyboard, if you wish.

IDE I/O

The only motherboard that will need this add-on card is an inexpensive VESA local bus motherboard. All other motherboards have a built in EIDE I/O. Figure 4-5 shows an EIDE I/O card, which supports four hard drives, two floppy drives, and I/O functions, such as a parallel printer port, a game adapter port for a joystick or flight controller, and two serial data ports.

This card has the 16550 fast UART, or *Universal Asynchronous Receiver Transmitter* IC normally included on faster motherboards with on board IDE I/O. This

component speeds up serial data transmission, particularly through a modem.

Obviously, a motherboard with these built-in functions eliminates the need for an add-on card, but if a motherboard IDE I/O fails, provisions on the motherboard allow you to add a card like this to restore the function.

Figure 4-5 AN EIDE I/O CARD

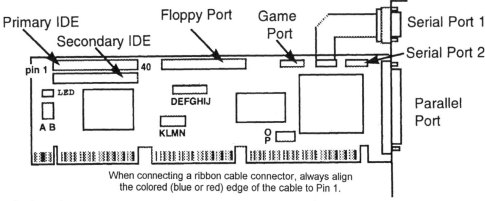

If your motherboard includes the IDE I/O function, do not buy this card. You will be spending about $20 to $40 unnecessarily. The only exception is if you need more I/O capability.

The Monitor

You must try out all types of monitors before you consider a purchase. The monitor you like may not work for anyone else. Everyone looks at monitors differently; that's why there are so many different types available. I will discuss a few parameters, however. The features most computer users want are *digital, non-interlaced,* and *size.*

The largest is not necessarily the best. I tried a 17″ monitor for about a week, then went back to a good digital Shamrock 15″ non-interlaced SVGA monitor. The 17″ monitor was ghosting on some of my faster moving applications, and gave me a headache. A 14″ monitor will probably give you a headache, too, because the image is so small. If you use your computer more than twice a week, do yourself a favor and get at least a 15″ monitor. Most people prefer a 15″ digital non-interlaced SVGA monitor. It combines all the

good features in an affordable package. If you have high definition graphics, such as Autocad drawings, multiple layer schematics, or PCB layout applications, a 17″ or larger monitor is necessary. Most other applications run very well on a good 15″ monitor. Disregard 14″ monitors.

Now lets discuss non-interlaced monitors. A *non-interlaced* monitor writes the screen with data in one pass. An *interlaced* monitor, like a television, writes the even numbered lines in one pass, then writes the odd numbered lines. It takes two passes to display one screen. Doing this causes a visible flicker on the screen, which often results in eye fatigue. Get the non-interlaced monitor.

A *digital* monitor can be preset to a number of different display control settings, any one of which can be automatically recalled with the push of a button. This is important if several people use the computer. Each can customize the display to his or her liking. You may like different brightness, contrast, and screen sizes in different programs, and can set the monitor to display your preferences at will.

Green monitors have energy saving features that shut them down when not in use for a time. This is an EPA-plus often ignored by computer buyers that saves money in utility bills, particularly when the computer is unattended and turned on occasionally.

Monitor prices vary by manufacturer. A 15 inch monitor should cost around $160 if it is digital, non-interlaced, and SVGA. The .28 dot pitch is mandatory. A 17 inch with similar specifications should run around $300. Expect to pay about $1000 for a digital 21 inch monitor. Remember, most computers sold in stores come with a small 14 inch monitor. Expect to have to spend money to replace it, when comparing system prices.

The Basic Components

These items and prices give you an idea of what it costs to build a basic computer. You have noticed it is much less than a packaged system. Now that you have prices for the basic computer, it is time to look at the add-on stuff you will include to make this system your own personal computer.

Personalizing Your Computer

Most computer users have unique operational needs. These may include requirements for adding pictures to presentations, faxing from within documents, and surfing the net. The proper combination of hardware and software allows you, the user, to perform virtually any task from your computer. What follows now is a brief look at the options available.

Talking To Other Computers

In a business environment where seemingly everyone in the company has a computer,

Local Area Networks provide the link between users. A *LAN* can be wired or wireless, depending on the needs of the company. Most home computer users have little interest in networking, unless they have more than one computer.

For this user, the ability to connect computers directly by cable is supported in DOS 6.22 and Windows 95. There are also third party programs that provide more enhanced functionality through direct cable connection than either DOS or Win95.

The Modem

Most home computers communicate via modem. This requires a modem and support software. If you purchase a modem, it *should* come with all the software that allows you to use it as a fax machine, an Internet access device, and a full-featured modem.

A basic 33.6 internal fax/modem costs about $40, and the external version is about $90. The 33.6 modem is the primary modem included in packaged systems. The faster 56k internal fax/modem can cost from $80 to $140, depending on the brand. The external version of 56k modems is priced between $120 and $150.

An external modem, like the one in Figure 4-6, lets you monitor what the modem is doing. The lights on the front panel show communication occurring. Another good thing about external modems is you can turn them off instantly. The additional cost is due to packaging and power supply requirements. For those looking for faster communication over the phone lines, the *ISDN* connection is state of the art. The *Integrated Services Digital Network* system was designed to replace standard analog phone lines with faster digital lines. Compare the 1 *megabit* per second transfer rate to the 33,600 *bit* per second rate for a good modem, and you can see why it is preferable. Other advantages of ISDN are clean digital voice, fax, and even high quality video transmission. ISDN modems are priced between $100 and $300, but expect prices to fall. Installation costs about $160. The service itself is $28 to $34 monthly, not unlike standard phone service.

Cable modem service, available from your cable supplier, is many times faster, however, and readily available. The cost ranges from $30 to $60, depending on your existing cable subscription. Unlike modem surfing, you are always *logged on*, and not using a telephone line, so you never get busy signals.

Figure 4-6 EXTERNAL MODEMS

CD-ROM

A CD-ROM drive is no longer an option; it has become a necessity for anyone who prefers easy software installation or enjoys computer multimedia entertainment. Forget dumping 10 to 30 floppy disks into your computer to load a software package. One CD holds the equivalent of 400 to 500 floppies.

The principal use of a CD-ROM drive today is running large multimedia packages. One or two of these programs loaded onto a hard disk could fill up a 1.2 Gigabyte hard drive completely. Most educational and reference material comes on CD-ROM now.

There are even CD-ROM drives available that can record. They are designed to fit in the same space a normal CD-ROM drive occupies. Some people use a *CD-R* drive to archive large amounts of data. This is a good idea, particularly if the data is in the form of video clips or other memory hungry applications, because large volumes of data, up to 650 Megabytes, can be stored on one disk. Companies that store data for long periods of time, including hospitals and legal practices, can benefit from the durable nature of a recordable CD-ROM disk. *Figure 4-7* shows an internal CD-ROM drive made to fit a 5.25 inch bay in your computer.

Figure 4-7 A 5.25 INCH INTERNAL CD-ROM DRIVE

Prices for CD-ROM drives are pretty consistent. The 16X IDE CD-ROM is available for about $40 to $50 with a IDE cable. The 24X drives are going for $70 to $80, and the 32X drives bring in about $85 to $95, depending on brand name. What's in a name? Check the features. The more expensive CD-ROM drives by NEC have a large cache buffer, which allows the drive to transfer data to your computer faster.

Ask around, and get the CD-ROM drive that fits your budget and requirements. Note: the 32X, 24X, 16X, and 10X mentioned are speeds. A 4X CD-ROM is 4 times faster than a single speed. See Chapter 1 for a review on CD-ROM speeds, and more information.

Another way to acquire a CD-ROM is through a *multimedia package*. The package normally includes a CD-ROM drive, a sound card, speakers, and several software titles bundled with the hardware. Multimedia packages vary widely in price, due primarily to the differences in the individual components. Note: unless the software titles particularly appeal to you, I suggest buying individual components. You will save money.

Multimedia Packages Without Software

Multimedia packages that do not include software titles are composed of the CD-ROM drive, a 16 bit sound card with amplified speakers, and an AC adapter for the speakers. They have installation software included, plus all required cables and instructions.

A package with a 32X IDE CD-ROM drive costs less than $175, and the same package with a 24X drive is less than $140. A packaged system is a good idea for the person who does not want to customize his sound card or speakers, and is a great idea for anyone who fears a complicated installation. Remember, however, that you can probably save between $25 and $50 by buying these items separately.

Multimedia systems have become commonplace in computers sold today. Unfortunately, the clone business is invading these systems. The clones in some "fast food" computers often have compatibility problems with some programs, leading to headaches later on. These show up when new software stretches the capabilities of the clone cards. The most affected clone card in this area is a sound card claiming to be "Sound Blaster compatible." I found out the hard way that there is no substitute for the real thing when it comes to sound cards.

Sound Cards

Many sound cards exist, and most are Sound Blaster compatible. Since all sound cards have to emulate Sound Blaster characteristics to be compatible with the largest variety of software, buy a Sound Blaster card. Then you will not have to be concerned about any compatibility problems between your programs and sound card.

Prices for sound cards oscillate around the Sound Blaster prices, so I will give you prices for the Sound Blaster family. Again, these prices are approximations, everything changes fast in the computer world. These are a few common Sound Blaster cards, and serve as representative performance levels of all sound cards available.

A 16 bit Sound Blaster Pro will cost around $35. The next step up is the surround sound version, at $45 or so. A jump to 32 voice performance costs around $50, and is called the AWE 32. The AWE 64 costs $89. The plug and play version of this card is slightly more expensive, but worth it from a configuration standpoint. Advantages of more expensive cards are discussed in Chapter 1.

Figure 4-8 shows a standard 16 bit Sound Blaster compatible sound card. This generic sound card is the most commonly available, and is primarily used by superstores in their fast food systems. It has some of the features available on the real thing, but lacks many of the more sophisticated features, like 32 bit stereo sound and universal game support. It is priced about $50.

Figure 4-8 A 16 BIT SOUND CARD

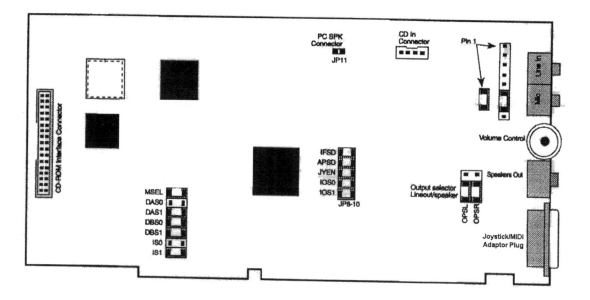

Printers

I have found recently that the printer market is shifting toward the inexpensive color ink jet

home printer. This family of printers has, in the last two years, dropped in price by several hundreds of dollars.

I bought an HP color ink jet printer about two years ago. I *thought* I paid an unbeatable price. I was wrong! The average price for a color ink jet printer with at least 300 dpi resolution is now under $200. This obsoletes everything except the better laser printers. I feel the two choices for home printers are a good ink jet printer, or a high quality laser. The amount of black and white printing you do should influence your decision. If you do mostly high quality black and white printing, get a laser printer. The speed of a laser printer is up to ten times faster than an ink jet, and the print quality can be up to four times better.

Consider price per copy when evaluating your printer needs. For black and white printing, a laser printer is much cheaper to operate. A toner cartridge will outlast several ink jet cartridges, and the cost per copy on an ink jet printer for identical copies is 5 to 6 times more expensive than with a laser printer.

The best reason to get an ink jet printer is color printing. If you have kids, get an ink jet. If you need presentation quality color printing for work or home use, the ink jet is the only way to go. Many ink jet printers will do near-photographic quality printing.

And don't forget price. The ink jet printers are cheap. The Epson Stylus color ink jet printer costs under $200 today. The average HP laser printer, on the other hand, lists in the same catalog for $389. Both are near the lower end of the price range in their respective disciplines, though it is not uncommon for laser printer manufacturers to run sale prices down to the $200 range. You should purchase the printer that suits your long term needs, since printers typically last a long time and are relatively expensive to replace.

Scanners

The family of *optical character readers*, commonly called *scanners*, is being expanded daily. As scanners become more popular, they also become more affordable. When scanners first became available to the masses, they cost upwards of $6000. Today's full page color scanners can be purchased for less than $200. Hand-held scanners are even more affordable. You can get a monochrome, hand-held scanner for about $35, and color for $90.

The most important thing to know about scanners is the difference between true and *interpolated* resolution. Many inexpensive scanners use interpolation software to *fill in the dots*, and advertise an interpolated resolution much higher that their actual performance. These scanners have true resolutions of 300 to 400 dpi, but report *interpolated* resolutions of up to 2400 dpi!

Most scanners come bundled with *Optical Character Recognition* software. OCR allows a scanner to recognize text characters in a scanned document. The text is imported into your computer for processing. You can then edit or fax the document as required. Obviously, anything you scan into a computer can be added to a prepared document, including pictures. This makes a scanner a very useful tool for the home office.

Your Computer's Protection

Here are some of the issues you must address in order to ensure a safe environment for your computer and peripheral equipment.

Software Safety

If you have ever experienced a hard disk crash but had not backed up your system, you know exactly what true horror is. You get to expend many hours trying to get back to where you were before the crash.

Another thing to think about, when considering such unspeakable disasters, is the possibility of a computer virus invading your otherwise perfect system. Every time you go online or insert a disk into your system, you risk infection.

The solution to either of these problems is having a recent tape backup of everything on your system. With large disk capacities, the safest and most cost effective way to keep an exact duplicate of everything on your system is tape. *Figure 4-9* shows an external tape backup system. This is my T1000, an 800 Megabytes per tape system mounted in an external case made for a completely different tape drive. Yes, now and then I tinker a bit.

Tape drives are available in internal and external types. The internal drives are much less expensive, at $40 to $80 less than the

external version. A HP T3000 tape drive will put up to 3.2 Gigabytes on one cartridge. This is true if the data on your hard drive can be software compressed 2:1. The average capacity is closer to 2.5 Gigabytes per tape.

What is software compression? There are several types of software compression used in backup systems. Each compresses data by eliminating the unused space in data packets.

To get an idea of what I mean, just eliminate the spaces in this line and see how much less space is required to store it.

Togetanideaofwhatimean,justeliminatethespacesinthi slineandseehowmuchlessspaceisrequiredtostoreit.

Figure 4-9 AN EXTERNAL TAPE BACKUP SYSTEM

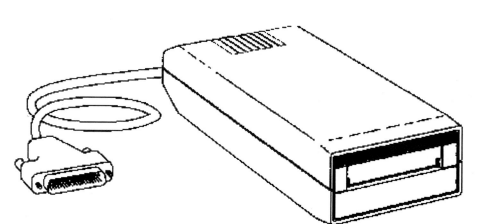

In addition to removing the *white space*, or blank portions in text files, data compression software searches for repetitive strings. During compression, each string is replaced by a single character, or token. When a program needs a portion of the compressed data, the compression software decompresses the data. Software compression is how most tape drives get 200 Megabyte capacity from a 120 Megabyte DC2120 tape cartridge.

For about $130, you can have a Hewlett Packard T1000 Travan tape drive, with up to

800 Megabyte storage per tape. As you may have guessed, the average storage capacity is somewhat less, and to get this capacity you must use longer Travan tapes.
The external versions of these tape drives are normally $40 to $80 more expensive. The reason is simple. The tape drive must interface to your system in some manner. An internal tape drive shares resources with one of your floppy drives, and even shares a control cable with the drive. An external drive, on the other hand, must have its own power supply and enclosure. It must also have an interface compatible with either a printer port or one of

your serial ports, or have its own add-in card. What you get with an external drive is more hardware and portability to other computers.

Protection from the Elements

Review Chapter 1 and determine what type of power protection you require. The minimum should be a good surge suppression power strip. A good strip always comes with an equipment replacement guarantee. If your area has power problems, consider a UPS. These topics are covered at length in Chapter 1.

Toys

Toys are nice things to have, but some toys become essential parts of your computer, and can both generate enjoyment and facilitate the work you perform. I have a color scanner, and use it to enhance documents I create by adding color pictures to them. I also have two game controllers, and a host of small accessories too numerous to mention. Accessories, like microphones, allow you to interact in exciting ways with your computer.

New toys come out all the time, like digital cameras, golf trainers, flight simulators, and more. For every new game, there is a new function added to existing game controllers. Examine options for playing on your computer, because all work and no play make any computer user less efficient.

You will be amazed when you compare your new computer's performance to the fast food variety with larger price tags. What will amaze you more, perhaps, is your newfound willingness and ability to jump in and modify your computer as new options become available.

You now have the list of the parts you need, and an idea of the prices to look for. Now, let's look at the tools required to build a computer. You will find the tools required to assemble your computer in nearly every household today, and if not, they are inexpensive to purchase.

"Looks like this is going to be easier than I thought." the novice computer builder thinks.

Figure 4-10 **TOOLS OF THE TRADE**

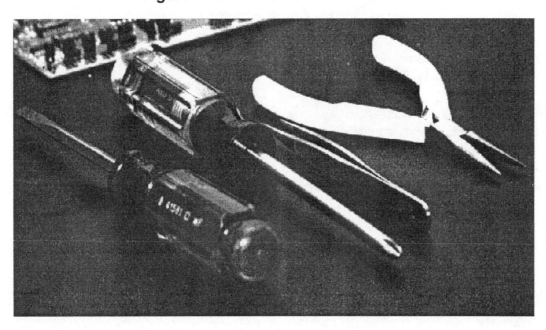

What To Watch Out For

When buying computer parts, there are a few pitfalls. Here are a few things to look out for.

When you first scope out a prospective source for parts, examine how things are packaged. Add-on cards, motherboards, memory, and hard disk drives all have static sensitive CMOS, or *complementary metal oxide* semiconductor parts installed on them, which are extremely sensitive to *electrostatic damage*, or ESD.

Components of this type should be packaged in static suppression packaging, such as sealed, dark gray, black, or pink polyethylene bags labeled "Danger, Static Sensitive Components." The motherboard and add-on cards should also be packaged inside a box.

The primary reason computer components are DOA or die within the first month is attributable to poor handling of some kind, usually the result of electrostatic damage.

Beware of missing or incorrect manuals or documentation. Check the manual against the parts to be certain you have all the proper hardware, software, and documentation.

Be certain you have proper manuals for each item you buy. The motherboard, hard disk, CD-ROM, and monitor each will come with a book. Other items may come with a one or two page handout. The modem will come with software and several other documents, such as a manual for the software and quick setup guides. The CD-ROM will come with driver software and a cable. The sound card should have a book, cables, and software. Exactly what comes with each item you buy varies widely, so be certain you open everything and check the packing list for omissions.

Check the motherboard for installed cache. There should be no empty IC sockets, unless

pipeline burst cache is installed. If this is so, there will be a single inline memory module installed on the board, and 9 empty IC sockets. You can either have pipeline cache *or* dip cache, but not both. If you have questions, ask the vendor before you leave the store.

Beware of places offering more than 3% cash discount. 3% is the amount normally charged a supplier if he accepts a charge card. Some get away with 2%. If possible without incurring an additional cost, charge it. You have more flexibility on returns or exchanges offered by the credit card companies.

Judge quality in the products you purchase by completeness of documentation, proper packaging, and good ESD protection and packaging practices.

One of my greatest fears is buying something I then have to send away for service. It is mandatory that any place where you buy components or systems have a service center. If not, you may not be able to easily exchange a defective item.

These are the things I look out for. If you purchase from a catalog, see the cautions I list for catalog ordering later in this book. The cautions follow the extensive list of computer magazines and literature, since this is where you will select the magazines from which you make your purchases.

High Performance Parts

Several components enhance your computer's performance. The most significant is pipeline burst cache in a Pentium or 6x86 machine. The improvement you see depends on processor speed, and may be up to 30% running 32 bit applications.

EDO RAM is extremely fast RAM. It will give you 10% improvement in 100 MHz or faster Pentium or 6x86 machines.

A fast video card, like the Diamond Stealth cards, will improve graphics programs, games, and multimedia speeds significantly.

Buying a video card with VRAM instead of DRAM gives you a 30-50% improvement in video card performance, depending on your software applications. Games run at rocket speed, especially 3D games and applications.

Of course, many clone chips are available in the microprocessor department. Expect the 5x86 processors to be much faster than the 486 chips, and the 6x86 processors to outgun Pentium devices in non-floating point apps.

One last thing: if you want the fastest machine in your performance range, and you have a 200 MHz Pentium or faster system, SDRAM is a must. The 10ns speed of this RAM beats the 60ns EDO RAM by a considerable margin. This RAM comes only in 168 pin DIMM configuration, so ensure your motherboard supports it. It is also about the same price now as EDO RAM.

These tips will wring out additional speed for enthusiasts who want to live on the edge.

Static Handling

When you get your computer parts home, do not handle them carelessly. The time to open the bags is while installing the components, and not before.

When this time arrives, handle all PC cards by the edges only, and, before you touch any of the components, touch the bare metal part of your case, to discharge any electrostatic voltage.

Electrostatic damage is not immediately terminal. Tiny junctions within an electronic component can be damaged enough that, over time,it degrades sufficiently to finally fail.

The spark you receive from a metallic surface after walking on carpet is enough to destroy or damage many electrical parts in your computer. The damage may be slight, but a failure can occur up to 6 months from the initial damaging spark.

I have an ESD-safe work area, because I build so many computers. You will not damage anything in your computer if you follow the simple guidelines above.

The documentation for your components may have additional advice, so follow all static control instructions you receive.

Read on. Chapter 5, Putting It All Together, will show you how to build your computer.

Your Notes

5 PUTTING IT ALL TOGETHER

Topics
Assembling your new computer
Setting up your system for first time operation
Testing for conflicts and correcting them
Performance optimization

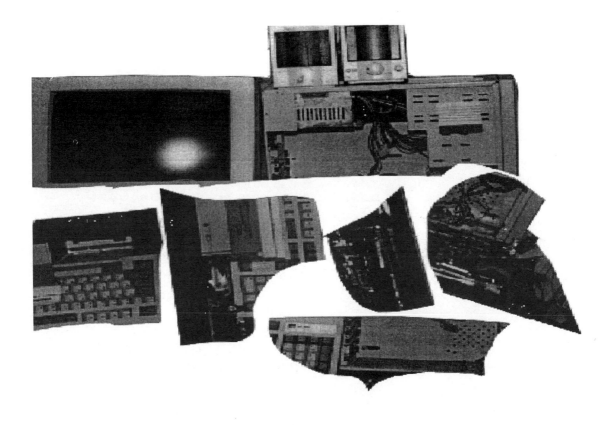

The first time I assembled a computer, I built it on a fine dining room table. The next time I came home with boxes of parts, I found my wife, in her infinite wisdom, had purchased a small card table with a soft vinyl cover. This was her way of convincing me the dining room table was inappropriate for use as a secondary computer testing site. I totally agree. For a few dollars, she gave me a spot of vinyl to call my own.

Choose your assembly site carefully. Make certain there is enough room to safely put your computer together, and that there is power available for first time operational tests. Ensure in advance the table can support the combined weight of the computer components and that it is a stable work station.

You have come a long way to get to this point in the project. You have a considerable pile of computer parts and accessories before you, and are going to make sense of it all. Look at *Figure 5-1*, which shows the pile of parts Lisa turned into a computer.

Figure 5-1 THE COMPONENTS OF A COMPUTER

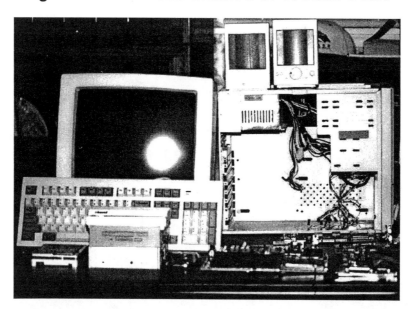

When you finish this chapter, you will be able to confidently and efficiently build your computer. The real benefits come when you put your computer to use, the whole time realizing you created that wonderful machine. I still get goose bumps when I think of the *MONEY* I have saved through the years by building and upgrading my own systems. Read on. The process goes fast from now on.

Assembling Your New Computer

The first step is inspection. Confirm you have everything you need. Inspect all components for damage and completeness of assembly documentation, and be certain you have all the interconnecting cables. Connect all cables to the add-in cards, to be certain you are not short anything.

The next step is component configuration. Your computer will be made of parts from a variety of manufacturers, as occurs in most computers today. Each component will have configurable options. Many components have hardware *jumpers* to select those options. A jumper connects two circuits together, and is like a switch. You can select options, such as clock speed on a motherboard or IRQ on an I/O card.

Read all documentation carefully, and preset all jumpers to the default settings called out in the documentation supplied with each card. The cards are normally already set to default positions that provide the fewest conflicts. You are just performing a final check of someone else's work, but it is better to find any configuration problems early.

The motherboard is the most critical. The documentation will tell you how to set the configuration for your CPU type. *THIS IS VERY IMPORTANT.*

Many CPUs run on different power supply voltages and clock frequencies. If you have any doubt of the correct motherboard jumper settings, the vendor will help. The supplied documentation should help you find the correct settings, if you read it carefully. There is always a pictorial diagram to follow if the instructions are too confusing.

Other cards may have configuration jumpers, but I have found that few use them today. The Plug and Play, or *PnP* motherboards and add-on cards set themselves up when you turn on the computer. Hopefully you have one or more of these components.

The PnP Pentium/6x86 motherboard in my computer has no jumpers because it "auto-detects" the CPU, cache, and RAM. The first time I turned on my computer, the configuration was loaded into BIOS on the motherboard. This setup is the best and easiest as manual configuration is not required.

Nearly all motherboards built after March 1996 have BIOS that supports both Intel and clone microprocessors, and auto-detects PnP add-in components. It is unlikely you will have to configure a motherboard, but if you do, the following information will help.

Remember, even if you have configuration jumpers, the default positions are generally the best. *Figure 5-2* shows a motherboard with configuration jumpers, each labeled *JP* followed by a number.

The jumpers on this motherboard set voltage to the CPU, clock frequency, VESA master or slave connector priority, and cache memory size. Some of these parameters change with each different type of CPU you can install.

If you have to set jumpers on the motherboard you selected, look at *Figure 5-2* on the following page. Your jumpers, if any, will be different. The documentation with your motherboard will help you perform any necessary configuration changes required by CPU type, RAM type, and cache size.

This is the most precise part of the entire computer building experience, and the only task that requires anything more than a pair of screwdrivers. *You might need a pair of tweezers or small needle nose pliers to move the jumpers.*

At this point the cards have been configured, either by you or the factory. Default conditions have been set by jumpers, and each component is ready to install. I normally perform one additional task. I find it easier to connect any ribbon cables to the add-on cards now. That way you do not have to fight the cable, case, and cards to install them while the card is inside the case, and you can see the connector pins better, and ensure the connectors mate properly with the cables.

A quick word about alignment of connectors to cables. Normally, the connectors on the add-in cards and motherboards have a "pin 1" designation. It is either an inverted triangle near the pin designated as pin 1, or a number 1. This pin aligns with the same type of designator on the cable connector. An added check is to look at the cable itself. Nearly all cables have a red wire on one end. This is pin 1 of the cable assembly. Power cables are the

exception. They are keyed, and can plug in only one way.

Figure 5-2 A MOTHERBOARD WITH CONFIGURATION JUMPERS

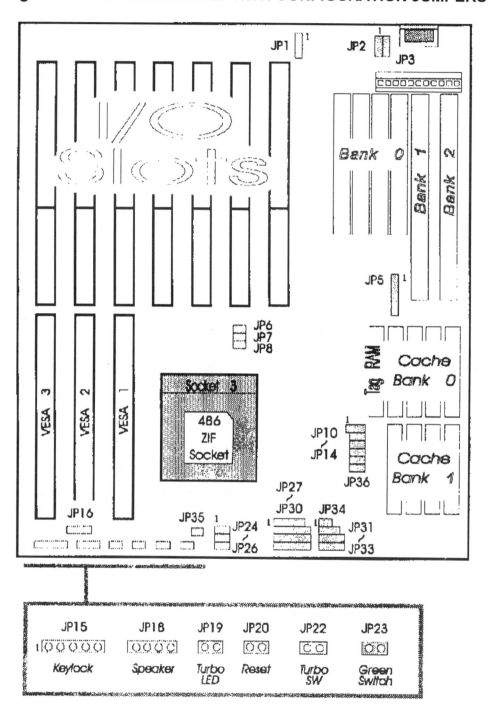

Cards with cables attached include a sound card, an IDE I/O card (if required), any tape controller card, and any CD-ROM add-on

card, such as a SCSI interface card. *Figure 5-3* shows an IDE I/O card with the cables attached.

Figure 5-3 AN IDE I/O CARD WITH CABLES

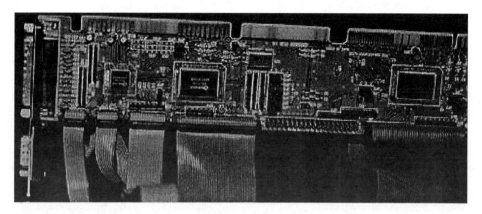

Note: this card has jumpers for DMA and IRQ settings, which we discussed in detail earlier, in the introductory chapter. Neither has to be moved from default, however, upon installation into the case. The documentation for the card depicts exactly how to connect each ribbon cable correctly.

Be certain to follow all connector polarities when installing the cables to the PCB. Pin 1 is normally identified by an inverted triangle mark on the connector or a red-colored wire on the cable. The PCB should have a triangle shaped mark showing pin 1, or a pin 1 designation. Consult the documentation for polarities if there is any uncertainty.

Motherboard Memory And CPU Installation

You may have purchased a motherboard with memory, cache, and processors installed. If so, skip this step.

If not, install the memory first. SIMM memory installs one way, as the module is keyed. To install a SIMM, place the module in a slanted position in the socket. To lock the SIMM in position, raise it to a vertical position, and you will feel it snap into place.

SIMM may have to be installed in certain *banks* on certain motherboards. If so, the documentation will assign certain pairs of

sockets as bank 0, 1, 2, and 3, if so equipped. You must fill bank 0, then 1, and so on, until you run out of memory or all banks are filled. I recommend buying memory in a size that will fill only one bank, so memory upgrades mean just filling another bank. If you fill all your banks with lower capacity memory, you will have to replace the smaller capacity memory in order to upgrade.

Example: You buy memory in 1x32 SIMM, which are 4 MB in size. You have two banks of two each 72 pin SIMM sockets on the motherboard. You fill the computer with 4 Megabyte SIMM, resulting in 16 MB of RAM. Now you must replace SIMM with larger capacity SIMM, in order to upgrade RAM. If you had purchased two 2x32 SIMM, with a capacity of 8 MB each, a RAM upgrade would require only adding more SIMM.

CPU Installation Tips

Handle the processor as you would an add-on card. You will find a *ZIF*, or Zero Insertion Force socket on your motherboard, that allows you to easily remove and replace the CPU for upgrades. With the motherboard documentation handy, install the processor and confirm any jumper changes necessary. To install the processor, lift up on the handle attached to the socket, drop the processor, in and return the handle to its original position. It's that easy.

Some CPUs have a heat sink, and occasionally a fan mounted on top for additional cooling. Installation of these processors is identical to the one mentioned above. If the CPU has a fan attached, the power cable mates with any of the power cables for hard drives that are in the case. The instruction manual gives details.

The only additional work you may have to perform on the motherboard is installing the SIMM cache memory, if you are installing pipeline burst cache. Most motherboards for Pentium and 6x86 processors will already have this installed. Installation is simple. The socket is keyed, and all you must do is press in the module. *Figure 1-1* in Chapter 1 shows a Coast SRAM pipeline socket next to the empty DIP SRAM sockets.

Let's recap. The add-on cards are configured. They have the cables installed as required. The motherboard has memory, cache, and the CPU installed. The motherboard is configured for installation. So, what's keeping you?

Motherboard Installation

Open the case and remove the hardware inside. Most cases have one side that folds down. That's where you install the motherboard. This is usually the right hand side, with the front of the case facing you. The other side is open. There will be 2 to 4 screws holding the fold-down side in position. Remove them now, and remove or lay down the side.

Discharge static by touching the case anywhere on the bare metal surface. Remove the motherboard from its ESD protective container and lay it on the open side. Rotate the motherboard until the round keyboard connector faces the rear of the case. The two power connectors on the motherboard should also be to the rear of the case.

Align the motherboard with the mounting holes on the case side, and install the plastic standoffs wherever possible. There should also be one or two metal standoffs in the hardware package.

Install one at the rear corner of the case side nearest the power connectors on the motherboard. There may already be one there. This is the primary ground for the motherboard. Refer to figures *5-4, 5-6,* and *5-9* for assistance.

Figure 5-4 INSTALLING THE MOTHERBOARD IN THE CASE

With the plastic standoffs attached to the bottom of the motherboard where they align with the slides on the case side, slide the motherboard into place. When the hole in the motherboard aligns with the ground standoff, secure the motherboard with a screw from the hardware kit. The plastic standoffs should lock into the case slides on the case. Refer to *Figures 5-6* and *5-9*.

The next steps apply to both types of cases.

Connect the cables from the turbo and reset switches, and lights for turbo, power, and hard disk operation. Connect the two power cables from the case to the motherboard. The two power cables have six wires each, of which two are black. When the power cables are properly installed, the four black wires should be alongside each other, at the center of the two power connectors.

Figure 5-5 shows the angle of the power cables relative to the connector. They have to be hooked over the connector, stood up vertically, then pressed down. This type of connector reduces the possibility of the cables accidentally becoming disconnected.

If not already installed, install the power switch in the case. Pay particular attention to how it is installed, as an error might injure you or others.

If there is any doubt in your mind as to the correctness of this step, return the case to the vendor and ask for help. This is important! The documentation should eliminate all doubt.

Refer to *Figure 5-4* to see how you install a motherboard in a case with no fold-down side. This is the worst case scenario, since the fold-down case style is much easier on which to install the motherboard.

On the cases without a fold-down side, installation is similar, but somewhat more cumbersome than the fold-down style. Install the plastic standoffs, then slide the motherboard into position, aligning the ground screw with the metal standoff. Screw the motherboard to the metal standoff.

Exercise care not to damage the motherboard while installing it in a case without a fold-down side. You have to carefully slide the motherboard in without hitting the hard drive and floppy disk installation bays.

Note: with this type of case, and many of the purchased computers have this type, it is more difficult to upgrade a motherboard. Often you are better off removing the hard disk or disks first, then removing and reinstalling the motherboard. If you have a choice, always purchase a case that has a removable or fold-down side.

All sizes of cases come either with or without a digital readout indicator for system speed. You will find it quite an experience programming the readout to properly indicate the processor speed of your system. The three-digit readout is programmed by selecting, from a bank of options, the digits corresponding to your system's speed.

Jumpers are removed or connected to select the row and column associated with each number in the readout. The documentation is accurate for every case I have used, but the process is time consuming and occasionally frustrating. I recommend purchasing a case that does **not** have this feature because of the annoyance associated with this task. Then, if you upgrade later and use the same case, you do not have to reacquaint yourself with this task.

Or, select an impossibly high clock frequency readout, like 250, and have your friends wonder if you own the next generation high-end computer! If your computer is fast enough, you might just be able to pull it off!

Figure 5-5 **CONNECTING THE POWER CABLES TO THE MOTHERBOARD**

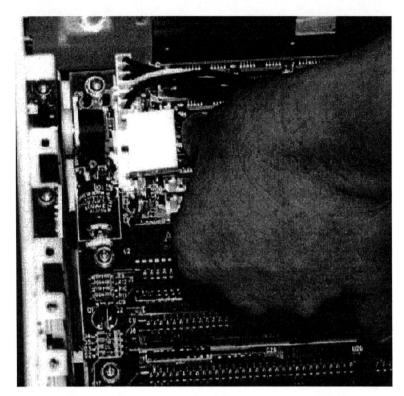

Reinstall the fold-down case side and check the rear panel cutouts for alignment with the add-on card slots. You can loosen the ground screw and realign the motherboard for closer fit if required.

Test the alignment by plugging in a card. Ensure that the mounting screw which holds the add-on card aligns properly, then tighten down the motherboard. Double-check the tightness of all screws.

This test ensures the motherboard will not accidentally short out if you plug in a card with the power on.

Press lightly on each corner of the motherboard after it is installed. Ensure no portion of the motherboard contacts the case beneath it. If it does, you should install another standoff in that area.

If there isn't a slide slot beneath the hole for a standoff on the motherboard, cut off the

portion of the standoff that hooks under the slide slot and install the standoff in the board anyway. It will not hold the board in position, but it will prevent it from accidentally contacting the case. Refer to *Figure 5-6*.

If you have to fashion a short standoff to prevent the motherboard from contacting the case, refer to this procedure. Note the installed position. Cut off that small portion of the standoff that normally slips under the case slide slot.

When you install the motherboard, it will be elevated by this standoff and unable to short to the case in the event you must plug in an add-on card with the power applied. You are performing this operation because some add-on cards allow you to plug them in with power applied, though this is not the normal practice.

Once the motherboard is installed in the case, the hardest part of this project is completed. Now let's install add-on cards.

Figure 5-6 THE PLASTIC STANDOFFS

Figure 5-9 TWO CASE SLIDES

Installing the add-on cards is quite easy. Be certain you have observed polarity on all cables you connected to the add-on cards. If there is any doubt, consult the documentation or your supplier.

Video Card Installation

Place the video card in the slot furthest away from the power supply. If it is a PCI video card, select the PCI slot furthest away, and if it is a VESA video card, use the VESA slot furthest away. The RAM on the video card can pick up noise from the power supply. *Figure 5-7* shows the installation.

Use care handling the video card. The RAM is sensitive to electrostatic shock. Ground yourself to the metal inside of the case once before unpacking the video card. Do this by touching any bright metal surface inside the case, preferably the power supply enclosure, if possible.

If your system has on board IDE I/O, skip the next step.

Figure 5-7 A VESA VIDEO CARD INSTALLATION

EIDE I/O Card Installation

Refer to *Figure 5-8*. It shows a local bus EIDE I/O card for a 486 motherboard. This is a VESA EIDE I/O card being installed. The cables are already in place, to facilitate installation, which is the only way to easily connect all the cables. The only cable still remaining to install on this card is the hard drive LED indicator. The documentation for the case will identify this two-conductor cable.

To complete the EIDE I/O installation, install the rear panel add-in slot with the other two communication ports. This is permanently connected to one of the cables you attached to the EIDE I/O card earlier. Refer to *Figure 5-10* for a quick look now.

Note: if you ever experience problems with a serial communications port on your system, and you have one unused port, you can easily reconfigure the system for the second I/O port.

The hardware jumpers covered in your documentation will show you how to easily swap the two ports, so you do not have to re-configure your software. It is much easier to reconfigure hardware settings than to peruse and change each software setting affected.

Some newer add-in IDE I/O cards, designed to replace defective on-board IDE I/O functions, have on-board BIOS which permits automatic configuruation. You are queried by the card during the first boot up after installation. You answer questions about your hardware, and the add-in card configures itself accordingly.

Figure 5-8 THE IDE I/O CARD INSTALLATION

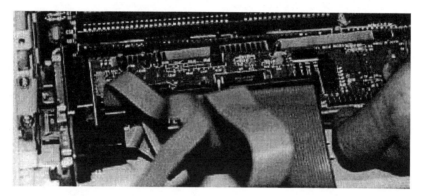

Figure 5-10 I/O INTERFACE REAR PANEL SLIDE

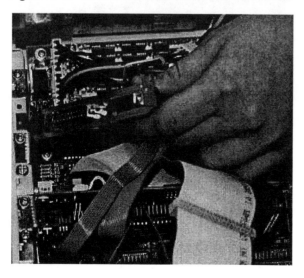

This add-in interface requires one unused slot in your computer. You should pick a position with an 8 bit slot, and not one of your faster slots. The 8 bit slots are the ones marked *ISA* in your motherboard's documentation.

Some motherboards have a slot position dedicated for this I/O slide. It is the one with the CMOS battery situated directly in the path of a potential add-in card, making the slot useless for any other purpose.

A basic computer requires only the add-on cards installed up to this point. Most people install a sound card, modem, and/or CD-ROM SCSI interface card as well.

You have completed the installation of all add-in cards, the motherboard, RAM, and CPU. You have connected all cables to the installed PC boards, including the motherboard. You have several cables hanging from the computer still, and a small pile of hardware remaining to install.

If you haven't done so already, connect the IDE and I/O cables to the motherboard with an on-board IDE I/O interface. Your motherboard documentation will show you where they go. Install the I/O interface as *Figure 5-10* depicts, and you are ready to move on.

Recheck the attached cables one more time before moving on; this is the best time, while some parts not yet installed are not in the way.

Let's install the remaining hardware now. We will start with the hard drive. Refer to *Figures 5-11* and *5-12* for installation and cable connections.

Figure 5-11 HARD DISK INSTALLED

Figure 5-12 HARD DISK CABLE

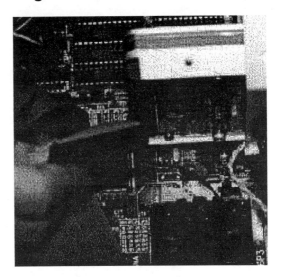

Configure the hard disk per instructions provided with it. Ensure the jumpers (shown in *Figure 1-4* in Chapter 1) are properly set. The default is "single hard drive." If you have multiple hard drives to install, you must set one up as master, and one as slave, using these jumpers. Make your boot drive the master.

Install the hard disk in the lowest 3.5 inch bay. Slide it into the bay until two holes align in the case and the hard drive. Install the short screws that came with the hard drive. Any other screws may be too long, and could damage the hard disk PCB.

Install two screws on the other side of the case in a similar manner. Each hard drive should have 4 screws holding it in.

Install the hard disk control cable from the IDE add-on card or motherboard as shown on *Figure 5-12*. Ensure that the polarity is correct. For multiple disk installations, a two-connector cable is available. It has two identical connectors on the hard disk side, so both drives can connect to the same cable. Be certain the master drive is the furthest from the end of the cable that connects to the IDE controller.

Installing the floppy drive is similar. There are two sizes of floppy drives, but I will not discuss the obsolete 5.25 floppy drive installation. Most people install only one 3.5 inch floppy drive, and a CD-ROM drive.

Refer to *Figures 5-13* and *5-14* that show installation of a 3.5 inch floppy drive and the cable that controls the drive. Note: the cable end furthest from the floppy control PCB or motherboard must be connected to the floppy disk (in a single floppy installation). The cable is coded to assign drive letter A to the floppy drive installed on that end of the cable.

If you install a second floppy drive, use the remaining connector on the same cable. The second drive will be assigned drive letter B.

Figure 5-13 THE FLOPPY DRIVE

Figure 5-14 THE FLOPPY CABLES

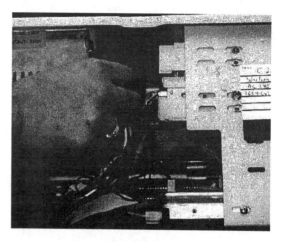

With the floppy and hard drives installed and configured, the remaining task is to install the CD-ROM drive. Review *Figures 5-15* and *5-16* for details on CD-ROM installation.

Figure 5-15 THE IDE CD-ROM

Figure 5-16 CD-ROM CABLES

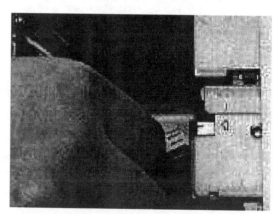

A typical IDE CD-ROM drive connects to the IDE interface through a cable identical to a hard drive control cable. The cable connects to the secondary IDE interface in an EIDE system. If you do not have the EIDE interface, you must give up the slave hard disk drive position to install an IDE CD-ROM. The CD-ROM documentation gives an example.

An SCSI CD-ROM needs an SCSI controller card or a SCSI sound card as an interface. The instructions for this type of installation are detailed, and are included with the purchase. Review the documentation for the interface card and the CD-ROM drive.

The power cables to the drives were not discussed earlier, but they are specified in the documentation for the hard drive, floppy drive, and CD-ROM drive. Confirm all the power connections have been made to these components.

The power connectors come in two sizes, and both sizes plug in only one way. With this task completed, it is time to hook up the monitor, keyboard, and mouse. If you have speakers for your CD-ROM drive and sound card, install them now as well.

Connect the keyboard at the round hole on the rear of the case. You can see the connector on the motherboard by looking into the left hand side of the case.

The mouse connects to the smallest of the I/O connectors you installed on the rear panel. If you installed an IDE I/O card, it is normally the top connector on this card, and has 9 pins.

For future reference, this configuration will default the mouse, as installed, on Com1. This is the first serial I/O port. You have two of these. The second one has a 25 pin connector. Both serial I/O ports can perform the same

functions, but, since a mouse normally comes with the smaller 9 pin connector, it is usually installed on COM1.

The monitor connects to the video card through the rear panel. Connect and screw down the interface cable from the monitor. If the monitor has a special power cable to connect to the case, install it now.

Connect the speakers to the sound card. The sound card has an interface cable that you connected between the sound card and the CD-ROM. This interface cable, a small cable with 3 to 4 wires, transfers digital sound information from the CD-ROM to the sound card for processing into analog signals that will drive the speakers.

Connect your printer to the printer port, if you have a printer. When you finish with this portion of the installation, you should have a system similar in appearance to the one pictured in *Figure 5a-1*, shown below.

Figure 5a-1 THE COMPLETED SYSTEM

Step by Step Installation

Most of you that evaluated the first edition of this book suggested the following step by step approach. Though information specific to the particular components you select for your system may differ from these directions, the pictorial nature of this presentation is very comfortable to many first time computer assemblers. These components are desirable to most of the individuals I queried, so the pictures presented here are representative of the most common system built today.

Step 1

Prepare the motherboard as described next. Install the cache RAM, as shown in *Figure 5a-10*, by pressing it down into the socket with your thumb. Install the SIMM RAM by placing it into the keyed socket and forcing it against the spring locks into an upright position, as shown in *Figure 5a-9*. The motherboard is now ready to install into the case, on the fold-down side shown in *Figure 5a-14*. Remove the 3 screws shown.

Figure 5a-10 PIPELINE BURST CACHE INSTALLATION

Step Two

Install the motherboard on the fold-down case. Review *Figure 5a-14*, for a back-side view, showing the plastic standoffs and the case slides. Review the section on motherboard installation on pages 96 through 100.

After performing these steps, you are ready to connect the remaining cables to the motherboard. Locate and install the IDE I/O cables to the motherboard, as shown in *Figure*

5a-11. These cables are keyed, with pin 1 of both the cable and connector identified clearly, as described on page 95.

Connect the remaining case cables for the power LED, reset switch, speaker, HDD activity LED, and any other applicable cables now. Since the options vary between cases and motherboards, you must use the installation documentation supplied with both. Refer to *Figure 5a-12* for one installation example.

Figure 5a-9 SIMM RAM INSTALLATION

After completion, the case side can be pushed back into normal position and secured with the screws previously removed. Refer to *Figure* 5a-13 for specifics. Note: ensure you do not pinch any wires as you reinstall the case side, **before** you tighten the mounting screws.

Figure 5a-14 THE FOLD-DOWN CASE SIDE

Figure 5a-11 IDE I/O CABLE INSTALLATION ON MOTHERBOARD

Figure 5a-12 THE REMAINING CASE CABLES

You have just finished the hardest part of the component installation phase. Remaining items plug into the motherboard or the case.

Step 3

Let's examine pictorially the remaining hardware to be installed. See *Figures 5a-13, 5a-4, 5a-5, 5a-7, 5a-8,* and *5a-17.*

Step 4

The remainder of the installation is simple. Install the cards pictured in the motherboard slots corresponding to the bus type. The short connectors with the pins close together are the 64 bit PCI connectors, and you only have one PCI card to install. When you install the PCI video card, place it in the slot furthest away from the power supply; away from the radiated heat and power supply noise.

Figure 5a-13 CASE SIDE REINSTALLATION

Figure 5a-4 A 16 BIT SOUND CARD

Figure 5a-5 A DIAMOND STEALTH 3D PCI VIDEO CARD

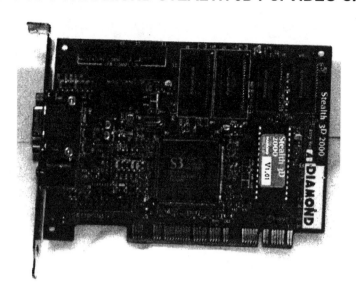

Figure 5a-7 AN EXTERNAL TAPE DRIVE AND ITS ACCELERATOR CARD

Figure 5a-8 AN 8 BIT SCSI CONTROLLER FOR A SCANNER, AND A 16 BIT SCSI CONTROLLER FOR A HEWLETT PACKARD CD-ROM RECORDING DRIVE

Figure 5a-17 (from top to bottom)
**CD RECORDER, CD-ROM DRIVE
3.5" FLOPPIES**

Next, install the 16 bit cards; the tape drive accelerator card, the SCSI CD writer card, and the sound card. If possible, allow some space between the cards.

The only 8 bit card to be installed is the SCSI adapter used to control the color flatbed scanner. Install it in the 8 or 16 bit slot nearest the bottom of the computer when the case is placed upright. Since this card is so small, it has the least requirement for cooling, and this slot is notorious for poor ventilation.

With all the cards installed, it is now time to install the remaining hardware; the hard disks, the floppy disks, and the CD-ROM drives. Review pages 103 through 105 for specifics, and study the pictures on those pages for the finer points.

Using the information in the beginning of this chapter and this pictorial step by step method, you have just built your own computer.

The sample system pictured and described here is a Pentium 166 computer with a full boat of accessories, including 2 printers and an external modem. When I started this book, it was just a Pentium 120, but times change.

Remember, the computer you choose may be anything the market has to offer, and the installation steps are basically the same.

This concludes the installation portion of this chapter. The next step is to power up and configure the computer as a complete system. You are about to turn on your new computer for the first time, and enjoy the benefits of your substantial efforts. Congratulations!!

Starting Your System For The First Time

Plug in the main power cable for your system to both the wall socket and your computer. Have the following documentation handy: the motherboard manual turned to the section on CMOS setup, the hard drive manual turned to the section on CMOS configuration data, and the phone book turned to the fire department's number. (Just kidding!!)

You have to tell your computer something about the components you installed. The CMOS setup stores the information, and uses it each time you turn on the computer. Turn your computer on. Look for any unacceptable signs, like smoke, arcing noises, or flashes of light. If you see or hear anything that suggests a problem, shut the computer off and recheck all connections, including power cables and the power switch connections. If everything is normal, press the required keys on the keyboard to enter setup mode. Often the computer screen will tell you which keys to press. The motherboard manual will certainly give the information.

The CMOS setup screen should come up. If it doesn't, and you get an error message about some configuration issue, refer to Chapter 7. Problems are discussed in detail, and can be quickly resolved.

If you have a blank screen, or the computer locks up during initial power up, repeat the process one time. If you get the same results, jump quickly to Chapter 7 (Murphy's Law), and we will analyze and fix the problem.

Once you are in CMOS setup, follow the motherboard documentation. Enter the date, time, hard drive information from the hard disk manual, and floppy disk size and type. Do not change anything in CMOS setup unless the documentation tells you to. We will optimize CMOS later in this chapter.

The CMOS directions are fairly simple. Follow them carefully, particularly when setting the hard disk's parameters. If you only have one floppy disk drive, make certain that you designate it as floppy drive A.

Note: CMOS setup is *volatile*, which means temporary. If the CMOS battery on the motherboard dies, the setup is lost. Make sure you write the CMOS setup down, and keep it inside your case. A floppy disk label is a good place to write it. Stick the label inside the case. Hopefully you won't need the information again, but it will be handy.

With CMOS setup configured, reboot the system with a DOS boot disk. The Microsoft DOS boot disk has the necessary files to prepare your hard disk for use, but use DOS version 6.0 or later. The disk should have a label which says *Disk 1 - setup*.

When you exit CMOS setup your computer will boot, or initialize from the floppy disk. You will receive a message allowing you to continue installing DOS or exit. The exit key is the F3 function key on the keyboard. Press this now, because you cannot install DOS yet, since DOS does not recognize your hard drive.

When setup returns you to the A> prompt, type *fdisk*. This calls the **fixed disk setup** program. The screen looks similar to this:

```
MS-DOS Version 6.22
Fixed Disk Setup Program
Copyright Microsoft Corporation   1983, 1993

FDISK Options:
Choose one of the following:

   1. Create DOS partition or logical DOS drive.
   2. Set active partition.
   3. Delete partition or logical DOS drive.
   4. Display partition information.
   5. Change current fixed disk drive.
       [Note: Number 5 shows up only if you have multiple hard drives.]


Enter choice:   [1]
Press ESC to return to FDISK options.
```

You must do two things to use your hard disk. Choose option 1 to create a DOS partition. Then return to the menu and choose option 2 to make the partition active. When asked if you want to use the entire disk for DOS, select 'yes'.

Note: if you wish to partition your hard disk into several smaller *logical* drives, now is the time to do it. If you partition the hard drive after formatting and installing software, you will destroy any installed software and data. Refer to the hard disk manual to investigate the benefits of partitioning before moving on.

After you finish, press the *ESC* key to return to the A> prompt. You are ready to format your hard disk and create the boot block.

High level formatting organizes the disk area into sections in a manner that allows data to be easily stored and accessed. A FAT, *File Allocation Table*, is created to index the stored data. Now, type *format C: /S*. This high-level formats the hard drive C and transfers the *system* files to the hard drive. The next time you boot up, you will be able to do so from the hard drive.

Try this test. Remove the floppy boot disk, and reboot your computer. To *soft boot*, hit

the *CTRL*, the *ALT*, and the *DEL* keys simultaneously. Your hard disk should boot, and you should have a message displayed asking for the date and time to be entered. This means your hard disk is successfully formatted and operational.

Now, reboot with the floppy disk. Install DOS according to the directions shown in the DOS setup program. You are on your way!

Install your software per the directions on the software package or documentation. It is best to install software in the following order:

> 1. **Microsoft DOS.**
> 2. **Microsoft Windows 3.1, Windows 95, or Windows 98.**
> 3. **DOS only applications, particularly backup programs.**
> 4. **Combination DOS and Windows applications.**
> 5. **Windows applications.**

Read your software documentation.

Software documentation is typically very good where installation issues are concerned. If you have any problems with software, the product support staff will help. I have even received good help from the software vendors.

Thoroughly Test Your System

The next few hours should be invested learning your system, and checking for any *glitches*. Test everything, from the speakers to the modem, by running the software you have installed. Anything that seems unusual, you should document. Keep an error log of your first 48 operational hours on the computer. Note the programs involved, the hardware being used, and the operations you are performing. Hopefully the log will be an empty sheet of paper, but if not, you have a good starting point to resolve the conflicts.

If you find problems, check the documentation on the programs involved. See if you might be doing something the program doesn't like. Look in the hardware documentation and be certain you are within the proper operational guidelines for the hardware involved. Glitches and conflicts are discussed and corrected in Chapter 7; Murphy's Law.

Example: you are typing in a word processor, and when you hit *ENTER*, the text reformats. Fix: check online help or the software setup and look for auto-format options that are on.

Example: you are testing sound card software in Windows, and the system locks up. You have to reboot to restore operation. Fix: you installed the Windows sound card software *before* the DOS software, and the DOS software modified your CONFIG.SYS and/or AUTOEXEC.BAT files, confusing the Windows setup. Reinstall the windows software for the sound card.

Let DOS programs have control over the AUTOEXEC.BAT and CONFIG.SYS routines by installing all DOS programs first. Windows will modify its Win.ini and System.ini files to run the DOS programs. Then, when Windows exits, it will restore the DOS settings. This is the primary reason to install DOS programs first.

Burn In Your Computer

If you can, leave your computer on for at least 24 consecutive hours. This *burn in* period allows hardware issues to surface. Ninety percent of all hardware failures occur within the first 24 hours of operation. It is unlikely that you will experience any problems, but if you perform this operation, you can be confident that you have reduced the chance of an unexpected failure considerably.

Start A Folder On Your Computer

Save all documentation, receipts, and other paperwork associated with your system. If you have a printer, enter the setup program and press the *SHIFT* and *PRINT SCRN* keys on the keyboard simultaneously. This will print a hard copy of the CMOS setup. Add it to the folder on your computer, and keep it in a safe place, along with other important paperwork. The folder will help if you decide to upgrade, because you will have all the information on your system in one place. Since you have documentation on everything you purchased, the folder is an excellent place to keep the documentation, along with receipts.

Now, let's look at a significant performance upgrade. It's time to look at the Pentium II.

Upgrading to a Pentium II

People involved with computers dream of a new system with leading edge performance read about in the computer magazines. Usually the super system we want is priced just out of reach, and we pass on the dream for now. "Maybe next year…"

One way to have the dream system is to perform a competitive upgrade, using most of the components in your existing system.

Let's look at one of the things that must change. Review *Figure 5b-1*, the Pentium II ATX case, rear view, with a slide-out motherboard mount.

Figure 5b-2 shows the case slide removed from the case. Removal consists of separating the case from its cover, then removing the one screw that retains the case slide. After doing so, lift up on the top of the case slide and pull rearward. It will come out easily.

Now, lay the case slide down on your work area with the inside facing upward. Place your motherboard over the case slide on the metal standoffs, aligning each standoff with a hole in the motherboard. Attach the motherboard to the case slide with the included screws. **If any standoff does not align with a hole in the motherboard, remove it, to prevent the possibility of shorting the motherboard to the case.**

Assemble the cards onto the case slide and the motherboard, as shown in *Figure 5b-3*. If you have built a computer before, you remember how difficult this action was with the older cases, since installing the add-in cards had to occur inside the tight confines of the case.

Check to ensure that all add-in cards are properly seated in their slots, and screwed down to the case slide. Confirm that both the RAM and Pentium II are seated tightly in their slots. Look once more to ensure that no possibility of a short exists between any component and the case. Now, set this assembly in a safe place, and prepare to install your drives in the case.

FIGURE 5b-1 Pentium II ATX CASE

FIGURE 5b-2 THE CASE SLIDE

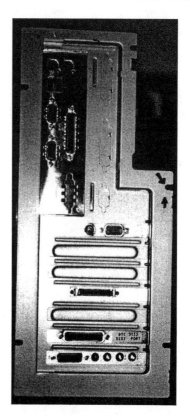

Figure 5b-3 PENTIUM II BOARD MOUNTED ON CASE SLIDE

The next step is installing the case-mounted drives, including the CDROM(s), the hard disk(s), and the floppy disk(s). Install them in the new case in the same manner that they were installed in the old case. Review *Figure 5b-4* for a sample installation.

Now, connect all cables to these components, including the power cables, while the case is uncluttered by the circuit boards and their cables. By now you realize that most of the difficulty in installation has been eliminated by the ATX case designers.

After connecting the cables to the drives, place the case in the upright position, allowing the cables to hang freely. *Figure 5b-5* shows exactly what you should see during this step.

Place the case slide on the two tracks, and gently slide it forward, until the motherboard power connector reaches the power supply cable. *Figure 5b-6* is a good example.

Figure 5b-4 DRIVES IN ATX CASE

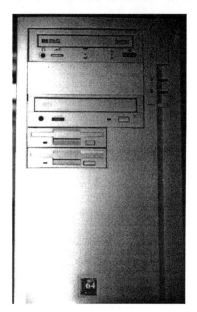

Figure 5b-5 CABLES AND SLIDE IN POSITION FOR CABLE CONNECTION

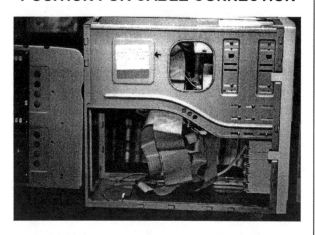

There are a few things to be aware of as you continue. As you connect cables between the hard disks, floppy disks, and CDROMs, be absolutely certain that you observe the proper orientation of the cables to the connectors.

All cables have a red mark on the cable and a triangular indentation on the connector designating pin 1. There is a corresponding mark on both the drive and the motherboard connector designating pin 1. **Failure to follow cable orientation will result in damage to either the motherboard or the drive.**

Some peripherals and motherboards have keyed slots to prevent incorrectly plugging in the cables. Most CDROMs and a few newer motherboards share this safety feature.

Also, be certain there are no cables on or near the power supply fan or the CPU fan.

Figure 5b-6 CASE SLIDE IN POSITION TO CONNECT CABLES

Now for the truth behind this adventure. My wife, forever in my shadow because I had the Pentium 200 MMX blaster and she had my leftover Pentium 120, decided to ditch a day of work. Instead of running over to the local department store, she visited the local computer parts vendors. Little did I realize, she was planning a coup.

She had my draft of this book, about $600, and a desire to make me suffer, so she brought home a brand new ATX case, and an AGP video card, compliments of the salesperson, who knew it would improve her video graphics performance by 100%. She wrapped up the package by purchasing a Pentium II 333 MHz processor, 128 MB of SDRAM, and the latest American-made Tyan motherboard.

She had the system up and running in less than 2 hours. After she burned my tail in a Norton Utilities benchmark contest, she showed me the system. She also duplicated the assembly at my request, so I could document the process for your benefit.

Figure 5b-7 shows her completing the assembly process by installing the case slide, after connecting the cables to the motherboard that control the drives, and connecting cables between the sound card and the CDROM. She wrapped it up by installing the cover.

Figure 5b-7 SEEING IS BELIEVING. FINAL ASSEMBLY AFTER CABLING

Of course, the system booted perfectly, since the new motherboard was PnP compatible, and had an auto-detect function for configuring the hard drives and CDROMs.

Figure 5-8 shows the completed system with the cover on, booting for the first time. Not bad for a couple hour's work!

Please take note of the small label under her left hand. That's where she wrote the CMOS settings for her hard disk, in case the auto-detect feature in CMOS failed to accurately configure her hard disk. The information she wrote down is on the hard disk, but invisible when the hard disk is installed.

One other thing to remember when you do such a complete upgrade is, if you have an external modem, be certain that you take note of which *com port* the mouse is set to before you disassemble the old system. Swapping the com ports between the mouse and modem will cause some annoyance in re-configuring them. The computer will auto-detect the modem and mouse, but **any applications you have already installed that remember where the mouse or modem was before will be confused.**

Figure 5b-8 STARTING THE PENTIUM II FOR THE FIRST TIME

Now, let's look at some ways to speed up your computer. Note: CMOS setup parameters are normally preset very conservatively, to allow use of slower processors and RAM.

Performance Tricks

Several performance improvements are available in your CMOS setup; however, care must be taken in each case. Thoroughly test your system after each change, and return the system to default values if any problems arise.

These tricks work only if you have a fast Pentium, 6x86 or Pentium II system.

The advanced CMOS settings for each computer vary considerably. These settings assume a minimum of a Pentium 166, and can be improved somewhat with faster processors.

DRAM R/W BURST TIMING: The default for this is x4444/x4444. You can halve the wasted time reading and writing to the DRAM if you have pipeline burst cache. *Change these numbers to x2222/x2222.*

DRAM RAS# Precharge time: *Bump this down to* 3.

DRAM RAS to CAS Delay: *Change to* 2.

DRAM R/W leadoff timing: *Change to 7/5.*

ENABLE block mode for IDE Hard Disks.

These settings are normally conservatively set by the manufacturers of the motherboards, and can be set to faster positions for the faster processors, like we are doing. The performance increase is significant.

Now let's speed up hard drive access time.

Determine the *mode number* associated with your hard drive. Mode 3 and 4 HDD are

extremely fast, but CMOS must know the hardware is installed. If your motherboard has auto-detect for mode, you are already set.

Pushing these items gives a Pentium 120 benchmark numbers better than those of a Pentium 133. Other ways to pick up speed cost money.

Pipeline burst cache, EDO RAM, SDRAM, and a good fast video adapter card with VRAM also speed up a fast machine significantly. CD-ROM caching software will turn a quad speed CD-ROM into a eight speed or better without any hardware changes.

The most important upgrade capability involves the processor, as prices of the faster processors steadily fall.

That is the best time to buy a processor-only upgrade. You can have today's $4,000 performance for few hundred dollars when the opportunity arises.

You have built the computer of your choice, and saved a bundle doing it.

You have found and debugged conflicts by reading documentation (or Chapter 7). You have even taken a look at hot-rodding your system without spending another dime.

Now, let's look into the future, and get an idea of how we can upgrade the system we have, when the time comes.

Read on, and discover Chapter 6, *Upgrade or Perish.*

6 UPGRADE OR PERISH

Topics
Upgrading older computers
Why upgrade?
When to upgrade or replace
Upgrades for newer computers
Software upgrades, when and why

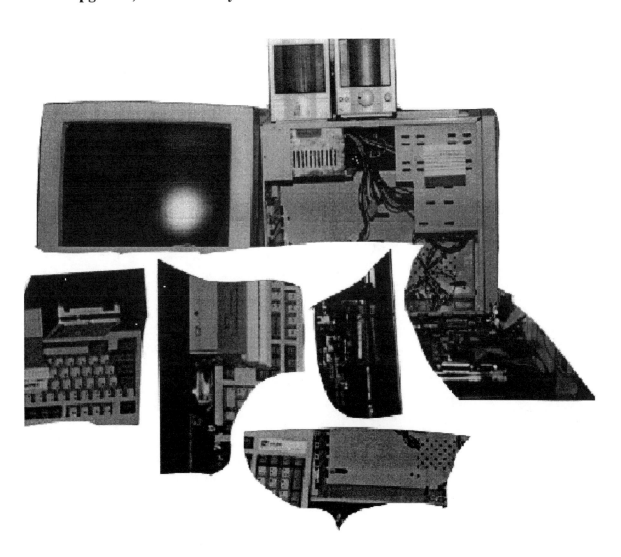

Upgrading Older Computers

When queried, most individuals would rather upgrade their existing computer than buy a new one. The reasons are varied, as are their unique applications and needs. The two computers I presently have are hybrids of the numerous upgrades I have performed.

Upgrading saves money; this is a fact. It gives you the performance of a new machine at a fraction of the cost. It's also a way to buy a new computer one piece at a time, allowing you to have a new computer without the immense bill normally associated with a purchase of that magnitude.

The title of this chapter was influenced by the actions of a friend. He is a published expert in the field of digital frequency synthesis and digital communication techniques. He also proudly owns and uses a 386-40 ISA computer. Now is the age of the Pentium II, but he still clings tenuously to the past. I have been leaving notes in his desk and e-mail with the message *upgrade or perish.* He pays me no mind, and just pumps out another book or technical document. This leads me to the most important subject in this chapter; upgrading older computers.

Several options apply to upgrading older systems. The upgrade can be a simple memory increase, monitor upgrade, processor upgrade, motherboard and add-in card upgrade, or my favorite, empty the case and start over.

The most common upgrade is the motherboard swap. Let's look at this upgrade step by step.

The Motherboard

If you read Chapter 5, you know how very important it is to have your CMOS setup information preserved. Imagine trying to read the setup information from an installed hard drive's top cover. Make a copy of your CMOS setup before you attempt any upgrades.

To access your CMOS setup, most computers have a startup message telling you which key to press to enter setup. The most common key is the *Del* key, followed by the *Esc* key.

When the CMOS screen is displayed, press the *shift* and *print SCRN* keys to print the setup information. If you don't have a printer, write down the information for the hard drive. You will need the number of cylinders, heads, sectors, landing zone, and precomp data.

If you know the mode information of your hard drive, include it. Scan all areas of your CMOS setup for information on hard disks, CD-ROM devices, and any other add-in devices, including pipeline cache and EDO RAM or SDRAM.

Shut off your computer and disconnect the power cables, monitor, keyboard, mouse, and any other cables on the rear panel. Mark the cables and the connectors for future reconnection. Use a permanent marker to avoid confusion when you disconnect these cables sometime later.

Remove the cover rear panel screws that hold the cover on. They are located at each outside corner and in the top center on the rear panel of a desktop case. The typical tower cover has one screw in each outside corner on the rear panel.

The next step is documenting the cables and connections to the motherboard. If you have the manual for the motherboard, this is unnecessary. I recommend that first time upgraders take a picture of the computer's interior in addition to documenting cable connection and placement.

If you don't take a picture, make a sketch of each card and cable's placement in the system.

Mark the interior cables and connectors to ensure correct replacement when the job is complete. Mark the cable and the connector on the same side, to ensure you do not install the cable backwards. I recommend leaving the cables connected to the hard drive, CD-ROM, tape drive, and floppy disk drives, if possible, and only disconnecting the opposite end of the cable.

Remove the cables for front panel switches and LED indicators. These can normally be traced back to the switch or indicator, so marking them may not be necessary. Remove the two power connectors on the motherboard, at the rear near the power supply. To be removed, they must be pulled up, then angled toward the center of the motherboard. Refer to *Figure 5-5* in Chapter 5, and read the paragraph immediately before the picture for clarification.

You are now ready to remove the add-in cards. Remove the screws that hold in the cards. They are screwed in at the rear panel through the add-in card retainers. Remove the cards one at a time, and place them in the trash. (Not really!) Ground yourself by touching the cover you removed. Place the add-in cards on this cover.

Find the one or two screws that retain and ground the motherboard. Remove them, and slide the motherboard from the case. The plastic standoffs will come free of the case slides, and the motherboard can be removed and placed on the cover with the other cards.

Refer to the documentation that came with the new motherboard, and insure the default jumper positions are correct for your processor, memory, and cache types. Compare the two motherboards at this time, and determine where each cable removed from the original motherboard will connect to its replacement. Refer to the section in Chapter 5

on motherboard installation for further information.

Check the mounting configuration on the new motherboard. Transfer the plastic standoffs to the new motherboard. Refer to Chapter 5 for the solution if one or more of the standoffs do not align with the case. Look at *Figures 5-6* and *5-9* in Chapter 5.

Transfer any RAM you intend to use onto the new motherboard. The documentation will tell you if you must install the RAM in a specific slot or bank. You are now ready to install the new motherboard in the case.

Install the motherboard by reversing the procedure you used to remove the original. Connect the power cables first, making certain the black wires are alongside each other, at the inside of the two connectors. If you incorrectly install these connectors, the black wires will be on the outside, and turning on the computer will send the motherboard to PC heaven.

Use the motherboard documentation to place the remaining cables in their correct position, then install the video card and all other add-in cards.

Note: If your new motherboard has on-board IDE I/O functions, do not install your existing IDE I/O card. This is the card that was connected to the hard disk, the floppy disk, and the extra I/O add-in rear panel slide. *Figure 1-2* in Chapter 1 shows the card. Instead, refer to the motherboard documentation and install the cables from the hard and floppy drives, then the I/O rear panel slide to the motherboard.

All internal components are now hooked up. Reconnect everything disconnected from the back panel, and replace the cover. *Never turn on anything plugged in to the wall socket with the cover removed, unless someone is with who knows CPR you.*

A motherboard powered up for the first time must have the CMOS configuration information updated. Using the motherboard documentation, turn the computer on and start the setup routine. Type in the date, time, and all CMOS information concerning the hard and floppy drives, and CD-ROM if required.

Exit the setup routine and allow the computer to reboot. Pat yourself on the back, then go to the bank with the hundreds of dollars you just saved.

Some people upgrade the video card to a PCI or VESA type when they upgrade their motherboard. I always install the motherboard first, then get the other goodies later. This allows me to thoroughly evaluate the motherboard alone, then check out the other parts later. It is no fun to do a complete upgrade and have one bad part hang up the system. Always keep your older components for a while, in case you need to use them as troubleshooting aids later. Then, sell them to a less fortunate friend.

Run your new motherboard overnight to burn it in. If anything is going to fail, it will probably do so in the first 24 to 48 hours of operation. Do a thorough test of your computer after 48 hours, to ensure you have a functional system. After performing these operations, you will know the project was successful.

Now, let's discuss why anyone would want to upgrade a perfectly operational computer.

Why Upgrade?

Occasionally upgrades are forced upon us. An example is a friend of mine's dilemma. He bought a version of Microsoft Office that slowed down his computer tremendously.

Why? The program requires 5 Megabytes of RAM to run effectively, and his computer only had 4 MB of RAM installed. A quick trek to the computer store and a modest purchase fixed his problem.

Another example. A client of mine likes multimedia packages. She bought a high end computer game with embedded video clips, but hated the horrible performance. The video was jerky and unrealistic. She had invested a bundle on a 6-CD game she couldn't play.

The reason: She had a single speed CD-ROM drive, which is good enough for data transfer, but not fast enough for good smooth video performance. Again, the solution was an easy upgrade she performed herself. The 32X CD-ROM drive she installed cost her very little money, and just 20 minutes of her time.

I have built more than 100 computers, ranging from DEC workstations and Tektronix information display systems in my years with Tektronix, to the faster Pentium II machines my clients occasionally require. I have noted the primary reason a computer becomes obsolete to the user is a change in software requirements. This single reason forces many good computers into a premature burial.

When is a computer obsolete? Never, if it fills the intended purpose. I've learned *a computer that fills it's required purpose is never obsolete.* If you never have the desire or need to upgrade your software, you may never want to upgrade your computer.

Why do software programmers write programs that have high hardware requirements? The primary reason is programmers aim their software at the fastest computers available. The faster machines show off the programs better than slow ones, and the programmers have more flexibility writing programs for faster machines. More memory in a computer means the programmer has even more flexibility with his program code.

It is hard to write programs with high levels of functionality for slow machines with small amounts of memory. The limitation of speed makes many visually oriented programs, such as Windows 95 and most multimedia programs, run slow or not at all. Most programs today must grab the user's attention and keep it, so they must be visually oriented and interact with the user. And, of course, programs like these consume memory. These reasons make programmers constantly strive for speed and functionality in their programming.

If you plan on upgrading or replacing your current system, be certain you are doing it for the right reason. Upgrading or replacing a system that performs to your requirements may not be a good idea, particularly if increased speed is not a concern. Save your money until your system fails to meet your requirements and a real need arises. Do not succumb to advertising literature telling you that you must have the latest and greatest software update unless you actually need the improvements the upgrade offers.

To Upgrade or Replace

When deciding between upgrading your system or replacing it entirely, consider the following items:

1. How old is your monitor? If it is a 15 inch SVGA monitor, it is worth saving. A 15 inch SVGA non-interlaced monitor is worth $150 to $200.

2. How old is the motherboard? If it is a 486 or older, the expense of replacing the motherboard, all the add-in 16 bit cards, and the memory will probably justify replacing the case and everything in it.

You can sell your 486 system to offset some of the cost. Also, if the monitor is not a non-interlaced SVGA monitor, you might want to replace it as well.

Generally, replace a 486 system if the monitor is not a SVGA non-interlaced monitor. The older monitors fall short in high quality visually oriented programs. Upgrading a 486 motherboard to a 6x86 or better may require replacing the RAM, due to the industry-wide migration from 30 pin SIMM to 72 pin. The add-in cards will have to be upgraded to PCI or AGP to work in a new Pentium or faster motherboard. This makes upgrading and replacing similar in price, assuming you plan to build the new system instead of buying a new one.

If you have an upgradable 6x86 or Pentium PCI motherboard, you probably also have a SVGA monitor. You can upgrade this system by replacing the processor alone, and get performance improvements of twice the speed or better. The price of a K6-200 MMX or 6x86MX-PR200 is around $60.

If you decide to upgrade the motherboard, a sneaky option is the 6x86 PCI motherboard upgrade. You will have to replace the motherboard to get BIOS which supports the 6x86, but the motherboard, cache, and a 233 MHz processor only costs about $150.

Then, you only have to add a $50 video card, and you have a complete PCI system. The IDE I/O function is built in. What this means is a complete upgrade (less RAM) will cost around $200, and your system will beat a comparable Pentium in performance and speed.

In the decision to upgrade or replace, consider the age of the components in your system. If you can live with a slight improvement in performance, upgrade the motherboard, and use the slower existing add-in cards from your original system.

If you want the full performance of a AGP or PCI system, it will be as cheap to buy a new case and build a PCI or AGP system inside it. Remember the Pentium II upgrade in Chapter 5. You can sell your old system for more than you will pay for the new case. The price of the case is the only addition to the price of buying new versus upgrading. I am assuming you will use the same floppy and hard drives.

Now, let's look into upgrading systems that are less than two years old.

Processor- or Motherboard-Related Upgrades

For some reason, most people shy away from upgrading the CPU. I find it the easiest and most beneficial upgrade you can perform. The CPU is a drop in upgrade for most newer motherboards.

This upgrade starts with a quick perusal of your motherboard documentation. Verify which processors your motherboard supports, and confirm the location of any jumpers, if any, you must move.

To upgrade a Pentium microprocessor-based motherboard, determine if its BIOS supports the 6x86 processor line. If it does, you can upgrade to beyond Pentium speed. If not, you may have to be satisfied with a little more than doubling your system performance.

Upgrading a Pentium system is similar to upgrading a 486 machine, though you have more options. The Cyrix 6x86 processor upgrades nearly double the comparable Pentium processor's speed. Confirm first that your motherboard supports the Cyrix processor. Of course, the faster Pentium processors are drop-in upgrades to most Pentium motherboards.

The Pentium motherboards also allow you to replace DIP cache with pipeline burst cache on a SIMM module. This cache is about 20 to 30 percent faster, depending on your CPU.

Another drop-in performance improvement is EDO RAM, which will buy you 10 to 15 percent improvement in overall speed. If you have 168 pin DIMM sockets, adding 10 ns SDRAM instead will give you an additional 10 to 20 percent improvement in speed over EDO RAM.

I have seen no improvement in using 60 ns RAM instead of 70 ns. Unless the 60 ns RAM is EDO RAM, the difference in speed of the RAM between 60 ns and 70 ns is insignificant.

Hardware Improvements on Newer Computers

Generally, everything you can add to a computer gets faster with time and technical evolution. The improvements in video adapter cards are significant in departments other than speed. You can upgrade to hardware MPEG video movie support with the replacement of your existing video card. Watch the ads. The price of this upgrade is falling fast.

CD-ROM drives are constantly increasing in speed. No sooner did I find a good deal on a 24X drive than the 32X drives hit the market. I just test drove a 36X recently. It is noteworthy to mention I saw no difference in performance

between my 24X and the 36X I evaluated, but software is currently being developed that will use the increase in speed.

Sound Cards

Since the new 64 voice sound cards are out in force, many gaming people have coded some extremely realistic games and multimedia programs that use the improvements. The sound card has come a long way, and an upgrade of this nature will give some people an extreme rush. Most programs, however, do not make use of the improvements. Be certain you will obtain measurable performance increases before making this upgrade by carefully reading the software documentation regarding hardware requirements.

Software Upgrades

When do you upgrade your software, and why? I have been asked this question many times. I upgrade when the newer version fixes a bug I wish to get rid of, or when new software offers something I can't live without.

The only other time I will upgrade is if the operating system I am using becomes obsolete. An example is DOS version 3 or earlier. Most DOS software requires DOS 4 or newer, and prefers DOS 5 or 6. You have to keep software for more than five years to run into a problem like this.

Upgrading software is an expensive process if you have 9000 Megabytes of software like me. Upgrade only if there is value to you in the result. Remember, if you keep upgrading software, sooner or later you must upgrade your computer. It's a never ending cycle.

Upgrading is the most inexpensive way to keep your computer current, if that is what you wish. I need to be on top of the current high end of computer technology, since I work with many people who need the latest in performance. I have not purchased a new computer since 1994, yet two of my computers are state of the art.

I sell most of what is removed from my computer as I upgrade. Every year or so, I put everything I have removed into a new case and build a system. I install the software I no longer use on it and transfer the software licenses to the person who buys the system. I refer the buyer to a local vendor who buys and sells equipment, and the person buys a used SVGA monitor for $110, and a keyboard and mouse pair for $15. They have a computer, and I have the money.

This action accomplishes two things: it keeps me from becoming a pack rat, and it reduces my upgrade costs. I found out my Pentium 200 cost about $600, after I subtracted revenue from selling the old stuff. The Pentium 200 has two 3.5 inch floppies, two 5.4 Gigabyte hard drives, an 800 Megabyte tape backup system, a 24X CD-ROM drive, a flatbed color scanner, and printer. Not bad for a mere $600!! Recently, our old Pentium 120 became a Pentium II 330 MMX with 128 MB of SDRAM.

As you can see, upgrading is the most inexpensive way to get a new machine, if your existing computer is fairly new. If you have a very old machine, I recommend selling it and applying the money toward parts for the new system. Note: be advised that computer software licenses must stay with the original software disks, and you cannot sell copies of your software. *You give up the right to use any software you sell.*

Let's move on to Chapter 7 and look at common trouble spots when building or upgrading computers.

Your Notes

7 MURPHY'S LAW

Topics
Common configuration conflict areas
Problems while upgrading
Problems while building new systems
Problems after installing software
Other compatibility issues

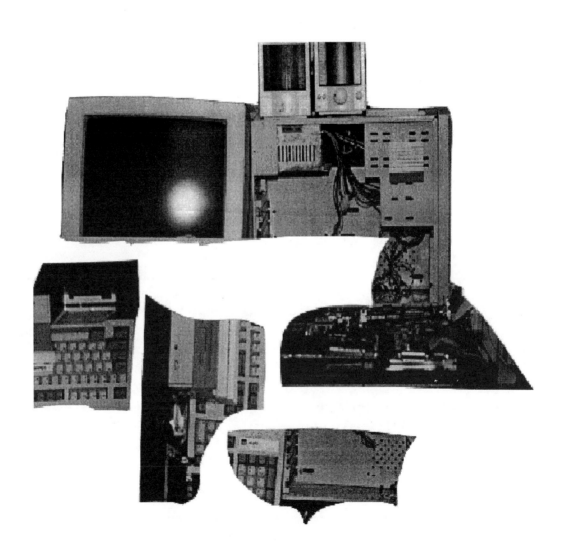

Common Conflict Areas

Hopefully you are reading this chapter for information only, and you have a successfully operating machine. Maybe you are intending to help an unfortunate friend ferret out a few bugs in his or her computer.

But, if you and Murphy are good friends, we know why you are here.

Murphy once said if something can possibly go wrong, it will. *He is right*. Occasionally, I will come across his magic working in a friend's computer, and sometimes it finds a way into mine.

I have seen a number of configuration issues in my time, and have read numerous books and articles on these issues. These are the most common problems and ways to deal with them.

DMA Conflicts

Let's look at the DMA channels and see who uses what. Remember from the introductory chapter that Direct Memory Access channels are required by many add-in cards, and no two items in the computer can share the same address.

DMA 0:
This signal line is internal to the motherboard, and is used to refresh memory. There is no conflict possibility with this line.

DMA 1:
This line is available, and primarily used by sound cards. You may have a conflict here if you default install a sound card, and then install a SCSI adapter for a scanner or other host device. This is an extremely common mistake.

DMA 2:
This line is for the floppy disk drives to share. You may also piggyback a tape drive here. Occasional conflicts occur if you try to use a tape drive and floppy drive simultaneously.

DMA 3:
This line is available, and is the primary choice for many Sound Blaster compatible sound cards. I found out the hard way that some IEEE controller cards and network cards use this line as a default.

DMA 4:
This is the DMA controller line. It is unavailable in most machines for other applications.

DMA 5:
Available for Sound cards and SCSI adapters. It is 16-bit stereo sound compatible. Watch for conflicts between sound cards and SCSI cards.

DMA 6:
Available for Sound Blaster compatible sound cards.

DMA 7:
Like DMA 5, available for sound cards and SCSI adapters.

There is quite a bit of flexibility in setting up DMA channels. Remember, when you set up DMA channels, set up the add on cards with the least amount of flexibility first. The least flexibility normally can be found on any 8 bit card and many network cards.

Make a point to set up VESA and PCI cards last, and be certain to configure all manually configurable cards before installing and configuring PnP add-on cards. If you have any conflicts attributable to DMA settings, the information presented here should fix the problem.

IRQ Conflicts

You have control over which device uses certain IRQ lines. Let's take a look. Remember from the introduction that Interrupt Request lines must also be unique between hardware add-on components.

IRQ 0:
The system timer uses this line. It is only available for the motherboard's use. If any conflicts are reported here, there is a problem with the motherboard.

IRQ 1:
This line is for the keyboard's use. The signal is available for the keyboard and motherboard only. Problems with this line may be caused by the motherboard or the keyboard.

IRQ 2:
Once used for EGA video adapters, this line is available. Watch for conflicts if your video adapter is backward compatible to EGA or if you are using IRQ 9. IRQ 9 often uses this IRQ to talk to the processor. Note: use this line for network cards. It is not an ideal choice for 16 bit stereo sound cards and may rob the card of stereo performance. Some systems assign this line to the programmable interrupt controller.

IRQ 3:
This line is normally assigned to COM2 and COM4. Some older 8 bit network cards came with this setting as the default. This is a conflict in most systems, and requires you to reconfigure the network card.

IRQ 4:
This line is normally assigned to COM1 and COM3. As with IRQ 3, this line can be configured on sound cards, network cards, and modems, so be aware of the numerous conflict possibilities.

IRQ 5:
This line was originally set up for a second parallel printer port. It is commonly used for sound cards, but most other devices can be set to this line. A tape drive may wind up being set to this line, particularly if it has a tape drive accelerator card.

IRQ 6:
The floppy drive controllers grab this line. Often, someone will use it for a tape drive or sound card, if concurrent floppy drive use never occurs. This can be a conflict area in some systems, particularly if a sound card is set to this line.

IRQ 7:
The primary use for this line is the first parallel printer port. Watch out for conflicts when background printing if you attempt to share this port with another add-on card.

IRQ 8:
Your motherboard uses this line for the real time clock. If something reports an error with this line, you must shoot the motherboard. Note: the CMOS uses this line also. System information programs report this line as *"CMOS and real time clock."*

IRQ 9:
Since this line shares with IRQ 2, it is a high priority line. A high speed network card will scream when set to this IRQ. Many 16-bit network cards are default set to this line.

IRQ 10:
Use this line for sound cards or network cards, particularly if all the lower numbers are utilized elsewhere.

IRQ 11:
SCSI cards often come set to this number. Multiple SCSI adapters may require the use of this line and others. Bump the network card

down to IRQ 10 if you have network and SCSI cards installed.

IRQ 12:
This is the default line for the on-board PS/2 mouse. Most computers do not use this type of mouse, so this line is available for network, sound, or any other add-on card use.

IRQ 13:
The numeric processor operation ties up this line. Any error associated with this line means, of course, shoot the motherboard. (Return to vendor.)

IRQ 14:
This is the secondary IDE hard disk controller line. If you have no IDE hard disk or adapter present in your system, it is an ideal setting for a SCSI hard disk controller.

IRQ 15:
The primary IDE hard disk controller lives here. As with IRQ 14, you may do anything with this line if on-board or add-in IDE controller functions are not installed in your computer.

These bits of information cover most of the conflicts seen in the DMA and IRQ areas. Conflicts found here may be an indication of defective components, but 99 percent of all conflicts are in the setup of the add-in cards or motherboard jumpers.

Make a list of these DMA and IRQ settings, and configure any items whose default settings conflict. Chances are this will solve any setup problems.

I/O Addresses

Input/output devices require unique addresses to operate. Two devices with the same address will not operate properly. The following list shows the addresses occupied by most add-in cards and resident operations.

These address schemes are the most common utilizations, and give you an idea of how to clear addressing conflicts. The addresses are in hexadecimal notation.

130h:
SCSI controller add-in cards often use this address.

140h:
SCSI controller add-in cards often use this address.

220h:
Sound Blaster emulation on compatible cards use this address. This is the default setting for the real Sound Blaster sound card.

240h:
This setting is the common alternative to Sound Blaster addressing.

278h:
With IRQ 5, this address is commonly the default setting for the secondary printer port.

280h:
This is a common choice for network, IEEE, and occasionally SCSI adapter cards.

2A0h:
This is a common choice for network, IEEE, and occasionally SCSI adapter cards.

2E8h:
Assigned as a default to COM4 as is IRQ 3.

2F8h:
Assigned as a default to COM2, as is IRQ 3.

300h:
Warning: steer clear of this setting if you use Windows 95. Sometimes used for network cards. Win95 uses this address, and causes conflicts with any devices set to this address.

320h:
This is a common network card setting. Avoid it if you have a SCSI adapter at address 330h.

330h:
This is a common choice for network, IEEE, and occasionally SCSI adapter cards.

340h:
This is a common choice for network, IEEE, and occasionally SCSI adapter cards.

360h:
Warning: Network cards set to this address will conflict with your primary printer port, unless you change the printer default from 378h.

378h:
This is the default primary printer port address.

3BCh:
This is a good alternative setting if you must move the primary printer port address default setting.

3E8h:
This address is assigned to COM3.

3F8h:
This address is assigned to COM1.

Occasionally, you will find intermittent or sporadic behavior. Be certain you check addresses for conflicts if any of these devices are inoperative or intermittent. The addresses normally are not a problem in systems with PnP cards installed.

Here's a problem I found in Windows 95 during the initial installation on a network machine. Remember the note about address 300h I mentioned earlier in this chapter? Yes, Murphy is alive and well. Things to avoid when installing Windows 95 on a network machine follow.

1. If your network card is set to address 300h, reset it to either 340h or 280h.

2. Avoid address 320h, since a SCSI device installed now or later at address 330h will screw up the system.

3. Avoid address 360h, to eliminate a conflict possibility caused by a parallel port interface installed now or later at address 378h.

Network installation under Windows 95 is automatic, and you will not realize you have a conflict unless you try to network soon after installation. If you are missing the *Network Neighborhood* icon, or if you simply cannot access the network, you may have this type of conflict.

If you have to reconfigure a network card for operation at another address, be sure you edit the *net.cfg* file in your system to reflect the changed address. You will find this file in your root directory on the drive your computer boots from, normally the C drive.

If you use Windows 95, you must go to the control panel and change the resource configuration under either the *Windows 95 network* or *System* icons.

Back to Home Use

Most conflicts in a home computer come from sound card installation or configuration issues. To determine if your sound card is causing the headaches you are experiencing, remove it from your system. If the system works, the sound card was the culprit.

If your sound card is giving you fits, here's how to find out why. The sound card is a resource hog. It needs three of your resources: a DMA channel, an IRQ line, and a unique hardware address.

When you install the software for your sound card, it should create a record of these settings in your Windows *system.ini* file. You will see a DOS record of the information in a line in your *Config.sys* file, too. Here are some examples.

Config.sys entry:

DEVICEHIGH=C:\PASTUDIO\MVSOUND.
SYS D:6 Q:7 S:1,220,1,5

This Pro Audio driver shows the DMA set to 6, the IRQ set to 7, and Sound Blaster emulation information.

Windows System.ini entry:

[mvproaud]
dma=7
irq=7

What's wrong with this picture? First look shows that DMA settings for Windows and DOS differ. Is this a conflict? Absolutely not! This card, like many other sound cards, is completely software configurable.

The nice thing about software configurability is the capability of different settings on the card for different operating systems. This actually *reduces* conflicts, since different operating systems have different resources available.

What does this mean? If your DOS settings cause problems in Windows, set the sound card to another DMA or IRQ setting in the Windows configuration. The DOS settings are restored, if you specify, when exiting Windows.

If you have a sound card you must configure with jumpers, be certain your configuration files reflect the exact configuration specified by the jumpers.

Upgrade Headaches

Some conflicts occur after upgrading one or more components. A new PCI motherboard and PCI video card may not like some of the older cards you transfer from your old motherboard. Generally, upgrades like this go flawlessly.

Try to isolate the questionable device or add-on card causing the conflict. If you are upgrading, you have a replacement for each new part. Try swapping in the original parts until the conflict is resolved.

When you find the offending component, try different configurations for DMA, IRQ, and I/O address, if possible. With the myriad of components available out there, occasionally one manufacturer's component may work with other brands. If you cannot satisfy the conflict between one component and the others, try a different brand. This nearly always works.

It is important to remember that a motherboard with on-board IDE I/O will *not* accept installation of an add-on IDE I/O card with the same DMA, IRQ, or I/O address settings. The default settings for both are the same. *Never* install an additional IDE I/O card without first setting the defaults differently. Remember, the only reason to install an additional IDE I/O card in your computer is if the function on the motherboard is either obsolete or defective.

Some video cards do not work well with certain brands of I/O card. You will have to get rid of one of the two. Of course, if your motherboard has on-board IDE I/O functions, the problem is already solved.

Remember, a PCI motherboard with on-board IDE I/O needs only a video card to run. When upgrading, start with only the one card installed, then add the others one at a time. You will quickly find the offending card.

Now, let's examine problems with new systems.

New systems have their share of problems, but not as many as older computers. With the enhanced bus and additional 16-bit configuration additions, there are considerably fewer conflicts, and many more configuration options available.

Most conflicts in new systems occur due to more than one device sharing the same DMA, IRQ, or I/O setting. These conflicts are easily remedied by confirming the default settings do not conflict, and ensuring that components are configured properly with the default settings.

What if your computer doesn't initialize? If all portions of Chapter 5 are followed, this is the least frequently occurring problem. Common causes for a computer not starting are unseated RAM, unseated add-in cards, and configuration BIOS not set properly.

Confirm that all RAM is seated properly. Remove and reinstall each RAM SIMM. Check the cards for proper seating. If you have on-board IDE I/O, confirm the plug-in cables are seated properly and installed correctly.

Try to boot up again. If this doesn't work, remove all add-in cards except the video card on motherboards with on-board IDE I/O. Leave the IDE I/O card installed on those motherboards without this option.

Try again. This time, the system should boot. Refer to Chapter 5 and complete setting the system up. Now, install the add-in cards one at a time to find the culprit. Try everything mentioned above to reconfigure the card to work; if you cannot achieve success, trade the card in for a new one or a different brand.

If the motherboard never enters the setup mode, either the motherboard, processor, or RAM are defective. Return the motherboard to the vendor, and he will test it. The processor and RAM can also be tested. You will return home with the problem solved.

Reassemble the system, and continue where you left off in Chapter 5.

Software Issues

You now have an error-free system, but little or no software has been installed. We can really mess up a system by improperly installing software, believe me. Software normally installs flawlessly, but you *must read and understand* the instructions to install it properly.

Beware of software that modifies configuration files without prompting you. Understand exactly what is being changed. Chances are, if your system is hardware filled, something else may be affected. The software you install today may reconfigure the add-in component you installed yesterday, particularly sound cards.

Software that modifies the Config.sys, Autoexec.bat, Win.ini, and System.ini files can cause unpredictable results. Always make a copy of each of these files and name them uniquely *before* installing a new software package, and make notes on which programs change the files.

The instruction set below assumes you have a single hard drive with no partitions. Change the paths to reflect your directories and disks as required. Be sure you can remember what you name the file copies, or write them down and save them in your computer's folder.

```
From the C: prompt type:

        copy Config.sys config.sav

        copy Autoexec.bat autoexec.sav

        copy c:\windows\win.ini c:\windows\win.sav

        copy c:\windows\system.ini c:\windows\system.sav
```

This creates uniquely named backup files of the configuration files new software installation might screw up. I assume you have a boot disk, so even if the Config.sys and Autoexec.bat files are modified to the extent that they do not allow you to start your computer, you can still boot up and copy over them with the saved files.

Most modern software has extensive error detection and corrective measures embedded within the programs. You will be able to fix most software problems after a few minutes of reading the manuals, but, since everything in life is nonlinear, some problems may escape the programmer's scrutiny. This is why the industry invented software hot lines, and put them in the documentation.

New versions, new operating systems, and initial releases of games typically have the largest number of errors.

Most problems will be small compatibility glitches with certain hardware packages, particularly involving sound card support. Video support is a close second when it comes to software incompatibility. The largest number of software compatibility problems are divided among these two hardware components.

We have looked at the primary sources of problems occurring in new and upgraded computers. A basic understanding of addressing and the conflicts associated with address, IRQ, and DMA sharing has been acquired. We have the knowledge to find and identify problem devices. We know what to do when the computer isn't feeling well.

Now is a good time to shift gears and look at diagnostic software. Chapter 8 gives pointers on putting your computer in top shape and keeping it there.

THE SOFTWARE TOOLBOX

Topics
Commonly utilized diagnostic software
Tune up hints

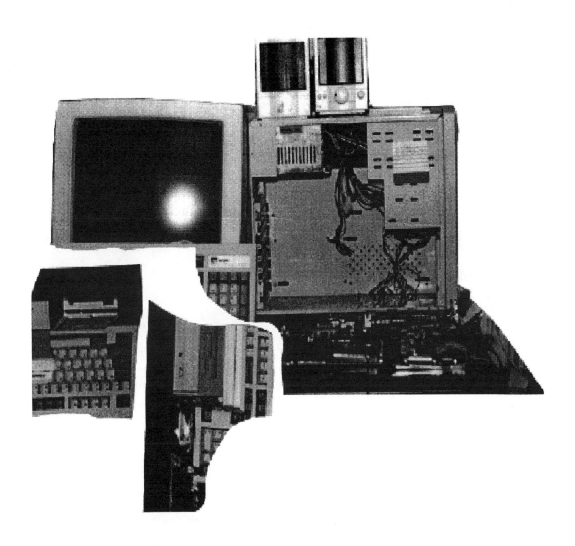

Diagnostic Software

Programs that fall into the category of *diagnostic software* generally do not top most software buyers' priority lists. *This is very unfortunate.* Without a good diagnostic program of some kind, you may become very unhappy someday soon.

Bad things can happen with computers. Some you may never notice, some make themselves the central focus of your life if you are in the middle of something important on your computer. Hard disks occasionally lose small bits of data, a common occurrence in systems that are shut off accidentally or turned off without properly closing programs.

Small bits of data may be the missing link in your important graphics application, or they may be part of a program you installed improperly. When you use the program again, or look for the missing data and can't find it, you will absolutely wish you had a good diagnostic program.

Occasionally you do something like this.

You put a floppy disk in a:

dir a:

You see nothing on the a drive you want to save. *Then you do it.* You are at the *c* prompt, but think you are erasing the floppy in the *a* drive.

Erase *.*

When you hit the *enter* key, everything at the root directory on the c drive is erased.

You just lost your Config.sys, Autoexec.bat, and many other important files.

Guess whose computer can't boot anymore?

If you had installed Norton Utilities and created a rescue disk, guess who would be back on line in minutes?

This is only one horror story. You will be able to create your own in time. You might do this a few times before you get a tool to recover data you accidentally lose.

There are many programs available to identify and correct the many little things that can go wrong while using and abusing your computer. I will discuss several I am familiar with in the remainder of this chapter, and will mention some cool tune up programs and their uses.

After reading this chapter, you will know which program suits your unique needs.

The Programs

I am going to list these in alphabetical order, since my preferences should not influence your decision on which best suits your needs. Remember, these are but a few of the many programs available. Check out your local dealer, and evaluate as many programs as possible before making your purchases.

Checkit Pro: Analyst

This extensive program details performance and diagnoses all aspects of your computer. A burn-in feature allows you to run unattended tests on your computer, a procedure I recommend you perform during the first 48 hours of continuous use. If your hardware is going to mess up, it will do so in the first two days of constant use.

Figure 8-1 shows some of the available features.

Figure 8-1 CHECKIT PRO BENCHMARK AND SYSTEM INFORMATION

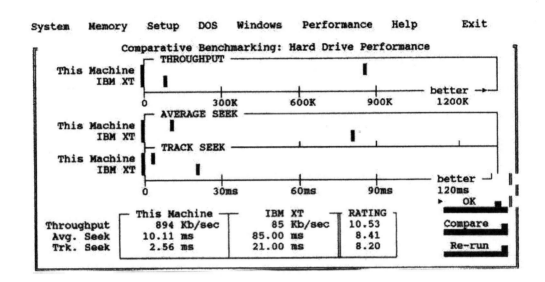

This program caters to new users and experienced personnel alike. The Windows version is the latest release, and is feature loaded. It can provide performance data, configuration data, benchmark your system and test all aspects of your hardware. *Checkit Pro* is available from **TouchStone Software**, at (800) 531-0450.

Com-And

Communications and… is shareware by Scott McGinnis, and you should evaluate it, especially if you are into on-line activity. You can find it on the Support ETC BBS by dialing (310) 439-7714.

Disk Technician

Prime Solutions, at (619) 274-5000, created Disk Technician, which is a superior method of detecting errors on, and recovering data from your hard disk. It will repair files by relocating data to a safe area on your hard disk. It can be configured to check your disk for errors on boot up, if you desire.

IniExpert

Windows configuration has always been an issue, particularly for new computer users. Programs use and abuse both the Win.ini and System.ini files. This program steps you through each line, allowing you to change anything, and giving you information on the significance of each line item.

The program also tracks any changes that programs make to these files. This is particularly important if a newly installed program adversely affects something you previously installed.

IniExpert is a product of Chattahoochee Software. Look them up on the Internet for more information, or call Computer Discount Warehouse, at (800) 330-4CDW.

Internet Suite

Speaking of Internet, this program rolls all aspects of surfing and peeking into one clean user friendly package. The user interface is the best I have used. This set of matched programs satisfies my appetite and increases my Internet mobility considerably. It is available from Shareware Express, at (800) 346-2842.

Microscope

I have never used this full featured program from Micro 2000, (818) 547-0125, but several people have written volumes of praise about it. It can analyze all aspects of your hardware, and report on DMA, IRQ, and I/O addresses, finding conflicts quickly.

It does a complete memory allocation test, shows CMOS contents, and allows you to modify CMOS setup.

MSD

Microsoft Diagnostics is a program resident in DOS. It gives a snapshot of all aspects of computer activity at the moment it is invoked. To initialize it, just type MSD anywhere in your computer, and it will work if a path to your DOS directory is spelled out in your Autoexec.bat file.

You can perform searches for subjects and files from MSD, and print out about 15 pages of detailed system information, including your Autoexec.bat, Config.sys, Win.ini, and System.ini files. MSD is available in MS-DOS versions 6.0 and later.

The Norton Utilities

Peter Norton put together a suite of diagnostic routines that dominates the market for superior and easy to use diagnostics. Both Windows and Windows 95 are supported. *Figures 8-2* and *8-3* show benchmarks using Norton Utilities.

Figure 8-2 BENCHMARKS USING NORTON VERSION 8 FOR WINDOWS

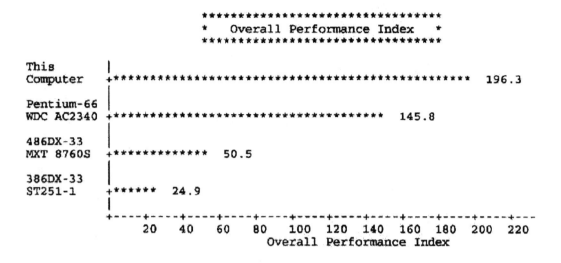

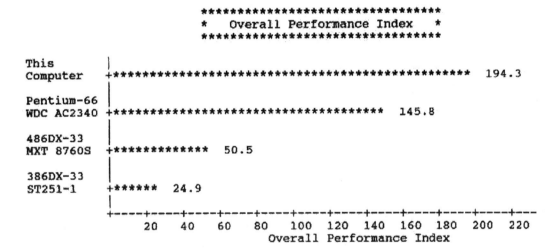

Now, let's look at the Windows 95 version of the same test. The Windows 95 version is a 32 bit program, and tests your computer's ability to use 32 bit code. The performance will be different than that presented by a 16 bit test program, even the 16 bit version of Norton Utilities shown above.

This program is representative of the type of programming becoming available as computer software experts become proficient at 32 bit program skills. 32 bit programming allows more flexibility to the programmers, since the programs run very fast on current machines, if your computer's operating system supports them. Examples of 32 bit operating systems are Windows 95 (a hybrid incorporating both 16 and 32 bit code), OS-2 WARP, and Windows NT.

Though 32 bit applications seem to be slow in coming, expect to see a virtual flock of new programs soon. The advantages will outweigh the wait. Watch for 32 bit games with embedded MPEG movies first, then full-featured upgrades to existing applications.

Figure 8-3 WINDOWS 95 VERSION OF NORTON UTILITIES BENCHMARK

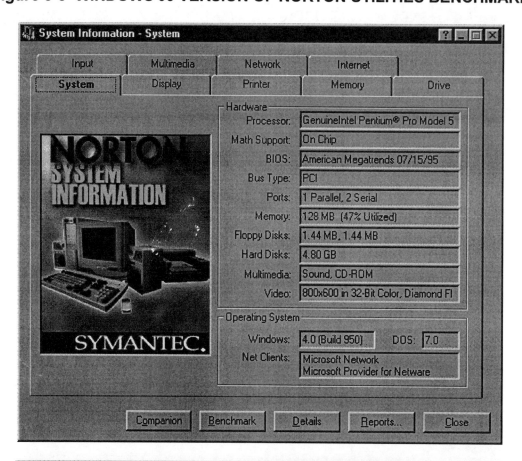

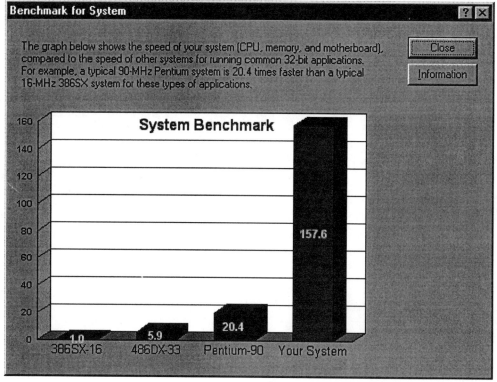

Figure 8-4a Pentium 200 benchmark, SDRAM

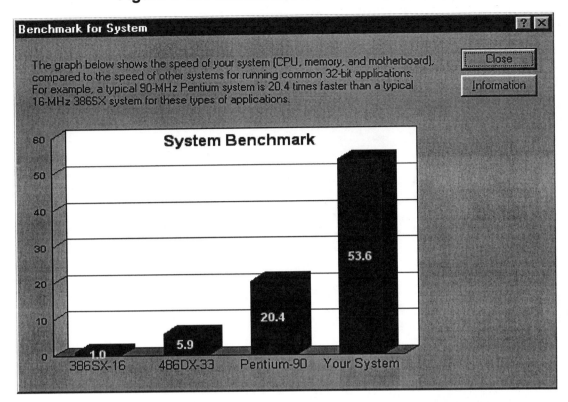

Figure 8-4b Pentium II-333 MHz benchmark, SDRAM

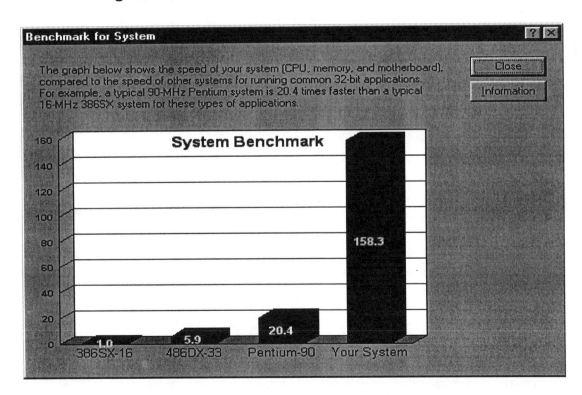

In addition to system information and benchmark testing, the Norton utility package provides comprehensive data protection. In Windows 95, you can protect the trash can from being accidentally emptied, which has saved many important files from destruction. The *image* program creates an exact duplicate of your file archive table, in case the hard disk area beneath it becomes damaged.

The speed disk program arranges files and directories in contiguous order, so fewer disk revolutions are required to store and retrieve data. There are many other features, and I will let you discover them for yourself.

Norton Disk Doctor is a program that I cannot do without. I'm constantly screwing up my system, though not intentionally. Trying some new and exciting global commands, I hang up even the most stable environments. Can you say *fatal disk error?*

Both Diskfix and Unerase have bailed me out of trouble when I tried something new and different to save time. I invariably find a way to hang my system with open folders, which creates nasty things called *widows and orphans.* Norton Utilities has restored my disk integrity, and sanity, on each occasion.

The most informative program, Ndiags, provides information on your CPU, memory, DMA, IRQ, and CMOS information. This information is necessary if you plan to upgrade your system.

Let's not forget the Norton Rescue Disk. When you install Norton Utilities, you have the capability of creating a rescue disk on a bootable floppy. This will allow you to boot your system and fix it, even if you damage the data on it.

The Norton Utilities package is available from Symantec Corporation, at (408) 253-9600.

PC Tools

If you need extensive and comprehensive utilities, this is the program you want. You can find and fix hard disk boot records and partitions, lost clusters, and damaged file archive tables. Like Norton Utilities, this lets you create an emergency disk.

PC Tools has an extensive virus scan and cleanup program that supports identification of more than 1,000 viruses.

PC Tools and Central Point Software have merged with Symantec, the creator of the Norton Utility package. Central Point Software can be reached at (503) 690-8090.

PC911

Normally considered a companion to First Aid for Windows Users, this program tracks all changes to PC configuration files. These two programs from CyberMedia at (800) 721-7824 offer a low cost alternative to some of the expensive utility programs previously mentioned.

QAInfo

Another writer once told me QAInfo is the most comprehensive source of PC configuration information. Along with QAPlus, it has been known as a technician's tool rather than a home computer jockey's workhorse. The times are changing. Hardware manufacturers often seek DiagSoft's expertise in software, rather than investing their resources. This makes DiagSoft's programmers among the best at diagnostic programs.

DiagSoft's programs cover more hardware than any program I have used.

QAPlus

The burn in portion of this program is worth the price. This program runs diagnostics and burns in your computer for you. It comprehensively and repeatedly tests your computer while you sleep.

What if you find something wrong, and don't know what to do next? QAPlus Windows version allows you to connect via modem to their *Electronic Technical Support Center.* You can electronically compose and send a test report. You will be notified by DiagSoft how to alleviate the pain associated with a sick computer.

The QA series of products is available from DiagSoft at (408) 438-8247.

QEMM

This memory manager from Quarterdeck Office Systems first interested me in the early '90s when I needed a more sophisticated method of controlling memory use. Embedded in it is a nice system information program called Manifest.

Quarterdeck Office Systems has several good utility programs on the market, including Sidebar and Internet Suite. The entire package is a cost effective and realistic support group for anyone interested in keeping their computer in top shape. Quarterdeck programs are available from local retailers or the Computer Discount Warehouse, at (800) 330-4239.

ScanDisk

This Microsoft DOS 6.2 utility is a basic diagnostic tool for hard disks and floppies. It performs basic analysis of file structure and analyzes the disk surface. If it finds disk surface errors, it can move the data to a safe part of the disk.

SpinRite

Gibson Research, (714) 362-8800 developed a program that can actually read and recover

data that DOS thinks is gone forever. This inexpensive program is a must.

SYSCHK

This shareware program, available on the BBS at (408) 945-0242, is an easy to use diagnostic program for the beginner and experienced user alike. The system information utility is simple and fun to use, and provides comprehensive information.

The Troubleshooter

AllMicro, at (800) 653-4933 has an inexpensive diagnostic program that allows you to bypass your computer's normal boot routine. It thoroughly tests all hardware, and allows you to print the results. If you have software conflicts, you can eliminate the hardware as the cause with this program.

What's-In-That-Box

Jeff Napier has created the ultimate PC tutor. He describes entertainingly the intricate goings on inside the case of your computer. More of an educational tool than a utility, this program gives the user an enjoyable trip through the inner workings of a PC. The program is available on CompuServe, just GO PCFF.

WinSleuth

This program, available at (714) 236-1380 is a low cost alternative. It performs all the tests the big guys do at a fraction of the cost.

WinProbe

The Landmark Company, at (800) 683-6696 makes the burn in program I like best. You can select as many tests as you like, and run them as many times as you like. This program is tops in the documentation department, and many companies like the technician form printout with the diagnostic information and a signature block.

These programs are but a small sample of what is available, mentioned because I have experienced them or had positive input from other users. You must select the programs that suit *you* best.

Tuning and Optimization

If you have purchased any one of the good diagnostic programs mentioned, you have the necessary tools to keep your computer in top operating system. Here are a few tips on how to do what is necessary.

First, create backup copies of your Config.sys and Autoexec.bat files. Use the technique mentioned in Chapter 7. Do the same with your Win.ini and System.ini files. Again, Chapter 7 gives real-life examples for you to follow.

Write down the names of the backup files, and keep them in a safe place. This will allow you to get moving again if a new program adds a conflicting line to any of your configuration files. To recover from a problem affecting any configuration file, just copy the saved backup file onto the existing configuration file. Make certain you rename the saved file the same as the original file you are replacing.

Second, review the performance tricks at the end of Chapter 5. Utilize any that apply to your system, and expect some increased speed and flexibility from your system.

Third, run memmaker, a DOS-based program, to increase the available DOS, or low, memory available to DOS and certain Windows programs.

Finally, utilize your diagnostic program (the program of your choosing) to perform a disk optimization on your hard disk. Select the option that allows you to optimize directories first and files second. This way, when your computer tells the hard drive to find programs, they are in one contiguous track or series of tracks.

Optimization takes the pieces of files scattered over the disk surface and places them in order, sequentially, on your hard drive. This means the hard drive travels a smaller amount to load programs into memory for utilization by the computer. Obviously, this saves time and wear and tear on your hard disk assembly.

Optimize your hard drive several times a year. This cleans up fragmented files, and returns your computer to optimal operating performance.

Moving On

Now, let's take a look at computer terminology. Read on. Chapter 9 will give you the power to communicate with sales personnel and software vendors, secure in the knowledge you will understand what they are saying. **You will be able to comprehend all the buzzwords and computer linguistics, and carry on an intelligent conversation with the best hardcore users.**

9 COMPUTER TERMINOLOGY

Topics
Buzzwords and their meanings
Other commonly utilized terms

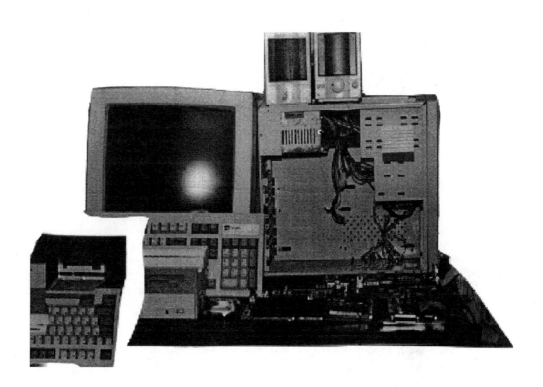

Buzzwords and their Meanings

The following tables start this chapter. Within them are the measurement units commonly applied to the computer terms you will be learning herein. You will acquire an understanding of many common terms used by the industry, and be able to use them to describe the system you wish to build or upgrade.

These terms by no means are the entire working glossary of the computer industry. They are the common descriptions most users and sales personnel are familiar with. You will be more capable of describing your needs, and determining whether or not the sales person is competent enough to help with them, after reading this chapter.

COMMON MEASUREMENT TERMS

ITEM	SYMBOL	ALSO EQUALS
bit	b	bits (symbol is lower case "**b**")
byte	B	Bytes (symbol is upper case "**B**")
b/s	bps	bits per second (lower case "**b**")
B/s	Bps	Bytes per second (upper case "**B**")
kb/s	kbps	kilo-bits per second (lower case "**k**")
Mb/s	Mbps	Megabits per second
MB/s	MBps	Megabytes per second
1 byte	1 B	8 bits
1 kilobyte	1 kB	1024 bytes
1 Megabyte	1 MB	1024 kilobytes
1 Gigabyte	1 GB	1024 Megabytes
1 Terabyte	1 TB	1024 Gigabytes
1 Kilohertz	1 kHz	1000 Hertz or 1000 cycles per sec
1 Megahertz	1 MHz	1000 kilohertz
1 Gigahertz	1 GHz	1000 Megahertz
1 Terahertz	1 THz	1000 Gigahertz

COMPUTER INFORMATION BY PROCESSOR TYPE

CPU TYPE	CLOCK SPEED	BUS BIT WIDTH	ADDRESSABLE MEMORY	CACHE RAM INT / EXT
XT (8086)	4.7-10 MHz	8	640 kB	0 / 0
80286	6-25 MHz	16	16 MB	0 / 64 kB
80386	16-40 MHz	32	4 GB	0 / 128 kB
486/5X86	25-133 MHz	32	4 GB	8 Kb / 256 kB
6X86/Pentium	60-233+ MHz	64	4 GB	16 kB / 512 kB
Pentium II	233-400+MHz	64-100+	1 Terabyte	32kB / 512 kB

(Yes indeed! The Pentium II is in a class by itself!)

Terms and their Definitions

Electronic terminology in general and computer related buzzwords in particular can be confusing, misleading, and even incomprehensible. This chapter exposes you to most of the commonly used terms, and provides definitions. After you finish this chapter, you will be able to communicate with anyone regarding any computer topic.

This glossary of terms and definitions is a good start on the road to computer literacy. It is placed in alphabetical, not historical order, to ease finding selective subjects of interest.

286

This is the original *AT* computer you hear so much about. It was a quantum leap from the 8 bit computers preceding it.

The original IBM 286 had an 80286 microprocessor and the capability of addressing 16 Megabytes of RAM. The most common processor speed was 12 MHz. I built a non-IBM equivalent, and was pleased to get an AMD 16 MHz clone processor.

The 16 bit internal and data bus made the XT machines slugs by comparison, and the 80287 math coprocessor made this the high speed machine of its time.

386

The 386 was the first processor in home computers to break the 32 bit barrier. The 386SX had an 80386 processor with a 32 bit internal and 16 bit external bus. The 386DX increased the external data bus to 32 bits.

For speed, the SX processor ran at 25 MHz, and the DX clocked at 33 MHz for the Intel version, with the most common clones running at 40 MHz.

The addressable memory size expanded to 4 Gigabyte, and a new 80387 math coprocessor was introduced. An SX version of the coprocessor also came out of the closet.

486

The 486 family of computers is still alive today, due to outstanding performance. Since nobody builds the 80486 microprocessor anymore, the 486 is being replaced by 5x86, Pentium, and 6x86 computers as the supply dwindles.

The 486SX computers house the 80486SX microprocessor. It is a 32 bit internal and external bus microprocessor running 25 MHz.

A 486SX2 computer boasts the faster 80486SX2 microprocessor, which runs at twice the SX speed, due to doubling the microprocessor clock. 50 MHz computers are not uncommon with this configuration.

The 486DX family added an 8 Kilobyte internal cache to the SX processors. The math coprocessor was also included within the microprocessor.

A 486DX computer has an 80486 microprocessor, which can move out at 50 MHz. The 486DX2 computers upgrade the processor to a 80486DX2 microprocessor running up to 66 MHz. The clock doubling technique utilized for the SX2 processors was used to double a 33 MHz clock, to give the DX2 the 66 MHz clock speed.

Someone found a way to quadruple clock speeds and build faster processors, so the 486DX4 computer became a reality. The most common processor speeds in this line are the 100 MHz and 120 MHz systems, and I have seen a 133 MHz processor.

8086

The IBM computer had to start somewhere. This was the processor of choice at the time. With an 8087 coprocessor, 640 Kilobyte of RAM, and a 10 Megabyte hard drive, this was the premier home computer for some time. If you opened an IBM PS/2 computer, this is what you would see. This processor supported 8 bits externally and 16 bits internally, and could address 1 Megabyte of RAM. It ran at a smoking 10 MHz.

8088

This 8 bit internal and external version of the 8086 found its way into most of the IBM XT computers. With the capability to address 1 Megabyte of RAM and operate up to 10 Megahertz, this system was the computer most people bought for home use.

AGP

Accelerated Graphics Port video cards use a proprietary bus structure, and provide significant improvements on 3-D video performance. They work in hand with the MMX instruction set to provide previously unheard of graphics speed.

Adapter

An adapter connects between two pieces of hardware and translates one form of connection to the other. It can be an interface cable, like a DB25 to parallel printer cable. It can be a 9 to 25 pin adapter for use with a mouse. It can be an add-in card whose purpose is interconnecting the motherboard bus to another device, like a hard disk.
The SCSI and IDE hard disk drive controllers are both adapters. So is a video add-in card.

Add-in Card

Add-in cards connect the motherboard to the devices you wish to operate with your computer. The video card, for example, connects the video monitor to the CPU through the motherboard. The sound card is an adapter which takes digital signals from programs and connects them to your speakers after processing them.

Address

Everything connected to your computer via an add-in card has a unique address, if it is an input or output device. This address is how your computer knows where to send data or where to receive information.

Memory locations are also addresses. Programs use memory addresses to find stored information to retrieve and process.

Addresses can be hardware addresses for a physical device or software data addresses in memory on a computer. The microprocessor treats them the same.

ANSI

The American National Standards Institute. This group controls specifications for many industrial applications, including the computer industry. The standards for displaying information, screen color, and positioning are part of this discipline.

The ANSI.SYS driver is often loaded as a line in your CONFIG.SYS file. If it is loaded, your computer can respond correctly to ANSI commands in the programs you execute. This DOS command is seldom seen in the Windows 98 environment of today.

Application

An application is a program or programs designed to execute a particular operation. For example, a word processor is an application designed to perform writing, editing, spell checking, and publishing functions.

AT Compatible

If a peripheral or computer provides the basic functionality of the same product in an original AT computer, it is AT compatible. This is a must for clone devices, so the buyer can have confidence his or her programs and accessories are compatible with the computer or add-on device. *IBM compatible* is another way of describing compatibility.

Autoexec.bat

This is one of the principal DOS configuration files. It is often utilized by installed programs to set up hardware or allocate memory blocks. You can use an ASCII editor, such as the DOS *edit* command, to add lines of code or change parameters in this file.

The Autoexec.bat file and all lines of code within it are executed in order of appearance. Some applications may be sensitive to the order in which commands appear in this file.

The most important feature of this file is the ability to set the *path* statement. You create paths to directories containing executable code here. Commands can be executed anywhere in your computer, if a path command to the executable code exists.

Example:
You exit from Windows. You are in the d:\windows directory on a two hard disk system. In your Autoexec.bat file, a path statement has the following line:

```
path=c:\norton
```

You type the command *sysinfo*, a Norton Utilities Version 8 DOS utility program.

Without a DOS path to the directory `c:\norton`, you would get a *bad command or file name* DOS error message, and the screen would laugh at you behind your back.

Base Address

Everything has a starting point. The first location in memory where a program resides is the base address of the program. Installed hardware devices also have a base address.

Batch Files

Like the Autoexec.bat file mentioned above, DOS recognizes filenames ending in *.bat* as batch files. These files are normally ASCII files written by the computer user to make life easier.

Example: you have an antivirus program and wish to run it occasionally, but do not want to waste a path statement to the directory *antivir* on a program operated once or twice a month. You enter the DOS editor by typing:

```
edit clean.bat
```

The file clean.bat will be created. Now start typing the commands.

```
cd c:\antivir
```

The first command changes your working directory to `c:\antivir`.

```
f-prot
```

This will execute an anti-virus program called f-prot.

Now, follow the DOS edit screen commands to save the file and exit the editor.

This is a simple batch program, but it will execute automatically if you type the command *clean* followed by the *enter* key.

BBS

Bulletin board services exist worldwide for your enjoyment. Not to be confused with the Internet, a bulletin board is normally a single computer or system you can dial up and obtain shareware from or engage in chat groups.

BBSes became popular long before the Internet, as a way groups could share files and information. Many companies still keep an open BBS to allow you to get the latest software updates and information.

One magazine that lists national BBS numbers every other month is the *Computer Shopper*, PO Box 51020, Boulder, CO, 80321-1020.

BIOS

You have seen this term used repeatedly throughout this book. The Basic Input/Output System is the ROM where your configuration platform resides, and is the first code to run when you turn on a computer.

The BIOS sets up hardware and software addresses and is the software interface between different devices in your computer. BIOS exists on your motherboard, and occasionally video adapters and other add-in cards, and provides interface services to and from the motherboard and these peripherals.

Boot

The act of initialization a computer undergoes when you first turn it on is called "booting up." The BIOS starts the boot process, and performs basic initialization.

The CMOS memory then executes configuration information to identify the hardware in your computer and perform basic tests on memory and other components as specified in CMOS setup.

Finally, the initialization files Config.sys, Autoexec.bat, and any other configuration files are run to set up components not specified in BIOS or CMOS. Normally, configuration files are modified by programs, so the programs know what hardware exists and can use it. This process occurs as the programs are being installed for the first time.

The computer is ready for use after this process is complete.

Bus

Unlike the Greyhound, this bus is the *pathway* that signals and data use to and from the microprocessor and all add-in cards and accessories in your computer. The bus transmits signals to control the video, disk, and I/O operations, connects the memory and the processor, and is used by programs to control all the above hardware elements.

Bus type is a primary reason some computers are faster than others. An 8 bit bus handles 8 lines of data simultaneously, and a 64 bit bus can handle 8 groups of 8 lines in the same amount of time. Imagine a ribbon cable, like the hard drive interconnecting cable. The more wires in the cable, the more data can be processed simultaneously.

Bit

The bit, or *BInary digiT*, is the building block for all information transmitted to or from any element in a computer. A bit can be a 0 or a 1, where 0 and 1 are opposite logic states. Computers communicate by building *bytes* consisting of 8 bits, and grouping the bytes in groups of two or more called *words*.

Byte

If you are mean to your dog, expect one of these. Or, in computer lingo, a byte is a group of 8 bits of computer information. The byte is the most common method to express memory size, hard disk capacity, and file size.

A kilobyte is 1024 bytes of information, often called a kB, or kbyte. A Megabyte is 1.024 million bytes of information, often referred to as MB or Mbyte, the primary measurement unit of hard drive, floppy disk, and memory capacity.

A recent addition to the measurement scheme is the Gigabyte, which is 1000 Megabytes of information or capacity. With 10 Gigabyte SCSI hard drives becoming commonplace, there may be another step in memory measurement coming soon: the Terabyte.

CGA

This was the *Color Graphics Adapter* in the first IBM color systems. The monitor and adapter combination was capable of 320x320 resolution and 16 colors, along with rudimentary text support.

If you have one of these around, its best current use is target practice.

CMOS

Complementary Metal Oxide Semiconductor is a process for integrated circuit manufacture. The devices are normally low power consumption, and ideal for battery operation. This makes them usable in portable computers, or *laptops*.

Two devices in your computer continue operating, even when the power is turned off and the plug is removed from the wall socket. The *CMOS clock* runs off the small battery on the motherboard, keeping the correct date and time, after you set them correctly.

Speaking of CMOS setup, a programmable integrated circuit saves the information you enter into the CMOS setup program, and reuses it each time you turn on your computer. This device also runs off the small battery. When you operate the computer, the battery is recharged.

Command Line and Command Prompt

When you turn on your computer, unless you enter a program automatically during the boot process, your screen displays a *command prompt*. This is the first character string on the *command line*. When you type, the characters appear after the prompt. The command prompt can be configured. A line in your Autoexec.bat file could read:

```
prompt = $P$G
```

This would give you a prompt designating the drive letter followed by the current path. If you were in the DOS directory on the first hard drive in your system, the prompt would be:

```
C:\DOS>
```

Now, for an enjoyable and easy to read screen in DOS, I have a prompt line in my Autoexec.bat file that looks like this:

prompt = `$e[0;37;44m$P$G`

This gives me a blue screen with white letters. A must for this option is a line in your Config.sys file reading:

device = `ANSI.SYS`

The special characters in this prompt command are available in the MS DOS version 6.0 or later manual.

As I previously indicated, the *command line* is where the commands you type are shown.

Config.sys

This is the configuration file that is executed after the BIOS and CMOS setup routines are processed. It precedes the Autoexec.bat file in order of execution. The hardware and software device drivers for video, CD-ROM, and sound add-in cards normally reside here.

You will have several lines in this file starting with *device =*. These are device drivers. They control programs like ANSI.SYS, EMM386.EXE, and several hardware drivers.

The DOS initialization programs are called out in the Config.sys file.

Controller Cards

Controller cards are synonymous with adapter cards. They process data to and from the CPU. See *adapter* and *add-in card*.

Conventional Memory

Often called low memory, this is the first 640 kB of RAM installed in your computer. DOS programs run in this portion of memory. Unfortunately, this area in memory normally houses all the device drivers and *TSR* programs running around in your computer. This reduces the maximum program size you can run under DOS.

Fortunately, Windows 95 and other programs break the 640 kB barrier. Programs such as MS-DOS memmaker also push some of the TSR programs and drivers into *upper memory*, and get some of the 640 kB back.

CPU

The *Central Processing Unit* is the main device on the motherboard. The CPU can be anything from an 8086 through a Pentium Pro and beyond. The CPU determines the bus architecture and system performance and speed. The computer's price is also determined by CPU type.

Note: The aforementioned are processors for IBM and compatible computers.

Current Directory

Your current directory is the spot in your system path you are indexed to. Every operation you perform runs on files and programs in the current directory. The current directory is searched first for commands you execute, then the path statement is searched until the program you executed is found.

Current Disk Drive

If you have a prompt that displays your current directory, it probably also displays your current disk drive. If you are in the root directory of the hard disk you normally boot from, your prompt may look like this:

```
C:\>
```

You can change your current disk drive by typing the drive letter, followed by a colon, then pressing the *return* key. Example: To change to the A drive, type *A:*

Your current disk drive will be the *A* floppy disk. The prompt will change to:

```
A:\>
```

Your current disk drive is the one first searched by any commands you execute. The *path* statement takes over afterward.

Device

Hardware connected to or inside your computer constitutes devices. Most devices are hardware, and either accept or transmit data. A video monitor accepts data, a keyboard transmits it. Both are devices.

Some software programs set drivers for *virtual devices*. The virtual device accepts input or gives output, but is merely a sub program and not hardware. This is common in sophisticated graphics programs that swap output and input with other resident programs.

Device Driver

Device drivers are software designed to configure hardware in your computer to perform certain tasks. You will find device drivers in your Config.sys file. *See Config.sys.* Some device drivers DOS uses are HIMEM.SYS AND ANSI.SYS.

Diagnostic Programs

These programs, discussed in Chapter 8, are tools to identify and correct problems. Diagnostic routines range from full blown burn in programs that test all operational parameters of your computer, to simple memory test routines. Review Chapter 8 for details.

Directory

When you first install DOS on a virgin hard disk, your first directory is created. The root directory is the first place on the hard disk programs and data are stored. The second directory is normally the DOS directory, created by your DOS installation disk to store the DOS program files. As you install other programs, they often create their own directories, or folders, to store the files required to run.

A DOS file system is like an upside down tree, with each branch representing a different directory, and the root directory is at the top of this inverted tree. As you add programs, branches grow on the tree.

Why have directories? First, there is a limit on how many files can exist in the root directory. If you have 512 or fewer files, you may never need any sub-directories. If you have 513 files, forget it. Many programs have more than 512 files.

Second, for organization of files within programs, directories and subdirectories are necessary. If each program has its own area to store information, identical filenames will not be overwritten.

Disk

Magnetic medium which rotates on a spindle, with read and write heads hovering over it, comprises a disk. Refer to the next two entries for information on the two primary types: hard disks and floppy disks.

Disk, Hard

Hard disks are multiple magnetic platters, with a handfull of read and write heads added, all sealed up in an enclosure with a circuit board for cache and sector translation attached.

This is an oversimplification, but a good analogy. The reason hard disks are sealed in a very clean medium is the small amount of area between the heads and platters. The smallest dust particle would jam between a head and one disk platter surface, destroying your recently installed DOOM 2 program.

Note: Hard disks are discussed in detail in Chapter One.

Diskette

Floppy diskettes are removable storage media which consist of a single magnetically coated vinyl platter installed in a jacket. The drive for a floppy disk has a spindle that spins the floppy disk, and read/write heads to transfer data to and from the floppy diskette.

Floppy diskettes are the most common way to transfer data to other computers.

Disk Controller

A disk controller is the IDE or SCSI interface between the hard disk and floppy disk drives and the CPU. It can be an add-in card or built-in circuitry on the motherboard.

DMA

Direct Memory Access is one way to transfer data between computer memory and a hardware device installed in the computer. DMA does not require CPU involvement, making the process extremely fast.

DOS Disk

A DOS disk is one that has been DOS formatted, and one that can be utilized for data storage and retrieval on a DOS based system.

DOS Memory

DOS memory is considered the first 640 kB of addressable memory in your computer. *See Conventional Memory.* It holds boot data, programs, and system information.

DOS

The *Disk Operating System* is software written to perform on a specific type of computer. In the case of MS-DOS, the program was written to operate on IBM and compatible PC systems.

Applications unique to the type of hard disk, monitor and adapter, file system, and input/output devices are written and developed into a complete operating system package.

Note: I mix upper and lower case in commands all the time; DOS recognizes commands typed in both cases, but many programming tools do not. Be careful.

DOS Boot Diskette

A floppy diskette with the necessary DOS system files required to launch DOS is called a boot diskette. It may be necessary to have one if something happens to the boot block on your hard drive.

A boot disk is an invaluable tool. The DOS manual describes how to make one for yourself.

Drive

The assembly that transports a floppy diskette, or the entire hard disk drive assembly, is often referred to as a drive. A CD-ROM transport system or tape transport system shares the same designation.

EGA

IBM introduced the *Enhanced Graphics Adapter* to improve graphics display quality in their computers. EGA offered a medium resolution alternative to the existing CGA system. EGA was compatible with both CGA and monochrome display units.

EISA

The *Extended Industry Standard Architecture* definition of the internal bus structure on an IBM or compatible PC redefined the existing standard. It offered higher speed and more features than the *ISA* bus.

The real improvement was definition of a 32 bit architecture completely different from the existing and proprietary IBM MicroChannel system; one the clone industry quickly adopted as the 32 bit standard.

EMM

The software that controls use and allocation of high memory in a PC is referred to as an *Expanded Memory Manager*. The specification is sometimes called *LIM*, for its developers, Lotus, Intel, and Microsoft.

The upper memory between the DOS memory (the first 640 kB) and 1 Megabyte can be included in the expanded memory. 64 kB of upper memory is set aside by the EMM as a map to the extended memory for certain programs to use. Extended memory usually starts at 1 Megabyte and runs up to the amount of RAM installed on the motherboard.

EMS

Not to be confused with its remote cousin, the female affliction, the *Expanded Memory Specification* is a standard. The EMS standard governs the hardware and software which comprises expanded memory.

ENTER

The *ENTER*, or carriage return key, signifies termination of a command line. It is often called the *RETURN* key.

Do not confuse the alphanumeric *ENTER* key with the numeric keypad *ENTER* key.. They have different functions in some programs. Normally, their functions are identical.

Environment

DOS sets aside a small amount of memory to store information. This information is available for use by other programs. Among the things in the DOS environment are the *Path* information, *Prompt,* and *Set* information for variable definition.

ESDI

The *Enhanced Small Devices Interface* is a definition of the standards applying to the interconnection of a type of high speed hard disk drive. It joins the currently utilized SCSI and IDE interface specifications.

Execute

When a program is running, it is being executed. A computer executes instruction sets when it runs software programs. An *executable file* is a file normally having a .bat, .exe, or .com filename extension. Files like this can be executed by typing the filename without the extension, then pressing the *ENTER* key.

Expanded Memory

Expanded memory is the portion of RAM set aside and managed by the EMM. This memory is normally used as a scratch pad for database and spreadsheet programs.

The EMM sets aside a 64 kB portion of upper memory between the DOS memory and 1MB.

This 64 kB of memory serves as an index to the larger portion of expanded memory above 1 MB. The expanded memory size is limited only by the motherboard capacity and the amount of RAM you have installed on the system. *It can be up to 1 Terabyte in current Pentium II systems.*

Extended Memory

In a 286 or higher computer, memory above one Megabyte is referred to as extended memory. Disk caching is a principal use for this memory.

If you install HIMEM.SYS in your Config.sys file, you can set aside a 64 kB portion of extended memory for DOS and other TSR programs.

File

A file is a portion of a program or data occupying space in memory or on a disk. Some files are complete programs, but most files are data resulting from program execution.

A file stored on a disk is identified in the *file archive table*, or FAT, by its starting location and size. This way the file can be accessed, modified, or deleted as required by you or program execution.

Filename

The filename is a group of ASCII characters you assign to a file to identify it. In a DOS system, a filename can be up to 8 characters with a 3 character extension identifying the type of file.

In Windows 95, the 8 character limit is trashed, and you have infinitely more flexibility naming files.

Filenames must be unique in the same directory, lest they be overwritten by another application.

Filename Extension

A string of 1 to 3 characters following the period in a filename is the filename extension. The extension normally describes the type of file, so applications can use it.

If you look in your Config.sys file, you will see several types of DOS filename extensions. EXE and COM files are ones DOS can load and execute. Filenames ending in SYS are DOS system files and DRV files are device driver filenames.

Fixed Disk

This doesn't mean a repaired disk. Refer to Disk, Hard.

Gigabyte

1024 Megabytes of memory, storage, or information is a Gigabyte. Hard disk drives and tape backup systems can have capacities in this range.

Hardware Interrupt

Interrupts alert the CPU of events requiring action. Hardware interrupts are asserted by a keyboard, mouse, hard disk, etc. to inform the microprocessor that software interaction is requested.

The action may be to open or close a file on the hard disk, accept movement information from a mouse, or input from the keyboard.

Hercules

Before IBM released the medium resolution EGA system for PC color displays, Hercules Technology came out with one. To this day, most video adapters are downward compatible to the Hercules format.

Hexadecimal

Unlike the standard base 10 counting system most humans use, computers often use a base 16 system called *hexadecimal notation*. Four bits of information, represented by 1, 2, 4, and 8, make up the base 16 number system. The 15 *numbers* that comprise the system are 0 through 9 and A through F. An 8 bit *byte*, represented by (8 4 2 1) (8 4 2 1) represents 255 different items, 00 through FF.

High Memory

HMA, or the *high memory area*, is the 64 kB area above the 1 MB address range that HIMEM.SYS creates. This area can be used by programs for storage of intermediate results during program execution. When this process occurs, you have more free *DOS* memory available for other applications.

Host Adapter

Add-in cards which interface between a hardware device, like a hard disk or video monitor, are referred to as host adapters. They process data to and from these devices and the memory, allowing the CPU to expend effort elsewhere. This speeds up execution of programs.

IBM-Compatible

If a computer or component provides the same function as the original component in an IBM computer, the device or computer is IBM-compatible. This means the software and hardware devices will behave the same in the *clone* and the original IBM machine.

IDE

The *Integrated Drive Electronics* standard for hard disk control is the most popular today. It regulates the definition of a high speed integrated drive and controller assembly, hence the name.

An adapter to transfer data to and from the hard disk is normally integrated into the motherboard, but is also available as an add-on card.

The IDE specification is part of the ATA standard. *AT-Attachments* is the specification used in the interface for hard disk drives to the IBM PC/AT bus.

I/O

Input/output is the ability of a computer to transfer data to and from internal and external devices. This capability can be inherent in both hardware and software.

I/O often refers to a special add-in card or function embedded in the motherboard. This function controls data transfer among devices inside the computer and outside, and includes interaction with other computers through a modem or external port.

IRQ

Interrupt requests are signals transferred over the bus between add-in cards and the CPU. They instruct the CPU to perform immediate action.

Normally IRQ lines are asserted to request the CPU coordinate transfer of data between add in devices and memory.

ISA

The 8 and 16 bit bus utilized by IBM and compatible computers is the *Industry Standard Architecture* bus. It can accompany a VESA or PCI system. Most computers have up to three ISA connectors, to ensure compatibility with older add-in cards.

LoadHigh

This statement describes the action of setting an executable file or device driver in the upper memory area or in high memory. With this command in your Config.sys or Autoexec.bat file, you can specify the start memory address the command must use.

Before you use this command, you must initialize a memory manager, like EMM386 or QEMM. The line to start the memory manager must precede this line in the batch file.

Local Bus

The VESA standard set down by the *Video Electronics Standard Association* is a high speed I/O to CPU interface that maintains compatibility with the ISA standard interface.

Logical Devices

Partitioning a large hard drive into smaller ones creates a logical device for each partition. DOS treats each partition as a physical device, not as a portion of one drive.

A logical drive is a partition as mentioned above. Other logical devices are RAM drives created in RAM and maintained by software control. Network drives are considered to be logical devices by your computer.

Loopback Adapter

This is a special connector wired to allow you to test communications ports without actually going on line.

Lower Memory

See DOS memory.

Math Coprocessor

The math coprocessor is integrated into 486DX and all faster microprocessors for IBM and compatible computers. The 486SX, 386, and earlier computers had an expansion slot to accommodate one if required.

The math coprocessor performs all the complex math operations, allowing the CPU to perform other tasks.

MCA

Micro Channel Architecture is the standard utilized in the IBM PS/2 computer line. It is an IBM trademark, and is incompatible with all other architectures past and present in any other system.

MCA systems use different adapters and add-in cards, none of which will work in anything else.

MCGA

Put simply, this refers to the *Multi-Color Graphics Array* system implemented in IBM PS/2 computers. It was noted for great gray-scale and improved resolution over CGA.

MDA

The first IBM computers had the *Monochrome Display Adapter*. The display was either green or amber. See *Target Practice*.

Megabyte

1024 Kilobytes of information, storage, or memory is a Megabyte.

Megahertz

This measure of frequency is in millions of cycles per second. Clock speeds are measured in megahertz.

Memory

Memory is any form of storage area for program use that resides in your computer. RAM, hard disks, floppies, and CMOS are types of memory. So are tape cartridges or CD-ROMs.

Cache is the fastest memory in your system, and the floppy disk is the slowest.

Microprocessor

See CPU.

MIDI

The *Musical Instrument Device Interface* is the industry standard driving the computer interface for musical devices. It specifies connections, hardware, and software protocol.

MMX

This term refers to the first significant extension to the 1985 era instruction set inside the CISC processor family. The addition of 57 new instructions accelerates calculations in graphics and audio applications, including 2D and 3D graphics, speech recognition and synthesis, and video processing and types of compression.

The performance expectations are an increase of 50 to 100 percent in speed while using multimedia programs and equipment.

Intel upgraded its entire product line to MMX in 1997, and introduced a cost-reduced Pentium Pro microprocessor later that year that included the MMX technology.

Modem

This name is an abbreviation for the actual function of the device. The *Modulator Demodulator* is an analog to digital and digital to analog converter.

The modem converts digital information from a computer to analog signals which can travel through the phone lines. It accomplishes the reverse upon receiving signals from another computer.

Motherboard

The heart and soul of a computer is the motherboard. Everything plugs into it, and the motherboard serves as the information pathway to and from the CPU and each device connected to it.

A motherboard typically has the CPU, RAM, cache, and IDE I/O function installed. Add-on functionality in the form of video support, hard and floppy disks, keyboards, and mice complete the computer.

Multitasking

Performing more than one operation at once is multitasking. This is normally a software process, where programs and data are quickly swapped between a reserved portion of memory and the active memory a microprocessor is using.

In a process like this, the software determines how long each operation remains on hold in reserved memory and how long the operation gets CPU attention. If you have a faster computer, you normally will never notice any slowdown in operation while your computer is performing multitasking operations.

The *foreground* process, the one you can see on the screen, is typically the one getting most of the CPU's attention. Examples of programs that use multitasking are Windows, Windows 95, and DESQview.

Network

When you connect more than one computer to another, you are establishing a network. Networking computers is an essential operation when common data and programs must be accessed by multiple users. The workplace is your most likely location to encounter a network.

Network Interface

An add-in card to interface between your computer and a network communications hub is called a network interface card. This add-in card processes digital signals from your computer and sends them to a common node all other users share with you.

Online Services

Online services are pay for use BBSes with advertisements. They do, however offer connectivity to a large number of useful and enjoyable sites. Shareware is available, and electronic mail, software support, online games, and chat groups are included.

America Online, CompuServe, Prodigy, and the Microsoft Network are examples of online services.

Page Frame

On a DOS machine, the location in memory between DOS memory and 1 MB where expanded memory is indexed is called Page Frame memory.

Parallel I/O

Transferring data using the parallel port is extremely fast. Eight or more bits of information can be sent simultaneously using the parallel I/O port on your computer. Data transfer rates of 100 kB are not unusual using this technique. The computer's parallel or printer port is the vehicle of transportation.

Parameter

Some commands allow you to specify how the program executes. This is done by setting different *parameters* in the command line. Example:

```
pkzip -ex -rp aargh.zip b:\*.*
```

The PKWARE program pkzip has been executed. The parameters -ex and -rp specify how the program will be executed.

PC

The first model designation IBM gave to its personal computer family was PC. The term has been adopted by all personal computer manufacturers who make IBM compatible computers and accessories.

The base IBM machine had 64 kB of memory, an optional tape drive instead of hard drives, and a monochrome display.

PC-Compatible

See IBM Compatible and AT Compatible.

PCI

The *Peripheral Component Interconnect* standard developed by Intel specifies a very fast interface between I/O devices and the CPU. The primary add-in cards using this interface are the video adapter and the IDE I/O cards.

PCMCIA

Portable computers brought with them a new specification. The *Personal Computer Memory Card Industry Association* I/O interconnect specification is the standard for interfacing memory, disk drives, modems, and network cards to portable computers.

Pentium

This 64 bit microprocessor is capable of operating beyond 233 MHz, and contains 16 kB of instruction cache and an internal floating point processor. It is the current mid-range processor, replacing the 486 of yesteryear.

Pentium II

The replacement for the Pentium Pro, this CPU has MMX instruction sets included, and the capabilities of both the Pentium and Pentium Pro. It is packaged more like an add-in card than a processor. Current versions run at speeds beyond 400 MHz, and have an L2 cache of 512 kB.

Peripheral

A device, like a scanner or printer, that is not necessary for the computer to operate. An internal tape drive or CD-ROM is a peripheral device, as are the external versions.

Physical Drive

The hard disk drive containing your partitions is a physical drive. Your floppy drives, tape drive, and CD-ROM drive are physical drives. The partitions on your hard drive, if any, are not physical drives. A physical drive is hardware, not a software managed partition on your (hardware) disk drive.

Port Address

The address in memory through which any hardware device allows access is its port address.

POST

When you turn on a computer, the first thing it does is a *Power On Self Test*, or POST. It runs diagnostic routines on various hardware components as specified in BIOS or CMOS setup. If errors are encountered, the test provides error messages or beep codes, or both.

Prompt

Your computer indicates when it is ready for commands by displaying a command prompt.

The prompt visual indicator can be changed using the DOS prompt command, as specified in your DOS manual.

PS/2

IBM recently released a new version of their *Personal System/2* computer. These systems had new bus and adapter designs, and were the current state of the art when introduced.

RAM

Random Access Memory is the primary storage computers use to store intermediate results. When a program is executed, data flows into and out of RAM during the processing portion of the program. Only after all operations are performed is the data stored on a hard disk or floppy drive.

RAM is identified by its storage capacity and speed. I have 16 Megabyte of EDO 60 Nanosecond DRAM in my computer. DRAM must be *refreshed*, or repeatedly written to with the same data, in order to retain information.

Cache memory is also RAM. Cache is extremely fast SRAM, which requires no refreshing, hence the speed. Eight Nanoseconds is the average Pipeline cache RAM's speed.

ROM

The ROM in your computer consists of one or more programmed EPROMS with setup information specific to your computer. The programs in ROM execute when you boot the computer. ROM stands for *Read Only Memory*, and it cannot easily be altered or erased.

ROM BIOS is the set of programs loaded in the ROM. Often, certain video adapters and add-in cards may have their own ROM BIOS.

Some computers today come with *FLASH BIOS.* This EPROM memory can be changed by running a software program. This is ideal as new BIOS is released to support more hardware devices and faster CPUs.

Root Directory

The first directory on a hard disk or floppy diskette is the root directory. See *Directory.*

SCSI

The *Small Computer System Interface* defined by these initials was the fastest thing around, until the high speed IDE drives became a reality. SCSI drives still hold the size record, with drives in the 10 Gigabyte range commonplace.

SCSI hard drives require a special interface to run in a PC. The interface supports many more drives than are possible with any other drive architecture.

SDRAM

SDRAM, Synchronous Dynamic Read-Only Memory, is the current standard for fast computer memory. It is nearly as fast as Pipeline Burst cache, at 10ns access speed. Significant improvements in application speed can be achieved with SDRAM in a Pentium 200, 200 MMX, or Pentium Pro system.

Serial I/O

Serial data transfer occurs one *bit* at a time, unlike parallel I/O, which transfers one *byte*, or 8 bits simultaneously. The good side of serial transfer is compatibility with modems and existing data transfer protocol.

Though it is fairly slow at 115 kB per second, it is the most common method of interconnection between computers for data transfer.

Communication occurs through one of the *serial ports* in your computer. The other ports can be used by a mouse or other serial device.

Shadow RAM

Many computers map BIOS information into faster RAM devices to speed up various operations. The RAM locations specified in CMOS setup as S*hadow RAM* are where this information is stored and executed.

Software Interrupt

An interrupt command from a program which requires CPU attention is a software interrupt. These can occur upon completion of part of a program or when device drivers are invoked.

Keyboard operations, drive access, and certain timing services are available to programs as software interrupts.

Sub-directory

Any directory within another directory is a sub-directory. Therefore, all directories other than the root directory are sub-directories.

Sub-directories allow programs to organize data and files by the application with which they are associated.

Target Practice

See *EGA and older monitors,* take thirty paces, turn and shoot!.

TSR

Terminate and Stay Resident programs are programs which remain in memory, so you can easily call up applications within them with a hot key or other command. Some device drivers fall into this category, like mouse drivers and the DOS *Setver* command.

UAR/T

These initials refer to the device commonly referred to as a *Universal Asynchronous Receiver/Transmitter.* This device converts parallel bus information into serial data for transfer using a modem. The device reverses the process upon receipt of serial data from a modem.

UMB

Upper Memory Blocks are made available by memory manager programs. They reside in the addressable memory area between DOS memory and 1 MB. TSR programs and part of DOS can be placed in upper memory to free up conventional memory for applications.

μP

See *CPU.*

Utilities

Programs that help with routine operations like backups, virus testing, file and hard disk testing are normally either utilities or diagnostic programs. *See Chapter 8 for diagnostic programs and utilities.*

VGA

Video Graphics Array is a high resolution graphics and text system that supports the previous IBM standards. It uses an analog video monitor as a display unit.

Video Adapter Card

The add-in card that interfaces the video monitor to the CPU is the video adapter card. Video adapters come in a wide range of performance and price ranges, and support all bus types.

Video Memory

This is a great hiding place for polymorphic viruses. It is often fast memory. Video memory speeds up graphics applications by taking the CPU out of the loop when processing video information.

Video memory can be DRAM, or the faster VRAM.

Windows

The first GUI program I used was Windows. It opened up the multitasking world to me. Windows supports multiple programs sharing the same resources.

Windows 95

The latest release of Windows is Windows 95. It has more resources available and 32 bit performance. Multitasking programs run smoothly under Windows 95.

Windows NT

Windows NT is the true 32 bit engine from Microsoft. It has become commonplace in power systems.

XMS

The *Extended Memory Specification* is the standard that defines control of any memory above DOS memory. When you load the HIMEM.SYS driver in the Config.sys file, XMS is set up. Other memory management programs and utilities can also set up XMS.

XT

This version of the IBM PC provided *extended technology*, enabling the user to add a hard drive to the machine. Up to 256 kB of memory could be installed.

These are the common buzzwords utilized today and their meanings. Look through them before you take that trip to the store, and you will better understand what the sales person is talking about. You will also have a better understanding of your computer needs.

This concludes the portion of this book living in the present. Let's jump ahead and look at what the future has in store in the computer industry.

Read on and enjoy Chapter 10, *Where Do We Go From Here?*

Your Notes

WHERE DO WE GO FROM HERE?

Topics
The future of in-home PC products
Subscription computer magazines
Free computer magazines
Catalogs of computer parts and accessories

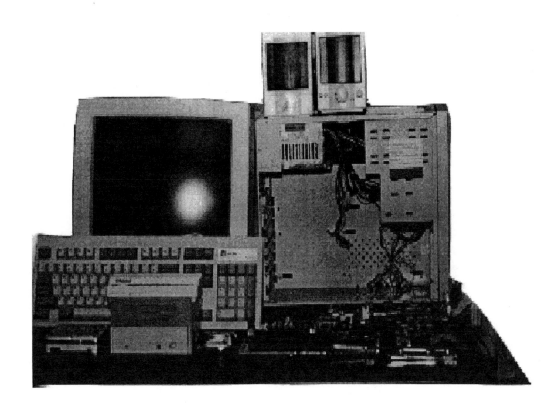

It's hot outside. The temperature has been rising as fast as memory prices have been falling.

When I prepared quotes on computer systems for this book a few weeks ago, the going price for 64 Megabyte of RAM was $60. I could get it for around $50, but I did not believe it would be fair to quote prices not *easily* available.

I found an advertisement in one of the magazines listed in this chapter with a price for 64 Megabyte of 132 pin 10 Nanosecond SDRAM for *less than forty dollars.* Not believing the reduction in price, I checked out some of my local component vendors. Sure enough, their advertising literature indicated similar reductions.

There is one certainty in computer and component prices: *They always go down.*

This chapter is devoted to *where the home computing industry is going,* and how you and I will be affected, both as consumers and proficient upgrade specialists. If you are reading this chapter, I'll bet you know more about building and upgrading computers than 99.9% of the other consumers.

My wild guesses are based on trends I have observed and hardware I have gotten my hands on. Some of these factors are good indications of the future in home computing. We are in for an E ticket ride if I am even close on my predictions.

Most of the advances affecting computers will occur in the peripheral devices. You can expect increased functionality from printers, FAX machines, and modems. Other improvements will occur in motherboard technology, as even faster bus speeds and microprocessors become available.

Speaking of microprocessors, expect sneakier processing schemes. For example, the Pentium Pro (Intel's boy wonder) uses a trick to change x86, or *complex* instructions into *reduced* instruction sets. Reduced instructions sets can be run in parallel. This makes the Pentium Pro a RISC microprocessor, after all, even though externally it looks like a CISC CPU. The Pentium II has the best of both!

Complex Instruction Set microprocessors are the type already familiar to you. They include everything from the Pentium on down to the 286. The section of Chapter 1 on motherboards gives a detailed description of the differences between CISC and RISC processors and systems.

Even the fastest microprocessor is limited by external bus speed, commonly called the motherboard clock speed. Look for vast improvements here, to get the most out of the faster processors. Example: A Pentium 150 MHz processor sitting on a 60 MHz bus performs no better than a Pentium 133 MHz processor using a 66 MHz bus, or CPU clock.

For the short term, rather than change motherboard architecture, most CPUs will probably increase internal cache size. The Pentium Pro has the L2, or secondary cache built into the chip already, and that is one reason it is so fast. The new MMX Pentium microprocessors from Intel have already doubled the Pentium's internal cache size.

Let's examine some of these future additions in more detail.

I've mentioned the addition of MMX technology to the Pentium line, but what is it exactly?

MMX is a set of additional instructions added to the existing Pentium's instruction set, that is designed to accelerate operations that commonly occur during multimedia tasks. What this means from the computer user standpoint is a considerable increase in speed and data throughput in these areas.

The benefits from these instructions go beyond the games and presentation graphics normally thought of as unused by the casual user, since so many programs use calculations commonly thought of as multimedia-related.

Some of the tasks that will see the 50 to 100 percent improvement are MPEG video, speech recognition, modem conferencing, all audio processing, and both 2D and 3D image processing.

The casual user with an office suite will see significant improvement, as will the heavy game player. Some of the MMX updated programs, like Microsoft Office and Macromedia Director, will provide 8 times the execution speed with this processor update.

Intel and other microprocessor developers are adding MMX technology to their entire product line. Intel is already incorporating MMX technology in the Pentium II processor line. The software developers are already taking advantage of the additional instruction sets in new revisions of existing programs and all new releases.

Last year, I got my first look at an experimental CD-ROM drive that can read two sided CD-ROM disks. It was about twice the size of the existing CD-ROM drive, requiring two 5.25 inch bays in a tower style case. The first thing I wondered is: Why?

CD-ROM drives exist that can handle six or more CD-ROM disks. The access time is at least 24X on the ones I have used. This system, I believe, makes a double sided CD-ROM disk unnecessary, or so I thought.

The real reason for research into double sided CD-ROM drives is not just for reading the disks, but for writing to them. With the drives rapidly approaching the access times of some hard disks, it is only a matter of time before your floppy or hard disk is replaced by a double sided CD-ROM writer. With CD-ROM writer media at or below the cost of a tape cartridge, the CD-R will become the standard for backup systems. Do you really need a floppy disk in this case? I think not.

The drive I looked at had a different method of data storage than conventional CD-ROM drives. A typical drive reads data in one continuous track, starting at the inside of the CD and spiraling outward. This one track recording method was not utilized in the new drive. The new drive stored data *exactly like a hard disk,* in concentric tracks.

Obviously, this type of CD-ROM drive is not intended to replace the existing type, *just as VHS never intended to replace BETA.*

The real future in CD-ROM technology is limited by laser color. The higher the frequency of light that can be used, the closer together the data can be packed. This is because a higher frequency of light has a smaller wavelength. Samsung has a green laser out that can store more than 100 minutes of MPEG video on one side of a laser disk. If you are counting, that is about five times the current amount.

The blue laser currently being worked on will more than double that storage. In Megabytes the storage capacity would be about 3 Gigabytes for the green laser and more than 6 Gigabytes for the blue.

Some laser disk drives have on-board cache to speed up access times. Look for larger caches, probably in the 10 to 20 Megabyte range, in the next few years. A CD-ROM with a large cache will be faster than a hard disk performing the same operations.

By now, you know color laser printers are available. They are extremely expensive currently, but so were color ink jet printers when I got one.

I have a special gift. I will go out and buy something when I think the price has bottomed out, only to have it drop 50% in price as I walk to the car with my new purchase. People hire me to buy things so they can get a good price after I make my purchase. I have been threatening to buy a color laser printer.

The modem in your computer is another area slated for vast improvement in the next year or so. Since the advent and increasing popularity of ISDN modems running at 128 k bps, the 28.8 k bps modems are rapidly approaching obsolescence. Internet cable will obsolete both, unless something even faster does.

For those unfamiliar with ISDN, the *Integrated Services Digital Network* is the digital alternative to your analog phone line. It replaces your analog phone line and modem with a digital system. Though the two copper wires coming out the back of your computer look not unlike standard phone cables, they are capable of up to 1 Megabit transmission rates with 8 to 1 compression.

Many phone lines are already ISDN compatible, since Ma Bell has been so influential in bringing out and supporting ISDN ready cables. If your area is compatible, the only costs are a one time set up fee, refunded after two years, and the modem. Now for the really fast alternative. Your computer has an interface in it that can probably communicate at 300 to 644 k bits per second. It is your parallel printer port.

The next generation of communications packages will make use of this port and your cable network. Parallel communication over video channels is being experimented with today, and serial communication over satellite is available already, *with 10 Megabit speed.*

Expect communications speeds in the Mega*byte* per second rate soon. Note the emphasis on *byte.* Parallel communication, as you remember, uses multiple lines to transfer data, so you can multiply existing speeds by at least a factor of 8.

Other communications breakthroughs to expect are digital cellular phones with modems embedded in notebook computers. Expect to be able to rent a system like this at airports when you pick up your rental car. No reason to buy if you only use the thing when traveling or on vacation.

Look for portable computers like this to continue to shrink in size considerably and to run on AA batteries. CPU speeds will not be that fast on such a system, but power consumption will be minimized.

As speech recognition becomes more commonplace, the need for a keyboard will be lessened. My wife talks to her computer all the time, and it does *exactly* what she tells it to do, just like me.

If you tell me, I will listen.
If you show me, I will see.
If you let me experience, I will learn.

This Chinese proverb describes the importance of *Virtual Reality Modeling Language* in the standardization of 3D simulations for use on the Internet. As modem speeds increase, the Internet will become a home tutorial system, which will aid tremendously in instruction of bedridden and home bound students. Interactive training already exists on CD-ROM.

In the *what will they come up with next* department, I want to talk a bit about the *DVD player*. This system, primarily designed for video playback, has found its way into the computer market.

Digital Versatile Disks are able to hold about 17 Gigabyte of MPEG 2 video. The players can be double sided and double layered, similar to a floppy disk drive's architecture.

The transfer rates have to be at least 1.1 Meg per second to provide the 8X performance specified. This drive, unlike the one I mentioned previously, will be compatible with existing CD-ROM technology.

The players became available in 1997, at about $300 for an entry-level unit. The recorders will be available to the public in 1999, if the Hollywood studios don't find a way to block recorder sales.

Motherboard innovations are coming up to speed. I read an advertisement recently about a dual Pentium II motherboard with 512 kB of pipeline burst cache. It had on-board SCSI hard disk control included. The motherboard price, without either CPU, was $175. Motherboard bus speed will increase significantly in the next few years. The newer processors will force the issue, but how do you get more speed from the bus?

Fiberoptic bus interconnections are proven in high-speed analog computers and some special purpose single board computers used in industrial applications. This will require expensive retooling and innovative bus design, but will be necessary in order to break the 1000 MHz barrier for CPU speed.

Back to the price of RAM. This single element of your computer will become a turning point if the price descends significantly.

Look for larger RAM installations in computers. Typical RAM installations today are 32 and 64 Megabytes. I expect a typical RAM installation to be 512 Megabytes by the year 2000. This, of course, assumes RAM prices will continue to decline.

These are a few predictions based on what I have seen. I know based on past performance that it will always be much cheaper to build your own computer and perform your own upgrades. Some things never change.

Following this page are lists of periodicals available with advertisements on computer parts and accessories. You will also find a list of free magazines. Be sure you enhance your qualifications on the questionnaire, in order to ensure a free subscription.

A list of catalogs that provide computer parts and accessories wraps up this chapter.

COMPUTER MAGAZINES

Here is a list of magazines that cater to the computer oriented individual. There are many others, and you will become aware of them if you read several of these.

Audio Forum
96 Broad St.
Guilford, CT 06437

Black Box Corp.
PO Box 12800
Pittsburgh, PA 15241

Byte Magazine
PO Box 558
Hightstown, NJ 08520

CD-I World
PO Box 1358
Camden, ME 04843-1358

CD-ROM Multimedia
720 Sycamore St.
Columbus, IN 47201

CD-ROM Today
PO Box 51478
Boulder, CO 80321-1478

CD-ROM Professional
462 Danbury Rd.
Wilton, CT 06897-2126

Compute!
PO Box 3245
Harlan, IA 51593-2424

ComputerCraft
76 N. Broadway
Hicksville, NJ 11801-9962

Computer Currents
5720 Hollis St.
Emeryville, CA 94608

Computer Graphics World
PO Box 122
Tulsa, OK 74101-9966

Computer Pictures
Montage Publishing, Inc.
701 Winchester Ave.
White Plains, NY 10604

Computer Shopper
PO Box 51020
Boulder, CO
80321-1020

Computer World
PO Box 2044
Marion, OH 43306-2144

Desktop Video World
PO Box 594
Mt. Morris, IL 61054-7902

Digital Imaging - Micro Publishing
21150 Hawthorne Blvd.#104
Torrance, CA 90503

Digital Video Magazine
PO Box 594
Mt. Morris, IL 61054-7902

Electronic Musician
PO Box 41525
Nashville, TN 37204-9829

High Color
PO Box 1347
Camden, ME 04843-9956

Home and Studio Recording
Music Maker Pub.
7318 Topanga Cyn Blvd. Suite 200
Canoga Park, CA 91303

Home Office Computing
PO Box 51344
Boulder, CO 80321-1344

Imaging Magazine
1265 Industrial Highway
Southampton, PA 18966

Insight Direct, Inc.
1912 W. 4th St.
Tempe, AZ 85281

International Spectrum
10675 Treena St.
Suite 103
San Diego, CA 92131

Internet
PO Box 713
Mt. Morris, IL 61054-9965

Kidsoft Magazine
718 University Ave.
Suite 112
Los Gatos, CA 95030-9958

LAN Magazine
PO Box 50047
Boulder, CO 80321-0047

MicroComputer Journal
76 N. Broadway
Hicksville, NY 11801

Micro Times Magazine
5951 Canning St.
Oakland, CA 94609

Musician's Friend
PO Box 4520
Medford, OR 97501

Nuts and Volts
430 Princeland CT.
Corona, CA 91719-1343

Open Computing
PO Box 570
Hightstown, NJ 08520-9328

PC Computing
PO Box 50253
Boulder, CO 80321-0253

PC Magazine
PO Box 51524
Boulder, CO 80321-1524

PC Novice
PO Box 85380
Lincoln, NE 68501-9807

PC Today
PO Box 85380
Lincoln, NE 68501-5380

PC World Magazine
PO Box 51833
Boulder, CO 80321-1833

PRE-
8340 Mission Rd.
Number 106
Prairie Village, KS 66206

Publish!
PO Box 51966
Boulder, CO 80321-1966

Video Magazine
PO Box 56293
Boulder, CO 80322-6293

Videomaker Magazine
PO Box 469026
Escondido, CA 92046

Voice Processing Magazine
PO Box 6016
Duluth, MN 55806-9797

Windows Magazine
PO Box 58649
Boulder, CO 80322-8649

MAGAZINES FREE TO QUALIFIED SUBSCRIBERS

Advanced Imaging
445 Broad Hollow RD.
Melville, NY 11747-4722

Automatic ID News
P.O. Box 6158
Duluth, MN 55806-9870

*AV Video Production
and Presentation Technology*
701 Winchester Ave.
White Plains, NY 10604
(914) 328-9157

Beyond Computing
1133 Westchester Ave.
White Plains, NY 10604

California Business
P.O. Box 70735
Pasadena, CA 91117-9947

CD-ROM News Extra
462 Danbury RD
Wilton, CT 06897-2126

Client/Server Computing
Sentry Publishing Co.
1900 W. Park Drive
Westborough, MA 01581-3907

Communications News
2504 Tamiami Trail N.
Nokomis, FL 34275
(813) 966-9521

Communications Week
P.O. Box 2070
Manhasset, NY 11030

Computer Design
Box 3466
Tulsa, OK 74101-3466

Computer Products
P.O. Box 14000
Dover, NJ 07801-9990

Computer Reseller News
P.O. Box 2040
Manhasset, NY 11030

Computer System News
600 Community DR
Manhasset, NY 11030

Computer Tech. Review
924 Westwood Blvd.#65
Los Angeles, CA 90024

Computer Telephony
P.O. Box 40706
Nashville, TN 37204-9919
(800) 677-3435

Data Communications
P.O. Box 477
Hightstown, NJ 08520-9362

Designfax
P.O. Box 1151
Skokie, IL 60076-9917

Document Management & Windows Imaging
8711 E. Pinnacle Peak Road, # 249
Scottsdale AZ 85255

EE Product News
P.O. Box 12982
Overland Park, KS 66212

Electronic Design
P.O. Box 985007
Cleveland, OH 44198-5007

Electronic Mfg.
P.O. Box 159
Libertyville, IL 60048

Electronic Publish & Print
650 S. Clark ST
Chicago, IL 60605-9960

Electronics
P.O. Box 985061
Cleveland, OH 44198

Federal Computer Week
P.O. Box 602
Winchester, MA 01890

Identification Journal
2640 N. Halsted ST
Chicago, IL 60614-9962

ID Systems
P.O. Box 874
Peterborough, NH 03458

Imaging Business
Phillips Business Info
P.O. Box 61130
Potomac, MD20897-5915
1-301-343-1520

InfoWorld
P.O. Box 1172
Skokie, IL 60076

LAN Times
122 E. 1700 S.
Provo, UT 84606

Lasers and Optronics
301 Gibraltar DR
Morris Plains, NJ 07950

Machine Design
P.O. Box 985015
Cleveland, OH 44198-5015

Managing Office Technology
1100 Superior AV
Cleveland, OH 44197-8092

Manufacturing Systems
P.O. Box 3008
Wheaton, IL 60189-9972

Medical Equipment Designer
29100 Aurora RD
Number 200
Cleveland, OH 44139

Micro Publishing News
21150 Hawthorne Blvd. # 104
Torrance, CA 90503

Mini-Micro Systems
P.O. Box 5051
Denver, CO 80217-9872

Mobile Office
Subscriptions Dept.
P.O. Box 57268
Boulder, CO 80323-7268

Modern Office Technology
1100 Superior Ave.
Cleveland, OH 44197-8032

Mr. CD-ROM
MAXMEDIA Dist. Inc.
P.O. Box 1087
Winter Garden, FL34787

Network World
161 Worcester RD
Framingham, MA 01701
1-508-875-6400

Network Computing
P.O. Box 1095
Skokie, IL 60076-9662

Network Journal
600 Harrison ST
San Francisco, CA 94107
(800) 950-0523

New Media Magazine
P.O. Box 1771
Riverton, NJ 08077-7331
(415) 573-5170

Office Systems
P.O. Box 3116
Woburn, MA 01888-9878

Office Systems Dealer
P.O. Box 2281
Woburn, MA 01888-9873

PC Week
P.O. Box 1770
Riverton, NJ 08077-7370

Photo Business
1515 Broadway
New York, NY 10036

The Programmer's Shop
5 Pond Park RD
Hingham, MA 02043-9845

Quality
P.O. Box 3002
Wheaton, IL 60189-9929

Reseller Management
Box 601
Morris Plains, NJ 07950

Robotics World
6255 Barfield RD
Atlanta, GA 30328-9988

Scientific Computing
301 Gibraltar DR
Morris Plains, NJ 07950

Software Magazine
Westborough Office PK
1900 W. Park Drive
Westborough, MA 01581-3907

Surface Mount Technology
P.O. Box 159
Libertyville, IL 60048

Sun Expert
P.O. Box 5274
Pittsfield, MA 01203-9479

STACKS
PO Box 5031
Brentwood, TN 37024-5031

CATALOGS OF COMPUTERS, COMPONENTS, AND SOFTWARE

CompuClassics
PO Box 10598
Canoga Park, CA 91309

Compute Ability
P.O. Box 17882
Milwaukee, WI 53217

Computers and Music
647 Mission ST
San Francisco, CA 94105

DAMARK
7101 Winnetka Ave. N.
P.O. Box 29900
Minneapolis, MN 55429-0900

Data Cal Corp.
531 E. Elliot RD
Chandler, AZ 85222-1152

Dell Direct Sales
11209 Metric Blvd.
Austin, TX 78758-4093

Digi-key Corporation
701 Brooks Ave. S.
Thief River Falls, MN 56701-0677

DTP Direct
5198 W. 76th ST
Edina, MN 55439

Edmund Scientific Co.
101 E. Gloucester Pike
Barrington, NJ 08007-1380

Global Computer Supplies
11 Harbor Park DR
Dept. 48
Port Washington, NY 11050

Global Office Products
11 Harbor Park DR
Dept. 30
Port Washington, NY 11050

Hello Direct
5884 Eden Park Place
San Jose, CA 95138-1859

IBM PC Direct
P.O. Box 12195
Bldg. 203/Dept. WN4
Research Triangle Park, NC 27709-9767
(800) 426-2968

JDR Microdevices
2233 Samaritan DR
San Jose, CA 95124

KidSoft Software Catalog
(800) 354-6150

MAILER'S Software
970 Calle Negocio
San Clemente, CA 92673

MicroWarehouse
1720 Oak ST
P.O. Box 3014
Lakewood, NJ 08701-3014

Momentum Graphics
16290 Shoemaker
Cerritos, CA 90701-2243

Mr. CD-ROM
P.O. Box 1087
Winter Garden, FL 34787
(800) 444-6723

Multimedia World
P.O. Box 58690
Boulder, CO 80323-8690

One Network Place
4711 Golf RD
Skokie, IL 60076

Paper Catalog
205 Chubb Ave.
Lyndhurst, NJ 07071

Pasternak Enterprises
P.O. Box 16759
Irvine, CA 92713

PC Connection
6 Mill ST
Marlow, NH 03456

Personal Computing
90 Industrial Park RD
Hingham, MA 02043

Power Up!
P.O. Box 7600
San Mateo, CA 94403-7600

PrePress
11 Mt. Pleasant AV
East Hanover, NJ 07936-9925

Presentations
Lakewood Bldg.
50 S. 9th ST
Minneapolis, MN 55402-9973

Processor
P.O. Box 85518
Lincoln, NE 68501
(800) 334-7443

Projections
Business Park DR
Branford, CT 06405

Queblo
1000 Florida Ave.
Hagerstown, MD 21741

Software Labs
100 Corporate Pointe, # 195
Culver City, CA 90230-7616

Soundware
200 Menlo Oaks DR
Menlo Park, CA 94025

South Hills Datacomm
760 Beechnut DR
Pittsburg, PA 15205

TENEX Computers
56800 Magnetic DR
Mishawaka, IN 46545

Tiger Software
800 Douglas Tower, 7th Floor
Coral Gables, FL 33134
(800) 888-4437

Tools For Exploration
4460 Redwood Hwy. Suite 2
San Rafael, CA 94903

United Video and Computer
724 7th Ave.
New York, NY 10019
(800) 448-3738

UnixReview
P.O. Box 420035
Palm Coast, FL 32142-0035

IN CONCLUSION...

This book has been enjoyable to put together, and I hope you get satisfaction from reading it.

More importantly, I hope this book has opened a door for you, as building my first computer did for me.

It always seemed to me that the price for a computer was about 30 percent out of my reach. One day, I found out I had the capability to build a computer, and suddenly I could afford one.

This book represents everything I have done or read on the subject, and everyone I have talked to or learned from has contributed. It is only a small subset of the knowledge available on computers, but it is the most important information for the new computer builder to know.

There are few books that actually instruct you how to put together a computer, and none that walk you through the process with the depth this book presents.

I have listened to about one hundred computer builders and people who upgrade their own systems, and they agree with me that the text and pictures in this book accurately convey the process.

The examples of systems I included are a great reference for anyone not sure of the exact configuration they desire.

Mike Harris
Shadows_Lair@MSN.COM

APPENDIX

RESOURCES ON THE WORLD WIDE WEB

BIOS	AMI (American Megatrends)	http://www.amibios.com
BIOS	Award	http://www.award.com
BIOS	Micro Firmware	http://www.firmware.com
BIOS	MR Bios (Microid Research)	http://www.mrbios.com
BIOS	Phoenix	http://www.ptltd.com
Chipsets	Intel	http://www.intel.com
Chipsets	OPTi	http://www.opti.com
Chipsets	SiS	ftp://ftp.sis.com.tw
Chipsets	UMC	http://www.umc.com.tw
Chipsets	VIA Technology	http://www.via.com.t7
Chipsets	VLSI	http://www.vlsi.com
Chipsets	Winbond	http://www.winbond.com
Computers	Acer	http://www.acer.com
Computers	Acorn	http://www.acorn.co.uk
Computers	ALR	http://www.alr.com
Computers	Amiga	http://www.amiga.de
Computers	AMS	http://www.amsnote.com
Computers	Apache	http://www.apache.com
Computers	Apple	http://www.apple.com
Computers	Appro	http://www.appro.com
Computers	Apricot	http://www.apricot.co.uk
Computers	Aris	http://www.aris.com.sg
Computers	Aspen	http://www.aspsys.com
Computers	AST	http://www.ast.com
Computers	Astro Research	http://www.astronote.com
Computers	Axil	http://www.axil.com
Computers	Be	http://www.be.com
Computers	Bull	http://www.bull.com
Computers	Chicony	http://www.chicony.com
Computers	Compaq	http://www.compaq.com
Computers	Convex	http://www.convex.com
Computers	Daystar Digital	http://www.daystar.com
Computers	Data General	http://www.dg.com
Computers	Datalux	http://www.datalux.com
Computers	Dell	http://www.dell.com
Computers	Digital	http://www.dec.com
Computers	Dolch	http://www.dolch.com/
Computers	Encore	http://www.encore.com
Computers	Epson	http://www.epson.com/prod/desktop/index.html
Computers	Everex	http://www.everex.com
Computers	Gateway2000	http://www.gw2k.com/
Computers	HAL	http://www.hal.com
Computers	HP	http://www.hp.com
Computers	IBM	http://www.pc.ibm.com
Computers	Integrix	http://www.integrix.com
Computers	Intergraph	http://www.intergraph.com
Computers	Jepssen	http://www.vol.it/jepssen/
Computers	Magitronic	http://www.magitronic.com
Computers	Micron Electronic	http://www.mei.micron.com
Computers	Mitsuba	http://www.mitsuba.com
Computers	Nec	http://www.nec.com
Computers	NeXT	http://www.next.com
Computers	Newchip	http://www.newchip.i

Computers	Nimantics	http://www.nimantics.com
Computers	Olidata	http://www.olidata.it
Computers	Olivetti	http://www.olivetti.it/opc/welcome.htm
Computers	Packard Bell	http://www.packardbell.com
Computers	Panasonic	http://www.panasonic.com/products/comperi/
Computers	Polywell	http://www.polywell.com
Computers	Power Computing	http://www.powercc.com
Computers	Pyramid	http://www.pyramid.com
Computers	RDI	http://www.rdi.com
Computers	Ross	http://www.ross.com
Computers	Samsung	http://www.sec.samsung.co.kr/Product/computer/
Computers	Sequent	http://www.sequent.com
Computers	Silicon Graphics	http://www.sgi.com
Computers	Siliconrax	http://www.siliconrax.com
Computers	Sony	http://www.sel.sony.com/SEL/
Computers	Stratus	http://www.stratus.com
Computers	Swan Technologies	http://www.swantech.com
Computers	Tadpole	http://www.tadpole.com
Computers	Tandy	http://support.tandy.com
Computers	Tera	http://www.tera.com
Computers	Toshiba	http://www.toshiba.com
Computers	XI	http://www.win.net/xi_comp
Computers	Zenith	http://www.zds.com
Controllers &I/O	Adaptec	http://www.adaptec.com
Controllers &I/O	Advanced Storage Cncpts	http://www.eden.com/~asc/
Controllers &I/O	Advansys	http://www.advansys.com
Controllers &I/O	Advantech	http://www.advantek.com
Controllers &I/O	American Megatrends	http://www.megaraid.com
Controllers &I/O	Atronics	http://www.atronicsintl.com
Controllers &I/O	Berkshire	http://www.berkprod.com
Controllers &I/O	Buslogic	http://www.buslogic.com
Controllers &I/O	Byterunner	http://www.byterunner.com
Controllers &I/O	Centennial	http://www.cent-tech.com
Controllers &I/O	CMD	http://www.cmd.com
Controllers &I/O	Comtrol	http://www.comtrol.com
Controllers &I/O	Crestor	http://www.crestor.com
Controllers &I/O	Cyclades	http://www.cyclades.com
Controllers &I/O	Digi Intl.	http://www.digibd.com
Controllers &I/O	DPT	http://www.dpt.com
Controllers &I/O	DTC	http://www.datatechnology.com
Controllers &I/O	Dynatex	http://www.zstarr.com/dynatex/
Controllers &I/O	Future Domain	http://www.adaptec.com/sales/#FD
Controllers &I/O	Gtek	http://www.gtek.com
Controllers &I/O	Infotrend	http://www.infotrend.com.tw
Controllers &I/O	Initio	http://www.initio.com
Controllers &I/O	Iwill (aka SIDE)	http://www.iwill.com.tw
Controllers &I/O	Mylex	http://www.mylex.com
Controllers &I/O	NCR	http://www.ncr.com
Controllers &I/O	New Media	http://www.newmediacorp.com
Controllers &I/O	Pathlight	http://www.pathlight.com
Controllers &I/O	Promise	http://www.promise.com
Controllers &I/O	QLogic	http://www.qlc.com
Controllers &I/O	Specialix	http://www.specialix.co.uk
Controllers &I/O	Symbios	http://www.symbios.com
Controllers &I/O	Tandy	http://support.tandy.com
Controllers &I/O	Tekram	http://www.tekram.coe
Controllers &I/O	TURBOstor	http://www.genroco.com/
Controllers &I/O	Tyan	http://www.tyan.com/yline.htm
Controllers &I/O	Winbond	http://www.winbond.com.tw
Controllers &I/O	Z-World	http://www.zworld.com
Input Devices	Acecad	http://www.acecad.com
Input Devices	ACT Lab	http://www.actlab.com
Input Devices	Advanced Input	http://www.advanced-input.com
Input Devices	Advanced Gravis	http://www.gravis.com

Input Devices	Alps Electric	http://www.alpsusa.com
Input Devices	BTC	http://www.btc.com.tW
Input Devices	Calcomp	http://www.calcomp.com
Input Devices	Casco	http://www.casco.com
Input Devices	CFX	http://cfx.com.au
Input Devices	CH	http://www.chproducts.com
Input Devices	Chicony	http://www.chicony.com
Input Devices	Contour	http://www.contourdes.com/
Input Devices	Cybernet	http://www.cybernet.com
Input Devices	DataHand Systems	http://www.datahand.com/
Input Devices	Datalux	http://www.datalux.com
Input Devices	Eurgonics	http://eurgonics.com
Input Devices	Evergreen	http://www.trackballs.com
Input Devices	Exos	http://www.exos.com
Input Devices	Focustaipei	http://www.focustaipei.com
Input Devices	Gefen	http://www.gefen.com
Input Devices	Genius	http://www.genius-kye.com/
Input Devices	Genovation	http://www.genovation.com
Input Devices	Glidepoint	http://www.glidepoint.com
Input Devices	The Glove	http://theglove.com
Input Devices	Gyration	http://www.gyration.com
Input Devices	Infogrip	http://www.infogrip.com/infogrip/
Input Devices	Interlink Electronics	http://www.interlinkelec.com/
Input Devices	JAG Tech	http://www.clearlight.com/~jagtech
Input Devices	Kernel	http://www.kernel.co
Input Devices	Keytronic	http://www.keytronic.com
Input Devices	Kurta	http://www.mutoh.com
Input Devices	Left Handed	http://www.lefthanded.com
Input Devices	Logitech	http://www.logitech.com
Input Devices	Memtron	http://www.memtron.com
Input Devices	Microsoft	http://www.microsoft.com
Input Devices	MicroSpeed	http://www.microspeed.com/
Input Devices	Mitsumi	http://www.mitsumi.com/
Input Devices	Mouse Burger	http://www.unipac-usa.com
Input Devices	Mouse Systems	http://www.mousesystems.com/
Input Devices	Mouse Trak	http://www.mousetrak.com/
Input Devices	Mutoh	http://www.mutoh.com
Input Devices	NMB	http://www.nmbtech.com
Input Devices	No Hands Mouse	http://www.footmouse.com
Input Devices	Paneltec	http://www.paneltec.com
Input Devices	Polytel	http://www.danish.com/polytel/
Input Devices	Primax	http://www.primax.nl
Input Devices	Sejin	http://www.sejin.com
Input Devices	Sicos	http://www.sicos.com/mice.htm
Input Devices	Spacetec	http://www.spacetec.com
Input Devices	Spec Research	http://www.spec-research.com
Input Devices	Star Track	http://www.am-group.com/zentech/
Input Devices	Summagraphics	http://www.summagraphics.com
Input Devices	Supermouse	http://www.supermouse.com
Input Devices	Sym Media	http://www.symmedia.com
Input Devices	Synaptics	http://www.synaptics.com
Input Devices	Sysgration	http://www.sysgration.com
Input Devices	Tandy	http://support.tandy.com
Input Devices	Texas Indstrl Periphs	http://www.ikey.com
Input Devices	Thrustmaster	http://www.thrustmaster.com
Input Devices	Trust	http://www.trust.box.nl
Input Devices	U&C	http://www.superpen.com
Input Devices	USAR	http://www.usar.com
Input Devices	Vector	http://www.mbws.com
Input Devices	Wacom	http://www.wacom.com
Input Devices	Wireless Computing	http://www.cpgs.com/wireless/
Memory	Centon	http://www.centon.com
Memory	Century	http://www.century-micro.com
Memory	Cypress	http://www.cypress.com

Memory	Dallas	http://www.dalsemi.com
Memory	Hsin Lin	http://www.hsinlin.com.tw
Memory	Hyundai	http://www.hea.com/products/semicond/
Memory	IDT	http://www.idt.com
Memory	Jaton	http://www.jaton.com
Memory	Kingston	http://www.kingston.com/
Memory	Memtron	http://www.memtron.com
Memory	Micro Memory	http://www.umem.com
Memory	Micron Technology	http://www.micron.com/mti/index.html
Memory	Newer Technologies	http://www.newertech.com/products/
Memory	Nutek	http://www.nutekmem.com
Memory	PNY	http://www.pny.com
Memory	Rambus	http://www.rambus.com
Memory	SIMM expander	http://www.minden.co
Memory	Simple Technology	http://www.simpletech.com
Memory	Sony	http://www.sel.sony.com/semi/memory.html
Memory	Visiontek	http://www.visiontek.com
Microprocessors	AMD	http://www.amd.com
Microprocessors	Analog	http://www.analog.com
Microprocessors	ARM	http://www.arm.com
Microprocessors	Cyrix	http://www.cyrix.com
Microprocessors	Evergreen Technologies	http://www.evertech.com
Microprocessors	Kingston	http://www.kingston.com/
Microprocessors	IDT	http://www.idt.com
Microprocessors	Intel	http://www.intel.com
Microprocessors	IBM (chips site)	http://www.chips.ibm.com
Microprocessors	Motorola	http://www.mot.com
Microprocessors	Nexgen	http://www.nexgen.com
Microprocessors	Quantum Effect Design	http://www.qedinc.com
Microprocessors	SGS-Thomson	http://www.st.com
Microprocessors	Texas Instruments	http://www.ti.com/sc/docs/x86/home.htm
Microprocessors	Zilog	http://www.zilog.com
Modems & Fax	Aceex	http://www.aceex.com
Modems & Fax	Aetherworks	http://www.aetherworks.com
Modems & Fax	Amquest	http://www.amquestcorp.com
Modems & Fax	Anchor	http://www.anchor.nl
Modems & Fax	Apex Data	http://warrior.com/apex/index.html
Modems & Fax	Angia	http://www.angia.com
Modems & Fax	Archtek	http://www.archtek.com.tw
Modems & Fax	Askey	http://www.askey.com
Modems & Fax	Asuscom	http://www.asuscom.com.tw
Modems & Fax	AT&T Paradyne	http://www.paradyne.att.com
Modems & Fax	Banksia	http://www.banksia.com.au
Modems & Fax	Best Data	http://www.bestdata.com
Modems & Fax	Boca Research	http://www.bocaresearch.com
Modems & Fax	Cardinal	http://www.cardtech.com
Modems & Fax	Com 21	http://www.com21.com
Modems & Fax	Comcorp	http://www.comcorp.com.au
Modems & Fax	Communicate	http://www.communicate.co.uk
Modems & Fax	Creatix	http://www.creatix.com
Modems & Fax	Digicom System	http://www.digicomsys.com
Modems & Fax	Dr. Neuhaus	http://www.neuhaus.de
Modems & Fax	Echo	http://www.echousa.com
Modems & Fax	Eiger labs	http://www.eigerlabs.com
Modems & Fax	Elebra	http://www.elebra.com.br
Modems & Fax	E-Tech	http://www.e-tech.com
Modems & Fax	EXP	http://www.expnet.co@
Modems & Fax	Gammalink	http://www.gammalink.com
Modems & Fax	Gavi	http://www.hwgavi.com
Modems & Fax	Genoa	http://www.genoasys.com
Modems & Fax	Hayes	http://www.hayes.com
Modems & Fax	Intertex	http://www.intertex.se
Modems & Fax	J-Mark	http://www.j-mark.com
Modems & Fax	K M Engineering	http://www.kme.com

Modems & Fax	Konexx	http://www.konexx.com
Modems & Fax	Logicode	http://www.logicode.com
Modems & Fax	Maestro	http://www.maestro.com.au
Modems & Fax	Max Link	http://www.askey.com
Modems & Fax	Maxtech	http://www.maxcorp.com/product/inde1.htm
Modems & Fax	Megahertz	http://www.megahertz.com
Modems & Fax	Min	http://www.kct.com
Modems & Fax	Motorola	http://www.mot.com/MIMS/ISG/Products/Modems/
Modems & Fax	MultiTech	http://www.multitech.com
Modems & Fax	NetComm	http://www.netcomm.com.au
Modems & Fax	Newcom	http://www.newcominc.com
Modems & Fax	Novalink	http://www.novalinktech.com
Modems & Fax	Olitec	http://www.olitec.com
Modems & Fax	Practical Peripherals	http://www.practinet.com
Modems & Fax	Psion Dacom	http://www.psiondacom.com
Modems & Fax	Quantum Data System	http://www.quantum.co.uk
Modems & Fax	Rockwell	http://www.rockwell.com
Modems & Fax	RSA	http://www.rsacode.com
Modems & Fax	Sidin	http://www.inrete.it/sidin/sidin.html
Modems & Fax	Smart Line	http://queen.shiny.it/indexbev.html
Modems & Fax	Spectrum sp	http://www.spectrumsignal.com
Modems & Fax	Tandy	http://support.tandy.com
Modems & Fax	TDK	http://www.tdksystems.com
Modems & Fax	Telindus	http://www.telindus.be
Modems & Fax	Trust	http://trust.box.nl/trust/products/xtel-it.htm
Modems & Fax	US Robotics	http://www.usr.com
Modems & Fax	Western Data	http://www.western-data.com
Modems & Fax	Wisecom	http://www.wisecominc.com
Modems & Fax	Zentech	http://www.zentech.com
Modems & Fax	Zoltrix	http://www.zoltrix.com
Modems & Fax	Zoom	http://www.zoomtel.com
Modems & Fax	Zyxel	http://www.zyxel.com
Monitors	Acer	http://www.aci.acer.com.tw
Monitors	Acula	http://www.acula.com
Monitors	ADI	http://www.adi.com.tw/
Monitors	AOC Spectrum	http://www.aocltd.com
Monitors	Artmedia	http://www.artmedia.com
Monitors	AST	http://www.ast.com/monitors.htm
Monitors	Barco	http://www.mindspring.com/~barco/
Monitors	CTX	http://www.ctxintl.com
Monitors	Daewoo	http://www.daewoo-display.com
Monitors	Datalux	http://www.datalux.com
Monitors	Daytek	http://www.daytek.com
Monitors	DIGIview	http://www.digiview.com
Monitors	Dotronix	http://www.dotronix.com
Monitors	EDL	http://www.edldisplays.com
Monitors	EIZO	http://www.eizo.co.jp/welcome/
Monitors	Hitachi	http://www.hitachi.com/Products/
Monitors	Hyundai	http://www.hea.com/products/monitors/
Monitors	IBM	http://www.pc.ibm.com/products/g2214431.html
Monitors	Iiyama	http://www.iiyama.coE
Monitors	Ikegami	http://www.ikegami.co.jp
Monitors	KDS	http://www.kdsusa.com/
Monitors	MAG	http://www.maginnovision.com
Monitors	Magnavox	http://www.magnavox.com/products/
Monitors	Maxtech	http://www.maxcorp.com/product/inde19.htm
Monitors	Miro	http://www.miro.com
Monitors	Mitac	http://www.mitac.com.tw/monitor.html
Monitors	Mitsubishi	http://www.mela-itg.com
Monitors	Nanao	http://www.traveller.com/nanao/
Monitors	NEC	http://webserver.nectech.com/
Monitors	Nokia	http://www.nokia.com/products/monitors/
Monitors	No Rad	http://www.noradcorp.com
Monitors	Pacom	http://www.pacomdata.com

Monitors	Panasonic	http://www.panasonic.com/products/
Monitors	Philips	http://www.philips.com/sv/
Monitors	Portrait	http://www.portrait.com
Monitors	Princeton Graphics	http://www.prgr.com
Monitors	Radius	http://www.radius.com
Monitors	JVC	http://www.jvc.ca/mon01.htm
Monitors	Samsung	http://www.sec.samsung.co.kr/monitor/
Monitors	Sceptre	http://www.gus.com/emp/sceptre.html
Monitors	Smile	http://www.smile.com.tw
Monitors	Sony	http://www.sel.sony.com/SEL/ccpg/index.html
Monitors	Tandy	http://support.tandy.com
Monitors	Tatung	http://www.tatung.com.tw/en/SERVICE/COMP/index
Monitors	Taxan	http://www.taxan.co.uk/
Monitors	Viewsonic	http://www.viewsonic.com
Monitors	VisionMaster	http://www2.kom.com/kc/visionmaster/
Monitors	Wen Technology	http://www.iiactive.com/wen/default.htm
Monitors	Wyse	http://www.wyse.com
Motherboards	Abit	http://www.abit.com.tw
Motherboards	Achme	http://www.achme.com
Motherboards	AIR	http://www.airwebs.com
Motherboards	American Megatrends (AMI)	http://www.megatrends.com/Motherboards/
Motherboards	Amptron	http://www.deltanet.com/users/amptron
Motherboards	A-Open	http://www.aopen.com.tw
Motherboards	Arvida	http://www.arvida.ca
Motherboards	Asustek	http://asustek.asus.com.tw
Motherboards	Biostar	http://www.biostar.net
Motherboards	California Graphics	http://www.calgraph.com
Motherboards	Chaintech	http://www.bdcc-nl.com/chain/chain.htm
Motherboards	DataExpert	http://www.dataexpert.com
Motherboards	DFI	http://www.dfiusa.com/motherbd.htm
Motherboards	ECS	http://www.ecs.com.tw
Motherboards	Edom	http://www.netindex.com/edom.htm
Motherboards	Epox	http://www.epox.com
Motherboards	FIC	http://www.fic.com.t7
Motherboards	Free Tech (aka Pride)	http://www.freetech.com
Motherboards	Fugutech	http://www.fugu.com.tw
Motherboards	Gemlight	http://www.gemlight.com.hk
Motherboards	Genoa	http://www.genoasys.com
Motherboards	GigaByte	http://www.giga-byte.com
Motherboards	Intel	http://www.intel.com
Motherboards	Iwill (aka SIDE)	http://www.iwill.com.tw
Motherboards	J Bond	http://www.jbond.com
Motherboards	J Mark	http://www.j-mark.com
Motherboards	Megastar (aka TMC)	http://megastar.kamtronic.com/
Motherboards	Micronics	http://www.micronics.com
Motherboards	Microstar	http://www.msi.com.tw
Motherboards	Microway	http://www.microway.com/
Motherboards	Mitac	http://www.mitac.com.tw/mboard.html
Motherboards	Mitsubishi	http://www.apricot.co.uk/products/g-oems.htm
Motherboards	M Technology	http://www.mtiusa.com
Motherboards	Ocean	http://www.ocean-usa.com/ocean/
Motherboards	Octek	http://www.oceanhk.com/ProductInfo/
Motherboards	Pc Chips	http://www.pcchips.com
Motherboards	QDI	http://www.qdigrp.com
Motherboards	See Thru	http://www.seethru.com
Motherboards	Shuttle	http://www.spacewalker.com
Motherboards	Soyo	http://www.soyo.de
Motherboards	SuperMicro	http://www.supermicro.com
Motherboards	Tyan	http://www.tyan.com
Motherboards	Vextrec	http://www.vextrec.com
Motherboards	Zida	http://www.zida.com
MMedia/CD-ROM	3DO	http://www.3do.com
MMedia/CD-ROM	8x8	http://www.8x8.com
MMedia/CD-ROM	Acer	http://www.acer.com

MMedia/CD-ROM	Advanced Digital Systems	http://www.ads-mm.com
MMedia/CD-ROM	Altec Lansing	http://www.altecmm.com
MMedia/CD-ROM	Animation Technologies	http://www.lifeview.com.tw
MMedia/CD-ROM	Aria	ftp://ftp.wi.leidenuniv.nl/pub/audio/aria
MMedia/CD-ROM	Aztech	http://www.aztechCA.com
MMedia/CD-ROM	Boffin	http://www.boffin.co
MMedia/CD-ROM	BTC	http://www.btc.com.tw
MMedia/CD-ROM	Casio	http://www.casio-usa.com
MMedia/CD-ROM	Chromatic Research	http://www.mpact.com
MMedia/CD-ROM	Connectix	http://www.connectix.com
MMedia/CD-ROM	Coreco	http://www.coreco.co-
MMedia/CD-ROM	Creative Labs	http://www.creaf.com
MMedia/CD-ROM	Crystal Lake	http://www.teleport.com/~crystal
MMedia/CD-ROM	DFI	http://www.dfiusa.com/cd-rom.htm
MMedia/CD-ROM	Digital Audio Labs	http://www.digitalaudio.com
MMedia/CD-ROM	Digital Vision	http://www.digvis.com
MMedia/CD-ROM	DyCam	http://www.dycam.com
MMedia/CD-ROM	Ensoniq	http://www.ensoniq.com
MMedia/CD-ROM	ESS	http://www.esstech.com/index.html
MMedia/CD-ROM	Frontier Design	http://www.FrontierDesign.com
MMedia/CD-ROM	Futurecho	http://www.futurecho.com
MMedia/CD-ROM	Genius	http://www.genius-kye.com/
MMedia/CD-ROM	Giltronix	http://www.giltronix.com
MMedia/CD-ROM	Goldstar	http://www.goldstar.co.kr
MMedia/CD-ROM	Gravis	http://www.gravis.co
MMedia/CD-ROM	H45 technologies	http://www.h45.com
MMedia/CD-ROM	Hitachi	http://www.hitachi.com/Products/Comprod/
MMedia/CD-ROM	Hsin Lin	http://www.hsinlin.com.tw
MMedia/CD-ROM	In Focus	http://www.infs.com
MMedia/CD-ROM	Interactive EFX	http://www.interactive-efx.com
MMedia/CD-ROM	IPC	http://www.ipctechinc.com
MMedia/CD-ROM	Jazz Multimedia	http://www.jazzmm.com
MMedia/CD-ROM	Kontron	http://www.kontron.com/progres/index.html
MMedia/CD-ROM	Koss	http://www.koss.com
MMedia/CD-ROM	Labtec	http://www.labtec.com
MMedia/CD-ROM	Logicode	http://www.logicode.com
MMedia/CD-ROM	Media Vision	http://www.mediavis.com
MMedia/CD-ROM	Mediatrix	http://www.mediatrix.com
MMedia/CD-ROM	Minolta	http://www.minolta.com/index.html
MMedia/CD-ROM	Mitsumi	http://www.mitsumi.com
MMedia/CD-ROM	Multimedia Labs	http://204.174.94.120/business/lifestyle/
MMedia/CD-ROM	Multiwave	http://www.multiwave.com
MMedia/CD-ROM	Nakamichi	http://www.nakamichicdrom.com
MMedia/CD-ROM	NEC	http://webserver.nectech.com/textadvmed/
MMedia/CD-ROM	Newcom	http://www.newcominc.com
MMedia/CD-ROM	Nikon	http://www.klt.co.jp/Nikon/
MMedia/CD-ROM	NSM Jukebox	http://www.nsmjukebox.com
MMedia/CD-ROM	NuReality	http://www.nureality.com
MMedia/CD-ROM	Ocean	http://www.ocean-usa.com/ocean/
MMedia/CD-ROM	Octek	http://www.oceanhk.com/ProductInfo/
MMedia/CD-ROM	Olympus	http://www.olympus.co.jp/indexE.html
MMedia/CD-ROM	OPTi	http://www.opti.com
MMedia/CD-ROM	Panasonic	http://www.panasonic.com/products/multimed/
MMedia/CD-ROM	Philips	http://www.philips.com/sv/
MMedia/CD-ROM	Pioneer	http://www.pgb.pioneer.co.uk/pioneer
MMedia/CD-ROM	Plasmon	http://www.plasmon.com
MMedia/CD-ROM	Play Inc.	http://www.play.com
MMedia/CD-ROM	Plextor	http://www.plextor.com
MMedia/CD-ROM	Polaroid	http://www.polaroid.com
MMedia/CD-ROM	Primax	http://www.primax.nl
MMedia/CD-ROM	Reveal	http://www.reveal.com
MMedia/CD-ROM	Roland	http://www.rolandus.com
MMedia/CD-ROM	Samsung	http://www.sec.samsung.co.kr/Product/computer/
MMedia/CD-ROM	SC&T2	http://www.platinumsound.com

MMedia/CD-ROM	SIC	http://www.sicresource.com
MMedia/CD-ROM	Sony	http://www.sel.sony.com/SEL/
MMedia/CD-ROM	SRS Labs	http://www.srslabs.com
MMedia/CD-ROM	Star Multimedia	http://www.starusa.com
MMedia/CD-ROM	Taiwan Multimedia	http://tmi.at-taiwan.com
MMedia/CD-ROM	Tandy	http://support.tandy.com
MMedia/CD-ROM	Teac (Main page)	http://www.teac.co.jp
MMedia/CD-ROM	Teac (US site)	http://www.teac.com
MMedia/CD-ROM	Terratec	http://www.terratec.com
MMedia/CD-ROM	Toshiba	http://www.toshiba.com
MMedia/CD-ROM	Trust	http://trust.box.nl/trust/products/xmm-it.htm
MMedia/CD-ROM	Turtle Beach	http://www.tbeach.com
MMedia/CD-ROM	Vertos	http://www.ecsusa.co-
MMedia/CD-ROM	Vine Micros	http://vinemicros.com
MMedia/CD-ROM	Wearnes	http://www.asiabiz.com.sg/wtk
MMedia/CD-ROM	Willow	http://willow.com/peripherals/
Networking	3Com	http://www.3com.com/
Networking	ACC	http://www.sys.acc.com
Networking	Accton	http://www.accton.com.tw
Networking	ADAX Inc.	http://www.adax.com
Networking	ADC Fibermox	http://www.adc.com
Networking	Agile Networks	http://www.agile.com/
Networking	Alcatel	http://www.adn.alcatel.com
Networking	Allied Telesyn	http://www.allied-telesyn.com
Networking	Amber Wave	http://www.amberwave.com
Networking	AMP	http://www.amp.com
Networking	Apple	http://www.apple.com
Networking	Asante'	http://www.asante.com
Networking	Ascend	http://www.ascend.com
Networking	AT&T	http://www.att.com/
Networking	Axis	http://www.axis.se
Networking	Banyan Systems	http://www.banyan.co$
Networking	Bay Networks	http://www.baynetworks.com/
Networking	Black Box	http://www.blackbox.com
Networking	Boca Research	http://www.bocaresearch.com
Networking	Cabletron	http://www.ctron.com
Networking	Cameo	http://www.cameo.com
Networking	Canary	http://www.canarynet.com
Networking	Cayman	http://www.cayman.com
Networking	Cellware	http://www.cellware.de
Networking	Chipcom	http://www.chipcom.com
Networking	Cisco	http://www.cisco.com/
Networking	Cnet	http://www.cnet.com.tw
Networking	Cogent Data	http://www.cogentdata.com
Networking	Compatible	http://www.compatible.com
Networking	Compex	http://www.cpx.com
Networking	Connectware	http://www.connectware.com
Networking	Cray	http://www.cray.com
Networking	Crosscom	http://www.crosscom.com
Networking	Cybex	http://www.cybex.com
Networking	Danpex	http://www.danpex.com/
Networking	Dayna	http://www.dayna.com
Networking	Develcon	http://www.develcon.com
Networking	Diamond Chip	http://www.dchip.com
Networking	Digital	http://www.networks.digital.com
Networking	D-Link systems	http://www.dlink.com
Networking	DPI	http://www.digprod.com
Networking	DTC	http://www.datatechnology.com
Networking	Dynatech	http://www.dynatech.com
Networking	Edimax	http://www.edimax.com
Networking	Efficient networks	http://www.efficient.com
Networking	Eicon	http://www.eicon.com
Networking	Ethercom	http://www.ethercom.com
Networking	Equinox	http://www.equinox.com

Networking	Eversys	http://eversys.com
Networking	Extended systems	http://www.extendsys.com
Networking	Farallon	http://www.farallon.com/
Networking	Fastcomm	http://www.fastcomm.com
Networking	Fibronics	http://www.fibronics.co.il/
Networking	FORE systems	http://www.fore.com
Networking	Gandalf	http://www.gandalf.ca
Networking	Global Village	http://www.globalvillage.com
Networking	Grand Junction	http://www.grandjunction.com
Networking	Hewlett Packard	http://www.hp.com
Networking	IBM (networking site)	http://www.raleigh.ibm.com/
Networking	IMC	http://www.imcnetworks.com
Networking	ICL	http://www.icl.com/products & FJICL/prodmenu.html
Networking	IMC networks	http://www.imcnetworks.com
Networking	Interlan	http://www.interlan.com
Networking	Interphase	http://www.iphase.com
Networking	Intel	http://www.intel.com/
Networking	Jolt	http://www.jolt.co.il
Networking	Katron (KTI)	http://www.ktinet.co
Networking	Kentrox	http://www.kentrox.com
Networking	Klever	http://www.klever.com/
Networking	LANart	http://www.lanart.com
Networking	Lantronix	http://www.lantronix.com
Networking	Linksys	http://www.linksys.com
Networking	Longshine	http://www.longshin.com.tw
Networking	Luxcom	http://www.luxcom.com
Networking	Madge	http://www.madge.com
Networking	Microcom	http://www.microcom.com
Networking	Microdyne	http://www.mcdy.com/
Networking	Microplex	http://microplex.com
Networking	Mitron	http://www.gus.com/emp/mitron/mitron.html
Networking	Morning Star	http://www.morningstar.com
Networking	MultiTech	http://www.multitech.com
Networking	Nbase	http://www.nbase.com
Networking	NetCorp	http://www.netcorp.qc.ca
Networking	Net Edge	http://www.netedge.com
Networking	Network Peripherals	http://www.npix.com
Networking	Networth	http://www.networth.com
Networking	Newbridge networks	http://www.newbridge.com
Networking	NHC	http://www.nhc.com
Networking	Novell	http://www.novell.com
Networking	Optical Data Systems	http://www.ods.com
Networking	Olicom	http://www.olicom.com/
Networking	OST SA	http://www.ost-us.co
Networking	Penril	http://www.penril.com
Networking	Performance Technologies	http://www.pt.com
Networking	Plaintree	http://www.plaintree.on.ca/plaintree
Networking	Plexcom	http://www.plexcom.com
Networking	Proteon	http://www.proteon.com
Networking	PureData	http://www.puredata.com
Networking	Racal	http://www.racal.com/
Networking	Racore	http://www.racore.com
Networking	Raritan	http://www.raritan.com
Networking	Retix	http://www.retix.com
Networking	Rockwell	http://www.rns.rockwell.com
Networking	Shiva	http://www.shiva.com
Networking	Sonic Systems	http://www.sonicsys.com
Networking	SMC	http://www.smc.com
Networking	Spider	http://www.spider.coe
Networking	Stallion	http://www.stallion.com
Networking	Standard Microsystems	http://www.smc.com
Networking	Startech	http://www.startechcomp.com
Networking	Symplex	http://www.symplex.com
Networking	SysKonnect	http://www.syskonnect.de

Networking	Telebit	http://www.telebit.com
Networking	Telindus	http://www.telindus.be
Networking	Thomas Conrad	http://www.tci.com
Networking	Transition	http://www.transition.com
Networking	Tribe	http://www.tribe.com
Networking	UB	http://www.ub.com
Networking	Vidasystem	http://www.groupbandmodem.com
Networking	Webster	http://www.webstercc.com
Networking	Whitetree	http://www.whitetree.com
Networking	Whittaker	http://www.whittaker.com
Networking	Xedia	http://www.xedia.com
Networking	Xircom	http://www.xircom.com
Networking	XLNT	http://www.xlnt.com
Networking	Xylan	http://www.Xylan.com
Networking	Xyplex	http://www.xyplex.com
Networking	Xircom	http://www.xircom.com
Networking	Zeitnet	http://www.zeitnet.com
Printers	Brother	http://www.brother.co.jp
Printers	Calcomp	http://www.calcomp.com
Printers	Canon	http://www.usa.canon.com
Printers	Citizen	http://www.citizen-america.com/
Printers	Colorocs	http://www.nav.com/colorocs/colorocs.html
Printers	CoStar	http://www.costar.com
Printers	Dataproducts	http://www.dpc.com/
Printers	Encad	http://www.encad.com
Printers	Epson	http://www.epson.com
Printers	Excellink	http://www.excellink.com/
Printers	Fargo	http://www.fargo.com
Printers	GCC	http://www.gcctech.com
Printers	Genicom	http://www.genicom.com
Printers	Hewlett Packard	http://www.hp.com/
Printers	IBM	http://www.can.ibm.com/ibmprinters/
Printers	Isis	http://www.printers-from-isis.com
Printers	JRL	http://www.jrl.com
Printers	Kodak	http://www.kodak.com/
Printers	Kyocera	http://www.kyocera.co.uk/
Printers	Lasermaster	http://www.lasermaster.com
Printers	Lexmark	http://www.lexmark.com
Printers	Mannesmann Tally	http://www.tally.com
Printers	Microcom	http://www.microcomcorp.com/
Printers	Mutoh	http://www.mutoh.com
Printers	NEC	http://webserver.nectech.com/textprint/
Printers	OKI	http://www.oki.com
Printers	Okidata	http://www.okidata.com/
Printers	Olivetti Lexikon	http://www.olivettilexikon.com
Printers	Panasonic	http://www.panasonic.com/products/comperi/
Printers	Printer Works	http://www.printerworks.com/index.html
Printers	QMS	http://www.qms.com
Printers	Ricoh	http://www.ricohcorp.com
Printers	Samsung	http://www.sec.samsung.co.kr/Product/computer/
Printers	Seiko	http://www.cgg.seiko.com
Printers	Sharp	http://www.sharp-usa.com
Printers	Star Micronics	http://www.starmicronics.com
Printers	Talaris	http://www.talaris.com
Printers	Tandem	http://www.tandem.com/prod/print.html
Printers	Tandy	http://support.tandy.com
Printers	Tektronics	http://www.tek.com
Printers	Texas Instruments	http://www.ti.com/printer/docs/printhome.html
Printers	Xerox	http://www.xerox.com
Scanners	3Dscanners	http://www.3dscanners.com
Scanners	Adara	http://www.adara.com
Scanners	AGFA	http://www.agfahome.com
Scanners	Ana Tech	http://www.anatech.scanners.com
Scanners	Artec	http://www.artecusa.com

Scanners	Astro Research	http://www.astronote.com
Scanners	Avision Labs	http://www.avision-labs.com
Scanners	Banctec	http://www.bti-ok.com/bti/index.html
Scanners	Bell Howell	http://www.bellhowell.com/scanners/
Scanners	Blackwidow	http://www.blackwidow.co.uk
Scanners	Envisions	http://www.envisions.com
Scanners	Epson	http://www.epson.com/prod/scanners/index.html
Scanners	Genius	http://www.genius-kye.com/
Scanners	Hewlett Packard	http://www.hp.com
Scanners	Howtek	http://www.howtek.co
Scanners	Ideal	http://www.ideal.com
Scanners	Imacon	http://www.imacon.dk
Scanners	Interactive EFX	http://www.interactive-efx.com
Scanners	Logitech	http://www.logitech.com
Scanners	Lumina	http://www.lumina2000.com
Scanners	MicroTek	http://www.mteklab.com
Scanners	Mustek	http://www.mustek.com
Scanners	Nikon	http://www.klt.co.jp/Nikon/
Scanners	Paktec	http://www.paktec.com
Scanners	Panasonic	http://www.panasonic.com/products/imaging/
Scanners	Plustek	http://www.plustek.com
Scanners	Polaroid	http://www.polaroid.com
Scanners	Primax	http://www.primax.nl
Scanners	Relisys	http://www.relisys.com
Scanners	Ricoh	http://www.ricohcorp.com
Scanners	SunRise Imaging	http://www.sunriseimg.com
Scanners	Suvil	http://www.suvil.com
Scanners	Trust	http://trust.box.nl/trust/products/xinp-it.htm
Scanners	Umax	http://www.umax.com
Scanners	Visioneer	http://www.visioneer.com
Scanners	WordWand	http://www.wordwand.com
Software	3Com	http://www.3com.com
Software	Adobe	http://www.adobe.com
Software	Apple	http://www.apple.com
Software	Autodesk FTP	ftp://ftp.autodesk.com
Software	Banyan	http://www.banyan.com
Software	Banyan FTP	ftp://ftp.banyan.com
Software	Borland	http://www.borland.com
Software	C|net Software Library	http://vsl.cnet.com
Software	Compuserve	http://www.compuserve.com
Software	Digital	http://www.dec.com
Software	Digital FTP	ftp://ftp.dec.com
Software	FTP: Inc.	http://www.ftp.com
Software	Hewlett-Packard	http://www.hp.com
Software	Hewlett-Packard FTP	ftp://ftp-boi.external.hp.com
Software	IBM	http://www.ibm.com
Software	IBM-MWave Multimedia	http://watson.mbb.sfu.ca/
Software	IBM Redbooks	http://www.redbooks.ibm.com
Software	McAfee FTP	ftp://mcafee.com
Software	Microsoft	http://www.microsoft.com
Software	Microsoft FTP	ftp://ftp.microsoft.com
Software	Novell FTP	ftp://ftp.novell.com
Software	Lotus	http://www.lotus.com
Software	Next	http://www.next.com
Software	Symantec	http://www.symantec.com/
Software	WinSite FTP	ftp://ftp.winsite.com/pub
Software	Ziff-Davis FTP	http://www.ziff.com
Storage	3M	http://www.3M.com
Storage	Advanced Digital Info	http://www.adic.com
Storage	Aiwa	http://www.aiwa.com
Storage	Amdahl	http://www.amdahl.com
Storage	Andataco	http://www.andataco.com
Storage	APS Technologies	http://www.apstech.com/
Storage	Artecon	http://www.artecon.com

Storage	Atronics	http://www.atronicsintl.com
Storage	Boxhill	http://www.boxhill.com
Storage	Centennial	http://www.cent-tech.com
Storage	Ciprico	http://www.ciprico.com
Storage	Conner	http://www.conner.com
Storage	Cutting Edge	http://www.cuttedge.com
Storage	CRU	http://www.cruinc.co
Storage	Digi-Data	http://www.digidata.com
Storage	Disctec	http://disctec.com
Storage	ECCS	http://www.eccs.com
Storage	EMC	http://www.emc.com
Storage	Eurologic	http://www.eurologic.com
Storage	Exabyte	http://www.exabyte.com
Storage	Filetek	http://www.filetek.com
Storage	Fujitsu	http://www.fujitsu.co.jp/index-e.html
Storage	FWB	http://www.fwb.com
Storage	H45 Technologies	http://www.h45.com
Storage	Hitachi	http://www.hitachi.com/Products/Comprod/
Storage	HP Colorado	http://www.hp.com/go/colorado
Storage	IBMStorage	http://www.almaden.ibm.com/storage/
Storage	Intek	http://www.intek.net/platmen.htm
Storage	Iomega	http://www.iomega.com
Storage	JVC	http://www.jvcservice.com
Storage	Maxtor	http://www.maxtor.com
Storage	Megadrive	http://www.megadrive.com
Storage	Micro Hut	http://www.microhut.com/
Storage	MicroNet	http://www.micronet.com/
Storage	Micropolis	http://www.microp.com
Storage	Mindflight	http://www.mindflight.com/
Storage	MTI	http://www.mti.com
Storage	Optical Access	http://www.oai.com/
Storage	Optima Technology	http://www.optimatech.com/optima/
Storage	Panasonic	http://www.panasonic.com/products/imaging/
Storage	Pinnacle	http://www.pinnaclemicro.com
Storage	Procom	http://www.procom.com
Storage	Reveal	http://www.reveal.com
Storage	Ricoh	http://www.ricohcorp.com
Storage	Quantum	http://www.quantum.com
Storage	Samsung	http://tongky.sec.samsung.co.kr/hdd/hdd.html
Storage	Seagate	http://www.seagate.com
Storage	SonyStorage	http://www.mmmg.com/industry/sony/dsp.htm
Storage	Storage Tek	http://www.stortek.com
Storage	Syquest	http://www.syquest.com
Storage	Tapedisk	http://www.tapedisk.com
Storage	Tandberg	http://www.tandberg.com
Storage	Tandy	http://support.tandy.com
Storage	Tecmar	http://www.tecmar.com
Storage	Texas isa	http://www.texasisa.com
Storage	Toray	http://www.toray.com
Storage	Tri-Plex	http://www.triplex.com/
Storage	Valitek	http://www.contagious.com/valitek/valitek.htm
Storage	Western Digital	http://www.wdc.com
Storage	Winchester	http://www.winsys.com
Storage	Xistor	http://www.xistor.coe
Storage	Xyratex	http://www.xyratex.com

INDEX